OXFORD EC LAW LIBRARY

General Editor: F. G. Jacobs
Advocate General, The Court of Justice
of the European Communities

EC AGRICULTURAL LAW

OXFORD EC LAW LIBRARY

The aim of this series is to publish important and original studies of the various branches of European Community Law. Each work will provide a clear, concise and critical exposition of the law in its social, economic and political context, at a level which will interest the advanced student, the practitioner, the academic, and government and Community officials.

Other Titles in the Library

EC Agricultural Law

J. A. USHER

OXFORD

UNIVERSITY PRESS

OXFORD
UNIVERSITY PRESS

Great Clarendon Street, Oxford OX2 6DP

Oxford University Press is a department of the University of Oxford.
It furthers the University's objective of excellence in research, scholarship,
and education by publishing worldwide in

Oxford New York

Auckland Bangkok Buenos Aires Cape Town Chennai
Dar es Salaam Delhi Hong Kong Istanbul Karachi Kolkata
Kuala Lumpur Madrid Melbourne Mexico City Mumbai Nairobi
São Paulo Shanghai Singapore Taipei Tokyo Toronto

with associated companies in Berlin Ibadan

Oxford is a registered trade mark of Oxford University Press
in the UK and in certain other countries

Published in the United States
by Oxford University Press Inc., New York

British Library Cataloguing in Publication Data
Data available

Library of Congress Cataloging in Publication Data
Usher, John Anthony
EC agricultural law / J.A. Usher
p. cm. — (Oxford EC law library)
Includes bibliographical references and index.
1. Agricultural laws and legislation—European Union countries. 2. Agriculture and
state—European Union countries. I. Title. II. Series
KJE6605 .U838 2002
341.7'5471'094—dc21
2001052323

ISBN 0–19–826882–3

1 3 5 7 9 10 8 6 4 2

Typeset by Florence Production Ltd
Printed in Great Britain
on acid-free paper by
Biddles Ltd., Guildford and King's Lynn

General Editor's Foreword

This new edition on the agricultural law of the European Community is of value both as a guide to a subject of great practical importance and because of the part which agricultural law has played, and continues to play, in the development of the Community legal system. Remarkably, it could be said of the first edition that it was the first extended work on the subject in the English language. The new edition will keep it at the forefront of the writing on the subject.

The book deals, systematically yet within a manageable compass, with the different regimes adopted for the whole range of agricultural products—and for fisheries. It explores the legal consequences of the common organizations of the market; it explains the financial mechanisms; it covers structural and guidance measures. The new edition takes account of important developments in recent years, most notably the World Trade Organization (WTO) Agreement on Agriculture and the international context of agricultural support, and of course the introduction of the single European currency.

Apart from the intrinsic importance of the subject, expounded concisely and with a clarity that belies its complexity, the book has a wider significance since it covers the network of constitutional and administrative issues underlying the relationship between directly applicable Community legislation and its detailed implementation in the Member States. As the most developed of Community policies, agriculture illustrates better than any other the contribution of the law to the resolution of those issues: in particular the scope and limits of the power of the Community institutions, on the one hand, and of the authorities of the Member States—their government departments and their intervention agencies—on the other.

Agriculture has been a fertile field for litigation, and has required the Court of Justice to develop fundamental principles of judicial review. It is above all in the agricultural case-law that the Court, drawing on the fragmentary indications in the Treaty and on the legal traditions of the Member States, has developed an impressive body of case-law, constructing general principles of law—notably proportionality, equality and the protection of fundamental rights—which have been erected into quasi-constitutional principles to control the Community legislature and the national authorities and to ensure so far as possible a fair and even-handed application of the law.

This book thus does more than provide a detailed but succinct analysis of an elaborate system of legislation; it also performs a wider function in illustrating the techniques by which the Community's legal order has evolved to provide a means of subjecting the legislative and administrative apparatus to the rule of law.

Francis G. Jacobs

October 2001

Preface

It is as true now as it was in 1988 when the first edition of this book was published to say that while the Common Agricultural Policy (CAP) may be well-known for the political and financial problems to which it has given rise, the legal issues underlying it have not been so widely discussed. Yet the CAP lies behind many of the institutional developments in the Community, it has been all too closely intertwined with the system of Community finance, and it is an area where the introduction of the euro has had a considerable impact, even in non-participating Member States. Agricultural markets formed the first 'single markets' within the EC, and agricultural legislation forms the background to much of the European Court's case-law on the relationship between Community law and national law. It is also in the context of agricultural disputes that the European Court has developed, and continues to develop, many of the general principles of Community law.

My own interest in the subject developed while I was a Legal Secretary at the European Court in Luxembourg from 1974 to 1978, when it became very clear that agriculture was the largest single cause of litigation before that Court. However, the genesis of the first edition of this book was a request by Professor Sir Thomas Smith to write a section on the CAP in the chapter on *Agriculture in the Stair Memorial Encyclopaedia of the Laws of Scotland*, under a contract which expressly permitted the material to be used in a monograph. This new edition has a similar history, following my revision of my contribution to the *Stair Memorial Encyclopaedia*, and I should like to thank Prof. Niall Whitty, the General Editor of that Encyclopaedia, the Law Society of Scotland, and Butterworths for permission to make use of that material in this new edition of my book. The present book is therefore, essentially a considerably expanded and revised version of that text, albeit with some difference of emphasis.

The CAP is an area which has recently been influenced by broader international agreements, notably the WTO Agreement on Agriculture, but it is also an area in which EC policy has in fact been found to conflict with WTO law. In the light of this, and of my personal experience in leading a series of seminars over the last ten years at the University of Amsterdam on the CAP and international agricultural trade, this new edition contains a chapter on the international context of agricultural support, and the legal consequences for the Community. On the other hand, unlike the WTO Agreement on Agriculture, this book continues to deal with the question of fisheries, which has become a separate chapter.

A traditional feature of the CAP has been the frequency and bulk of the legislation to which it has given rise. Since the first edition of this book in 1988, major changes have occurred in 1992, beginning the move from product support to producer support, in the mid-90s as a result of the WTO Agreement on Agriculture, and in the late 90s as a result of the Agenda 2000 programme, anticipating enlargement to include Central and East European countries, not to mention the issues arising from the introduction of the euro in 1999. This helps to explain why a new edition has not appeared earlier. Indeed, whilst writing the original version of my text on milk quotas for the *Stair Memorial Encyclopaedia*, I was driven to suggest to the editors that the experience resembled that of chasing a moving target through thick fog. However, a particular feature of the new generation of EC agricultural legislation is that it tends to set prices and quotas for several years into the future, and while it may be too much to expect that it will remain totally unamended, my hope is that this new edition will be appearing at a time when we may look forward to a few years of relative stability with regard to EC agricultural legislation. Nevertheless, it should be emphasized that this book is concerned with the underlying principles of EC agricultural legislation and the issues arising therefrom, rather than with its day-to-day detailed implementation.

Finally, and with some wistfulness, I may observe that the first edition of this book turned out to be the last of my books to be typed for me by a secretary— and such of the original text as remains has now gone through three changes of word-processing format. Most importantly, however, as in the first edition, may I take this opportunity to thank my family for their patience and encouragement.

John A. Usher

Edinburgh   *July 2001*

Contents

Table of Cases
(In Numerical Order)

Cases before the European Court of Justice

Opinions of the European Court of Justice

Table of Cases
(In Alphabetical Order)

Cases before the European Court of Justice

Opinions of the European Court of Justice

Cases before United Kingdom Courts

Table of Community Treaties

EC Treaty

1972 Act of Accession

Greek Act of Accession

Spanish and Portuguese Act of Accession

Table of Community Legislation

Regulations

Other Acts

Table of WTO Agreements

Agreement on Agriculture

General Agreement on Tariffs and Trade

General Agreement on Trade in Services

Table of UK Legislation

Table of U.K. Statutory Instruments

Table of Abbreviations

MMB	Milk Marketing Board	psr	produced in specific
NEAFC	North-East Atlantic		regions
	Fisheries Convention	QB	Queen's Bench
OECD	Organization for Economic	SDR	Special Drawing Right
	Cooperation and	SI	Statutory Instrument
	Development	SSI	Scottish Statutory
OJ	Official Journal of the		Instrument
	European Communities	TAC	total allowable catch
PDO	protected designation of	TS	Treaty Series
	origin	UMR	usual marketing requirement
PGI	protected geographical	VMS	vessel monitoring system
	indication	WTO	World Trade Organization

1

Agriculture in the EC Treaty

Introduction

'It is inconceivable that any common market should be established in Europe which did not include agriculture':[1] this book is concerned with the legal consequences of that approach to European integration. On the other hand, agriculture is an area where the trade of developed countries appears to be conducted on a highly artificial basis reflecting the system of support used in their internal markets. The reality is that agricultural trade is an area where developed countries have not been willing to allow free reign to market forces. Using OECD figures[2] which compare agricultural support in terms of producer subsidy equivalent, whether it takes the form of price support or the form of a subsidy as such, the average level of support in the OECD member countries in 1999 was the equivalent of a producer subsidy of 40 per cent—which makes the Community figure of 49 per cent seem not far out of line. It is hardly surprising therefore that the EC Treaty contains some special rules relating to agriculture. However, it is also in the sphere of agriculture that many of the fundamental institutional, financial, and legal developments in the history of the Community have occurred.

Thus, it was in anticipation of the introduction of qualified majority voting in the Council of Ministers with regard to agricultural legislation under art 37(2) and (3) of the EC Treaty, at the end of the second stage of the original transitional period (ie 1 January 1966), that the French government pursued its 'empty chair' policy in the second half of 1965, resulting in the so-called Luxembourg Accords of January 1966; yet it was also in the context of agricultural legislation that the system of delegating discretionary powers to the Commission subject to consultation with a management committee representing the Member States was evolved. Financially, it has been argued that it is only 'the accident of history which led to the establishment of the CAP in a particular form' which resulted in the adoption of the 'own resources' system of financing Community expenditure with the core principle of 'financial solidarity' or common financing.[3] Be that as it may,

---

[1] Spaak Report (1956) 44 as translated by E Neville-Rolfe in *The Politics of Agriculture in the European Community* (1984) 185.

[2] OECD, *Agricultural Policies in OECD Countries: Monitoring and Evaluation 2000* (2000).

[3] H Wallace, 'A European Budget Made in Strasbourg and Unmade in Luxembourg' (1986) Yearbook of European Law 263.

agricultural expenditure consumes the greater part of the Community budget, even if in percentage terms the proportion diminished from 80.6 per cent at the time of United Kingdom accession to 48 per cent in 1999[4] for the Guarantee Section[5] and just under 5 per cent[6] for the Guidance Section.[7]

Legally, the introduction in the late 1960s of common organizations of agricultural markets based on a single Community market was one of the factors which enabled the Common Customs Tariff to be introduced eighteen months early in July 1968,[8] and the regulations creating those common organizations expressly reproduced the provisions of the EC Treaty relating to the free movement of goods, and applied them to trade in the relevant agricultural products at a time when the basic Treaty rules had not become fully effective. Moreover, it is in the context of such common organizations that the European Court's theories on the relationship between national law (and the powers of national legislatures) and Community law have largely been developed.[9] Finally, it may be observed that agricultural disputes have been the most frequent source of litigation before the European Court[10] and, hence, hardly surprisingly, the source of many of the general principles of Community law.[11] The aim of this book is, essentially, to examine the legal issues to which the common agricultural policy gives rise, rather than to discuss aspects of that policy itself, although this is an area where it is not always possible to separate the law from the policy to which it gives effect.

Definition of agricultural goods

The characteristic distinction between the ECSC and Euratom Treaties, on the one hand, and the EC Treaty, on the other, is that the former only apply (or, in the case of the ECSC, applied) to the goods, activities, and persons expressly listed therein, whereas the EC Treaty is limited only by reference to the scope of the other two Treaties.[12] However, the agricultural provisions of the EC Treaty are an exception to this generalization, at least with regard to the definition of agricultural goods. Art 32(1) of the EC Treaty provides that the common market should extend to agriculture and trade in agricultural products, and defines 'agricultural products' as products of the soil, of stock farming, and of fisheries, and products of first-stage

---

[4] European Commission, *The Agricultural Situation in the EU: 1999 Report* (2001) at 145.

[5] See Chapter 5 below.

[6] The author's calculation from the figures on p 156 of European Commission, *The Agricultural Situation in the EU: 1999 Report* (2001).

[7] See Chapter 5 below.

[8] An account of the interrelationship is contained in E Neville-Rolfe, *The Politics of Agriculture in the European Community* (1984) 239–242.

[9] See Chapter 7 below.

[10] According to the running totals recorded in the annual *Synopsis of the Work of the Court of Justice* (Official Publications Office of the EC, Luxembourg).

[11] See JA Usher, *General Principles of EC Law* (1998).

[12] Art 305.

processing directly related to these products. By virtue of art 32(3) a specific list of the products subject to the agricultural rules of the Treaty is contained in Annex I (originally Annex II), but the Council was empowered to decide what products should be added to this list within two years of the entry into force of the Treaty. This power was exercised in Council Regulation 7a[13] which, however, is not without controversy. The two-year period expired on 31 December 1959, and although the regulation is dated 18 December 1959, it was not published in the Official Journal of the European Communities until 30 January 1961. Under art 254 of the EC Treaty, publication is an essential requirement for the entry into force of a regulation, and in the Case 185/73 *Hauptzollamt Bielefeld v König*[14] it was there-fore argued that Regulation 7a was invalid. This argument was rejected by the Court of Justice on the ground that the late publication of the regulation had no significance save as to the date from which it could be applied and take effect.

Of more lasting importance is the fact that in its judgment in the *König* case the Court of Justice gave a purposive interpretation of the phrase 'products of first-stage processing directly related' to basic agricultural products, holding that what was relevant was the economic relationship between the basic product and the processed product, rather than the number of processing operations involved. It was held that there should be a clear economic interdependence between the basic products and processed products, but that where processed products have undergone a productive process, the cost of which is such that the price of the basic agricultural raw materials becomes a completely marginal cost, they do not fall within the definition. Applying this economic criterion, the Court held that the fact that ethyl alcohol of less than 80° strength would be diluted with water (not an agricultural product!) after distillation did not prevent its being included in the list in Council Regulation 7a.

Whilst the definition in the *König* case sets the overall limits on what may or may not be included in the lists of agricultural products, the lists themselves are highly specific, using the terminology of the 1950 Customs Cooperation Council Convention on Nomenclature for the Classification of Goods in Customs Tariffs, the same nomenclature as the original version of the Common Customs Tariff (CCT). The Annex was not amended when the terminology of the International Convention on a Harmonized Commodity and Coding System was introduced into EC law with effect from 1988, although the regulations governing individual organ-izations of the market do use the current terminology. There are two major legal consequences of this system. The first is that products falling within the definition in the *König* case will not be treated as agricultural products unless they are specifi-cally listed in Annex I of the EC Treaty or Council Regulation 7a, and the second is that in interpreting these lists regard may be had to the other headings of the Common Customs Tariff and to the accepted aids to the interpretation of that tariff.[15]

[13] OJ 1961, p 71 (sp edn 1959–1962, p 68).   [14] [1974] ECR 607.
[15] See JA Usher, 'Uniform External Protection: EEC Customs Legislation before the European Court of Justice' (1982) CML Rev 389.

Hence in Case 77/83 *CILFIT Srl v Ministero della Sanita*[16] it was held that whilst wool was indisputably grown on sheep, it did not fall within the concept of 'animal products not elsewhere specified or included' under CCT heading 05.15 b, which was included in Annex I of the Treaty, since a note to chapter 5 of the tariff specifically stated that it did not cover animal textile materials, and wool was the subject of a separate chapter 53 of the tariff which was not included in Annex I of the Treaty.

In so far as Annex I was based on the 1950 Customs Cooperation Council Convention on Nomenclature for the Classification of Goods in Customs Tariffs,[17] reference has been made in interpreting Annex I of the Treaty to the explanatory notes to that convention, as in Case 61/80 *Cooperatieve Stremsel- en Kleurselfabriek v Commission*.[18] There, in the absence, as the Court of Justice pointed out, of any Community provisions explaining the concepts contained in Annex I, those explanatory notes were followed in so far as they indicated that animal rennet should be classified under heading 35.07 as an enzyme or prepared enzyme rather than under headings 05.04 or 05.15, which are included in Annex I, as a gut, bladder, or stomach of an animal, or as other animal produce, even though the rennet there at issue was extracted from calves' fourth stomachs.

With regard to the overall scope of the concept of agricultural products, particular attention may be drawn to the products of fisheries. After the accession of the United Kingdom in 1973 the view was put forward that art 102 of the Act of Accession (1972), which laid down a time limit for the adoption of fishery conservation measures, conferred a new competence on the Community.[19] However, the Court of Justice affirmed in two cases[20] that sea fisheries had always fallen within the scope of the common agricultural policy, and that art 102 merely confirmed that conservation measures were included in the Community's powers. Indeed, it may be observed that 'fish, crustaceans and molluscs' are expressly included in the list in Annex I. This may be contrasted with the WTO Agreement on Agriculture, which expressly excludes fish and fish products.[21]

Readers of Annex I might, however, be interested to see that the last item on the list is cannabis (in the form of 'true hemp'). Of the items not included in the list, on the other hand, particular attention may be drawn to cotton, with regard to which the accession of Greece, followed by that of Spain and Portugal, resulted in the adoption of special measures. Although Annex I itself was not amended to include cotton, specific provisions were introduced under Protocol No 4 to the Greek Act of Accession, on the grounds of the great importance that cotton

---

[16] [1984] ECR 1257.

[17] Brussels, 15 December 1950; TS 29 (1960); Cmnd 1070.

[18] [1981] ECR 851 at 869.

[19] See eg E Hiester 'The Legal Position of the European Community with Regard to the Conservation of the Living Resources of the Sea' [1976] Legal Issues of European Integration 55.

[20] Case 61/77 *Commission v Ireland* [1978] ECR 417 and Case 141/78 *France v United Kingdom* [1979] ECR 2923.

[21] Art 2 and Annex I.

production represented for the Greek economy and 'recognising the specifically agricultural character of this production'. To avoid discrimination, these provisions apply throughout the territory of the Community, and the aims are to support the production of cotton in regions where it is important for the agricultural economy, to permit producers to earn a fair income, and to stabilize the market—aims remarkably similar to those of the common agricultural policy itself.[22] The basic system of support is a production aid, paid through cotton ginning undertakings, to cover the difference between a guide price and the world-market price (concepts familiar in common organizations of agricultural markets), subject to quantitative restrictions (also now familiar in common organizations). The link with agricultural organizations was further confirmed by Council Regulation 2169/81,[23] the basic implementing regulation, which used as the management committee[24] in the cotton sector the already-existing management committee for flax and hemp created by Regulation 1308/70[25]—hence, an express link with the first sentence of this paragraph.

There is a double reason for the importance of the definition of 'agricultural products' in the EC Treaty: certain of the general rules of that Treaty do not apply to agricultural products, even if the basic principle laid down in art 32 is that they do, and conversely certain special rules apply only to agricultural products. However, in practical terms it has not always been possible to operate a clear distinction between agricultural goods, and non-agricultural goods which nevertheless incorporate an agricultural element. Hence a series of regulations may be found, currently exemplified in Council Regulation 3448/93,[26] laying down the trade arrangements applicable to certain goods resulting from the processing of agricultural products. The effect of these regulations is that certain provisions of the special agricultural legislation, particularly trading rules relating to levies and refunds, may be applied to processed products not defined in Annex I of the EC Treaty in order to take account of the basic agricultural products considered to be comprised in those processed products.

Definition of agricultural producers and agricultural holdings

Whilst the Treaty defines agricultural products, it mentions 'persons engaged in agriculture'[27] and 'producers'[28] without defining those terms, and does not even mention 'agricultural holdings'; nevertheless, these terms have been widely used in

---

[22] As set out in art 33 of the EC Treaty.
[23] OJ 1981 L211/2; now repealed and replaced by Council Regulation 1554/95 (OJ 1995 L148/48).
[24] See Chapter 9 below.   [25] JO 1970 L146/1.   [26] OJ 1993 L318/18.
[27] Art 33(1)(b).   [28] eg arts 34(3) and 37(3).

the secondary legislation. A simplistic definition would be to say that an agricultural producer is a person producing agricultural products as defined in the Treaty, and that an agricultural holding is land used to produce such products, but this is not really sufficiently specific when it becomes necessary to categorize farmers who also carry out processing operations or have other part-time employment, or to categorize land which is also used for processing operations or part of which is used for non-agricultural purposes.

The argument that an agricultural producer is simply a producer of an agricultural product defined in the Treaty was put to the European Court in Case 139/77 *Denkavit v FZA Warendorf*,[29] in the context of a regulation which, following the revaluation of the German mark in 1969, allowed Germany to grant compensation 'in the form of direct aid to agricultural producers', to make up for the fact that such producers would receive fewer DM when Community prices expressed in units of account were converted at the new parity.[30] The applicant company produced feeding stuffs and fattened calves on substitute milk-based fodder which it produced itself, but under the German implementing legislation the breeding and keeping of livestock was deemed to be agricultural only if a defined quantity of livestock was kept in a defined area of land, whereas the applicant company, having bought its calves, entered into contracts with other farmers to have them fattened, thus not using any agricultural land of its own. In response to the applicant's argument that it should, nevertheless, in Community law, be regarded as an agricultural producer, the Court emphasized that the concept of agriculture (as opposed to that of agricultural products) was not precisely defined in the Treaty, and concluded that 'for the purposes of the agricultural rules derived from the Treaty, it is for the competent authorities where necessary to define the scope of such rules in relation to persons and in relation to subject-matter'. On the particular legislation at issue, the Court took the view that although the expression 'agricultural producer' was broad enough to include the production of agricultural products by any method whatever, the regulation conferred a power rather than a duty on the German authorities, and the distinction which the German authorities had chosen to make could be objectively justified and was, therefore, not a discriminatory exercise of their discretion.

A more specific Community definition used to be found in the context of structural (ie guidance) policy. Here, Council Regulation 797/85,[31] reproducing the terminology of the 1972 directives which it replaced,[32] provided in art 2(1) for aid to be granted to agricultural holdings when the 'farmer' practises farming as his main occupation, and, whilst the Member States were required to define this concept further, art 2(2) provided that the definition must require such a farmer to earn more than 50 per cent of his income from farming and to devote

---

[29] [1978] ECR 1317.

[30] This may be contrasted with what happened in 1971, when the German and Dutch currencies floated upwards, leading to the introduction of monetary compensatory amounts. See Chapter 5 below.

[31] OJ 1985 L93/1.   [32] See Chapter 8 below.

less than half his total working time to work unconnected with the holding. However, in Case C-403/98 *Monte Arcuso v Sardinia*,[33] it was held that when the regulation required Member States to define what was meant by a 'farmer practising farming as his main occupation' and the Italian definition failed to include companies, a company practising farming could not invoke the Community legislation in the absence of national implementing measures. This definition has now disappeared following the replacement of Council Regulation 797/85[34] and its successors by Council Regulation 1257/1999 'on support for rural development' from the EAGGF[35] which simply refers to 'farmers' in this context. On the other hand, art 1(4) of Council Regulation 3508/92[36] on an integrated administration and control system for certain Community aid schemes defines a farmer as 'an individual agricultural producer, whether a natural or legal person or a group of natural or legal persons, whatever legal status is granted the group and its members by national law, whose holding is within Community territory'.

However, even before the change in the legislation on support for rural development, farmers not falling within the former definition could still be eligible for national aids within certain limits, and this appears to have been the background to Case 152/79 *Lee v Minister for Agriculture*,[37] where the applicant was an office clerk as well as being a part-time farmer. Furthermore, in the context of the 1972 directives, it was clearly held in Case 312/85 *Villa Banfi v Region of Tuscany*,[38] that the concept of a 'farmer' is not limited to human beings and that a legal person carrying on a farming activity is not excluded if it complies with the other criteria—indeed, it would be a breach of the prohibition on discrimination between producers laid down by art 34(3) of the Treaty to exclude a producer who was a legal person from the scope of the structural legislation.

The dividing line between producer and processor was at issue in Case 107/80, *Adorno v Commission*,[39] where the applicant sought the annulment of a Commission decision refusing to grant aid for an investment project under Council Regulation 355/77 on common measures to improve the conditions under which agricultural products are processed and marketed.[40] The applicant ran a farm comprising two holdings traditionally devoted to wine-growing and capable of producing high-quality wine, and his investment project involved the creation of a new wine-making centre at the farm to improve the processing of his grapes into wine. The Commission rejected his claim on the basis that it fell within the scope of one of the 1972 structural directives benefiting farmers, Directive 72/159 on the modernization of farms,[41] and that it therefore could not fall within the scope of the regulation benefiting processors; however, the applicant fell outside the income criteria laid down by that directive. In its judgment, the Court effectively

---

[33] 11 January 2001.   [34] OJ 1985 L93/1.   [35] OJ 1999 L160/80.
[36] OJ 1992 L355/1.
[37] [1980] ECR 1495. See the Opinion of AG Warner at 1514.
[38] [1986] ECR 4039.   [39] [1981] ECR 1469.   [40] OJ 1977 L51/1.
[41] JO 1972 L96/1.

rejected the contention that a person who was also a producer was necessarily excluded from the processing regulation, holding that 'projects for improving the processing and marketing of agricultural products from the same farm as that in which the investment is to be made are in no way excluded from the scope of the Regulation if they are capable of making an effective contribution towards standardizing processing and marketing structures'.[42] On the other hand, in the Court's view, even though the applicant was a producer his project was not concerned with improving production conditions for basic agricultural products but with improving the processing and marketing of those products, so that it did not, in any event, fall within the scope of the 1972 directive.

Similar problems of definition have also arisen in the context of 'holdings' and 'farms', both terms being used in Council Regulation 1257/1999 on support for rural development from the EAGGF.[43] The basic question was put in Case 85/77 *Santa Anna v INPS*,[44] in relation to an Italian undertaking marketing eggs, day-old chicks, and fattened poultry, produced on a holding of some 3 hectares. The dispute before the national court related to the question whether the undertaking should have to pay social security contributions covering its employees as an agricultural undertaking (apparently liable to pay at lower rates) or as an industrial undertaking. In its reference for a preliminary ruling, the Italian court asked if there was a Community concept of an 'agricultural holding' and whether the Member States were obliged to follow this concept. The court again noted that the Treaty contained no precise definition of agriculture, and still less of an agricultural holding, so that it was for the Community institutions to work out such a definition where appropriate. After observing that the phrase was widely used in secondary legislation, the court stated that 'the definition of these words is far from being uniform throughout these rules . . . but on the contrary varies according to the specific objectives pursued by the Community rules in question';[45] it therefore concluded that it was impossible to find in the provisions of the Treaty or in the rules of secondary Community law any general, uniform Community definition of 'agricultural holding' universally applicable in all the provisions relating to agricultural production. On the other hand, it may be observed that art 1(4) of Council Regulation 3508/92[46] on an integrated administration and control system for certain Community aid schemes defines a holding as 'all the production units managed by a farmer situated within the same Member State's territory'.

Whilst, therefore, the meaning of the phrase 'agricultural holding' may depend on its context, it would appear that the fact that part of the land is used for non-agricultural purposes does not necessarily take it outside the scope of Community agricultural legislation. In Case 152/79 *Lee v Minister for Agriculture*[47] the applicant had bored for water on his land and installed a pump and an underground pipe to a drinking trough for cattle, but he had also inserted a T-junction in the pipe,

[42] [1981] ECR at 1485.   [43] OJ 1999 L160/80.   [44] [1978] ECR 527.
[45] [1978] ECR at 540.   [46] OJ 1992 L355/1.   [47] [1980] ECR 1495.

leading to a tank acting as a reservoir for a water-supply in houses built on his land for sale. The basic issue was whether this fell within the scope of the former Directive 72/159 on the modernization of farms,[48] and the European Court held that that depended on whether the provision of a water-supply was carried out principally in order to service dwelling-houses or whether a *part* (emphasis added) of that work related to the modernization of a farm; a question which it was for the national court to decide.

It may finally be observed that the dairy quota scheme depends on a combination of the concepts of a 'producer' and of a 'holding'. Under the original Council Regulation 857/84,[49] a producer was defined as a person farming a holding selling milk or other milk products directly to the consumer and/or supplying what was in effect a wholesale purchaser. A holding in turn was defined as all the production units operated by the producer and located within the geographical territory of the Community. However, whilst the initial allocation depended on the activities of the producer, subsequent transfer is defined in the Community legislation in terms of the holding. Though the quotas are allocated to producers, the legislation has from the outset enabled them to be transferred with the land. According to art 7(1) of Regulation 3950/92,[50] as amended by Regulation 1256/1999,[51] reference quantities available on a holding are to be transferred with the holding in the case of sale, lease, or transfer by inheritance, taking account of the areas used for dairy production and, where applicable, of any agreement between the parties. The same is to apply to other cases of transfers involving comparable legal effects.[52]

Application of general rules of the EC Treaty

The basic principle laid down in art 32(2) of the EC Treaty is that the rules laid down for the establishment of the common market are to apply to agricultural products save as otherwise provided in arts 33 to 38. These exceptional cases are considered below,[53] but it is a distinctive feature of the European Community that the common market which it creates extends not only to industrial products but also to agricultural products, whereas the European Free Trade Association, for example, expressly excluded agricultural products from the system of free trade which it created.[54] Indeed, Council regulations establishing common organizations of the market before the end of the transitional period (1 January 1970) reproduced the basic Treaty provisions concerned with the free movement of goods, expressly prohibiting charges equivalent to customs duties and measures equivalent to quantitative restrictions in trade between Member States, and it has long been held by the European Court of Justice that these concepts have exactly the

---

[48] JO 1972 L96/1.   [49] OJ 1984 L90/13.   [50] OJ 1992 L405/1.
[51] OJ 1999 L160/73.   [52] See Chapter 4 below.   [53] See p 13–19.
[54] Convention establishing the European Free Trade Association art 21.

same meaning when used in secondary agricultural legislation as they have when used in the Treaty itself.[55]

To some extent, the agricultural regulations went beyond the express Treaty provisions, as where they prohibited Member States from imposing charges equivalent to customs duties not only in trade between Member States but also at the external frontiers of the Community with regard to goods imported from third countries.[56] The Treaty itself does not expressly prohibit such charges on direct imports from third countries, and for goods not covered by agricultural common organizations of the market, such a prohibition was developed by the Court of Justice as case law, notably in Cases 37, 32/73 *Sociaal Fonds voor de Diamantarbeiders v NV Indiamex*,[57] where it held that it was incompatible with the concepts of a Common Customs Tariff and a common commercial policy for Member States unilaterally to alter the level of external protection through such charges.

After the end of the transitional period, the reproduction of the provisions of the EC Treaty in agricultural regulations became otiose, as was pointed out by Advocate General Warner in relation to a 1970 regulation on the common organization of the market in wine,[58] as these provisions have been held to be of direct effect, that is, since that date they give rise to rights enforceable by individuals before national courts. Hence the modern versions of the agricultural regulations do not reproduce the basic Treaty provisions. The status of a Regulation codifying the provisions governing a common organization of the market without expressly repeating the Treaty provisions relating to the abolition of customs duties and quantitative restrictions was considered by the Court of Justice in Case 83/78 *Pigs Marketing Board v Redmond*[59] in relation to Council Regulation 2759/75 on the common organization of the market in pigmeat.[60] The Court held that the provisions of the Treaty relating to the abolition of tariff and commercial barriers to intra-Community trade and in particular arts 28 and 29 on the abolition of quantitative restrictions and of measures having equivalent effect on imports and exports are to be regarded as an integral part of the common organization of the market.

On the other hand, it is clear that the Council and Commission cannot prevent the application of the basic rules of the EC Treaty to agricultural products except to the extent that arts 33 to 38 so provide.[61] This is illustrated in Cases 80, 81/77 *Société les Commissionnaires Réunis Sàrl v Receveur des Douanes*,[62] where France imposed levies on imports of Italian wine, claiming to be so authorized under Council Regulation 816/70 on additional provisions for the common organization of the market in wine.[63] Whilst art 31(1) of that regulation repeated the basic prohibition on the levying of charges equivalent to customs duties, art 31(2) contained

---

[55] See eg Case 34/73 *Variola SpA v Amministrazione italiana delle Finanze* [1973] ECR 981.
[56] See eg Case 84/71 *Marimex SpA v Italian Ministry for Finance* [1972] ECR 89.
[57] [1973] ECR 1609.
[58] Cases 80, 81/77 *Société les Commissionnaires Réunis Sàrl v Receveur des Douanes* [1978] ECR 927.
[59] [1978] ECR 2347.   [60] OJ 1975 L282/1.   [61] EC Treaty, art 32(2).
[62] [1978] ECR 927.
[63] JO 1970 L99/1 (sp edn 1970 (I), p 234).

a derogation to the effect that 'so long as all the administrative mechanisms necessary for the management of the market in wine are not in application producer Member States shall be authorized in order to avoid disturbances on their markets to take measures that may limit imports from another Member State'. The French view was that the relevant 'administrative mechanisms' were not in application in Italy, and the fundamental question referred to the Court of Justice was whether this provision was compatible with the EC Treaty. In its judgment the Court held that in order to justify the establishment of charges having equivalent effect to customs duties after the end of the transitional period, it must be shown that arts 33 to 38 contain a provision which expressly or by necessary implication provides for or permits such charges. After considering those articles, the Court found that there was no such provision; indeed, it found that under the original art 44 (now repealed), even during the transitional period, in so far as the abolition of customs duties and quantitative restrictions between Member States might have resulted in prices likely to jeopardize the attainment of the objectives of the common agricultural policy, Member States could only, subject to certain conditions, introduce a non-discriminatory system of minimum prices, and that it would be manifestly contrary to the Treaty to allow greater restrictions after the end of the transitional period.

The Court concluded from this that, at all events after the end of the transitional period, the powers of the Community institutions in agricultural matters should be used with the unity of the market in mind, to the exclusion of measures breaching the prohibition on customs duties and quantitative restrictions and charges and measures having equivalent effect. It went on to hold that art 31(2) of Regulation 816/70, in so far as it permitted Member States to levy charges having equivalent effect to customs duties in trade with other Member States on the products covered by the regulation, was incompatible with the original art 13(2) (now repealed) and arts 32 to 38 of the EC Treaty, and hence invalid. It would appear to follow from this decision that the treatment of agricultural products under the Treaty may not be as exceptional as is sometimes thought, and in particular that it may be difficult to give special treatment to a certain national interest simply by clothing it in Community legislation. Indeed, the Court has since held expressly that the Commission cannot, even by approving expressly or by implication a measure adopted unilaterally by a Member State, confer on that state the right to maintain provisions which are objectively contrary to Community law.[64]

It should however be borne in mind that it is not just the Treaty rules on the free movement of goods which apply in the agricultural sector. Personal rights of free movement also apply, so that citizens of Member States have the right to exercise the Treaty freedom of establishment for themselves and their businesses in the agricultural and fisheries sectors in another Member State, even where the relevant Community legislation appears to allot quotas on a national basis, as is clearly shown

---

[64] Case 288/83 *Commission v Ireland* [1985] ECR 1761.

in Case C-48/93 *R v SoS Transport ex p Factortame*[65] in relation to the common fisheries policy. There, UK legislation which required owners of fishing vessels, or major shareholders in companies owning fishing vessels, to be resident in the UK if the vessel was to be registered as British was found to be a clear breach of the Treaty freedom of establishment. Indeed, at the broader international level, the Community system of allocation of licences for the import of bananas under Council Regulation 404/93 on the common organization of the market in bananas[66] was found by the WTO appellate body to infringe, inter alia, the General Agreement on Trade in *Services* (emphasis added).[67]

The question remains however as to how far the basic Treaty rules apply in the absence of a common organization. Under art 34(1) of the EC Treaty, common organizations of the market should have been established by the end of the transitional period. For most products this was in fact done, notable exceptions being alcohol, potatoes, and sheepmeat (for which an organization was eventually created in 1980). At the end of the transitional period there was a widely held view that by virtue of arts 37 and 38 and the original art 45 (now repealed) of the Treaty national organizations of the market could be protected until they had been replaced by common organizations of the market. Art 37(3)(a) in particular provides that a national market organization may only be replaced by a common organization if the latter offers Member States which are opposed to it and have a relevant national organization 'equivalent safeguards for the employment and standard of living of the producers concerned'.

This view was accepted both by the Commission and by Advocate General Warner in the *Charmasson* case,[68] but not by the Court of Justice. In that case, a trader was challenging a French quota system applying to the importation of bananas into France. There was not at the time any common organization of the market in bananas. Whilst the Court held that a simple quota system could not amount to a national organization of the market, it did state its view on the position of a national organization of the market after the end of the transitional period. The view accepted by the Court was that as the common organizations of the market should have been introduced by the end of the transitional period, the protected position of national organizations could also only last until the end of that period. Hence, national organizations of the market become subject to the general rules of the Treaty, notably those on free movement of goods; and in the *Charmasson* case, it was held that the original art 33 (which may now be regarded as being subsumed in art 28) on the elimination of quotas would be applicable. This doctrine was reaffirmed in an action brought by the Commission against France[69] for breach of a Treaty obligation in subjecting exports of potatoes, even within the Community, to the requirement that an officially certified export declaration must be presented. Following earlier case law, the Court held such a requirement, even

---

[65] [1996] ECR I-1029.   [66] OJ 1993 L47/1.   [67] WT/DS27/AB/R.

[68] Case 48/74 *Charmasson v Minister for Economic Affairs and Finance* [1974] ECR 1383.

[69] Case 68/76 *Commission v France* [1977] ECR 515.

if purely formal, to be a measure having equivalent effect to a quantitative restriction, on the basis that arts 33 to 38 could not justify a unilateral derogation from art 29 prohibiting measures having equivalent effect to quantitative restrictions on exports, even if no common organization had been introduced.

The effect of this case law was clearly reaffirmed in Case 288/83 *Commission v Ireland*[70] with regard to Irish measures restricting the import of potatoes in free circulation in other Member States (that is, potatoes which have been imported from non-Member States on payment of the appropriate duties etc, and are therefore under arts 23 and 24 of the EC Treaty entitled to internal free movement in the Community). It was there stated that 'agricultural products in respect of which a common organisation of the market has not been established are subject to the general rules of the common market with regard to importation, exportation and movement within the Community'.

Exceptions from the general rules

Leaving aside certain transitional provisions, the only derogations in favour of agricultural products from certain specific rules of the EC Treaty are to be found in arts 36 and 38. Art 36 provides that the rules of competition are to apply to agricultural products only to the extent determined by the Council within the framework of the common agricultural policy, and specifically enables the Council to authorize the granting of certain forms of aid. Whilst the Community competition rules as such are not the subject of this book,[71] it should be observed that the relevant chapter of the EC Treaty[72] relates not only to the practices of private (and public) undertakings but also to the payment of state aids,[73] and in practice the role of art 38 is to allow import charges to be imposed on agricultural products in so far as state aids may be paid by the exporting Member State.

The basic rules were laid down by Council Regulation 26 of 4 April 1962,[74] which treats the practices of private and public undertakings differently from the payment of state aids. With regard to the anti-competitive practices of private and public undertakings, art 1 of the regulation provides in principle for the application of the general rules contained in arts 81 to 86 of the EC Treaty to the production of or trade in agricultural goods. There is, however, an exception to this laid down by art 2 of the regulation, which provides that art 81(1) of the Treaty, prohibiting certain agreements, decisions, and concerted practices of or between undertakings, is not to apply to agreements, decisions, and concerted practices which are either an integral part of a national market organization or are necessary

---

[70] [1985] ECR 1761.
[71] See eg R Lane, *EC Competition Law* (2000).
[72] ie the EC Treaty, Title VI, chapter 1 (arts 81–89).
[73] Arts 87–89.
[74] JO 1962, p 993 (sp edn 1959–1962, p 129).

for the attainment of the objectives of the common agricultural policy. In particular, art 81(1) does not apply to agreements, decisions, and practices of farmers,
farmers' associations, or associations of such associations belonging to a single
Member State which concern the production or sale of agricultural products or
the use of joint facilities for the storage, treatment, or processing of agricultural
products, and under which there is no obligation to charge identical prices, unless
the Commission finds that competition is thereby excluded (rather than simply
restricted) or that the objectives of the common agricultural policy are jeopardized.
The Commission is given exclusive power to determine which agreements etc fall
within this exception. With regard to the attainment of the common agricultural
policy, this effectively means that arts 81 to 86 of the Treaty are read subject to the
specific provisions of the legislation establishing common organizations of agricultural markets. This legislation has had the effect of severely restricting price
competition, being, as will be seen, based on 'common' prices, although the current
moves towards producer support rather than product support may leave greater
scope for price competition and may, to give a random example, require non-
members to abide by the rules of producer organizations, as under art 5 of Council
Regulation 104/2000 on the common organization of the market in fishery and
aquaculture products.[75] It is not, however, permissible for undertakings further to
restrict the degree of competition left open to them, as is evident from the cases
involving alleged concerted practices in the sugar market.[76] On the other hand,
these cases do also show, in relation to the Italian market for sugar at the relevant
period, that a combination of Community and national rules may leave so little
room for manœuvre that the conduct of undertakings is incapable of appreciably
impeding competition.[77] With regard to the other markets at issue in these cases,
however, the applicants were not able to show that their practices were 'necessary'
for the attainment of the objectives of the common agricultural policy.[78] Similarly,
in Case 71/74 *Frubo v Commission*,[79] which concerned an agreement relating to
the import of fruit into the Netherlands from outside the Community, the Court
took the view that such an agreement could not be necessary to achieve the first
two objectives of the common agricultural policy; that is, to increase agricultural
productivity and to ensure a fair standard of living for the agricultural community.
This statement is of particular interest, since the applicants' claim was that their
agreement helped attain the other three objectives of the common agricultural
policy, and the Court seems to have followed AG Warner's view that the objectives
of that policy 'are inseparable from each other'. By way of contrast, when assessing
the validity of Community legislation in the light of these objectives, the Court

---

[75] OJ 2000 L17/22.
[76] Cases 40–48, 50, 54–56, 111, 113, 114/73 *Suiker Unie v Commission* [1975] ECR 1663 at 1949,
1950.
[77] Ibid, at 1924.
[78] Ibid, at 1948, 1951, 2020.   [79] [1975] ECR 563.

has consistently held that priority may be given to one objective over the others,[80] and has upheld legislation serving only one of those objectives.[81]

The approach of the Commission to Regulation 26/62 when enforcing the competition rules may be illustrated by its decision in the *Meldoc* case,[82] involving an agreement between Dutch dairy undertakings. The Commission pointed out that since Council Regulation 804/68[83] had replaced national market organizations in the dairy industry the agreement would not be justified as being an integral part of a national market organization. With regard to the attainment of the objectives of the common agricultural policy, the Commission declared that the means to be employed in the dairy sector were stated in Regulation 804/68, whereas the agreement there at issue, which gave rise to a quota system, a compensation scheme, consultations on sales and prices, and measures designed to inhibit imports from other Member States, amounted to an attempt to set up a private intervention system very different from that for which the regulation provided. Having, thus, concluded that the agreement did not fall within the first sentence of art 2(1) of Regulation 26/62, the Commission took the view that the second sentence of art 2(1), stating, 'in particular', the agreements to which art 81 did not apply, merely referred to a particular form of the arrangements exempted under the first sentence, and this could only be invoked in relation to agreements so exempted.

With regard to practices claimed to form an integral part of a national market organization, there is the further problem of knowing what is a national market organization. In the *Charmasson* case[84] the Court of Justice defined it as 'a totality of legal devices placing the regulation of the market in the products in question under the control of the public authority, with a view to ensuring, by means of an increase in productivity and of optimum utilisation of the factors of production, in particular of manpower, a fair standard of living for producers, the stabilisation of markets, the assurance of supplies and reasonable prices to the consumers'—in effect, therefore, an organization pursuing the same aims as those laid down by art 33 of the EC Treaty for common organizations, albeit at the national level. With regard to such national organizations of the market as still survive, the Commission appears to have developed a system of requests for clearance by the national authorities concerned, as for example with the French market in new potatoes.[85]

As an exception, art 2 of Regulation 26 has been strictly construed, particularly with regard to the concept of agricultural products. Thus an exclusive purchasing obligation with regard to rennet, which is not listed in Annex I to the EC Treaty despite being extracted from calves' fourth stomachs, did not fall within the exception even though it was used in the manufacture of cheese, which is listed in Annex I.[86]

---

[80] Case 5/73 *Balkan v HZA Berlin-Packhof* [1973] ECR 1091.

[81] eg Case 138/78 *Stölting v HZA Hamburg-Jonas* [1979] ECR 713.

[82] Decision 86/596 of 26 November 1986 (OJ 1986 L348/50).

[83] JO 1968 L148/13.

[84] Case 48/74 *Charmasson v Minister for Economic Affairs and Finance* [1974] ECR 1383 at 1396, 1397.

[85] Decision 88/109, OJ 1988 L59/25.

[86] Case 61/80 *Cooperatieve Stremsel- en Kleurselfabriek v Commission* [1981] ECR 851.

Nor did a price-fixing arrangement relating to cognac and the wine from which it was distilled, on the ground that spirits are expressly excluded from Annex I, despite their economic importance for agricultural producers in the area concerned.[87] Furthermore, it should be emphasized that Regulation 26/62 does not create an exemption from the prohibition of an abuse of a dominant position set out in art 82 of the EC Treaty. Thus, in Case 27/67 *United Brands v Commission*,[88] which concerned an abuse of a dominant position in the market of bananas, the fact that an agricultural product was involved made no difference to the application of the normal competition rules.

In the matter of state aids, on the other hand, Council Regulation 26 of 4 April 1962[89] does not apply the substantive Treaty rules to agricultural products. Art 4 of the regulation merely provides for the application of the first and third paragraphs of art 88 of the EC Treaty, providing for the review of existing systems of aid by the Commission and requiring the notification of new aids. Hence the application of the substantive state aids rules to trade in agricultural products depends on the terms of the regulations establishing common organizations of the market for the products in question. In fact, most common organizations of the market do provide for the application of arts 87 to 89 of the EC Treaty within their scope and 'save as otherwise provided in this Regulation'.[90] According to the Community Guidelines for state aid in the agriculture sector published by the Commission in February 2000,[91] the sectors not covered by a common organization and therefore not subject to the substantive state aid rules are potatoes (other than starch potatoes), horsemeat, honey, coffee, alcohol of agricultural origin and vinegars derived from alcohol, and cork.[92] For the products subject to common organization and which therefore are also subject to the state aid rules, the Guidelines make it clear that aid measures must contain some incentive element or require some counterpart on the part of the beneficiary, and that aids granted solely in the basis of price, quantity, unit of production, or unit of the means of production are considered to be operating aids incompatible with the common market.[93] Taking account of the requirements of art 6 of the EC Treaty, introduced by the Treaty of Amsterdam, that environmental protection requirements must be integrated into the definition and implementation of Community policies, the Guidelines also require that all state aid notifications contain an assessment of the environmental impact of the activity aided, even if the aid scheme is not specifically concerned with environmental issues.[94]

Whilst the Treaty provisions on state aids have themselves been held not to be of direct effect in the sense of creating rights enforceable by individuals before national courts, it was argued in Case 78/76 *Steinike und Weinlig v Germany*[95] that

[87] Case 123/83 *Bureau National Interprofessionnel du Cognac v Clair* [1985] ECR 391.
[88] [1978] ECR 207.   [89] JO 1962, p 993 (sp edn 1959–1962, p 129).
[90] See eg Council Regulation 1766/92 (OJ 1992 L181/21) on the common organization of the market in cereals, art 19.
[91] Corrected version published in OJ 2000 C232/17.
[92] Para 3.8.   [93] Para 3.5.   [94] Para 3.9.
[95] [1977] ECR 595.

their incorporation in a directly applicable regulation did render them so enforce-able. However, the Court of Justice, following Advocate General Warner, held that the inclusion of the state aids rules in an agricultural regulation did not alter their nature and scope; as Advocate General Warner pointed out, the effect was to lift the bar to their application which would otherwise have resulted from art 36 of the Treaty. In the result, it is therefore for the Commission to enforce the state aids rules within the common organization of agricultural markets, and this has led it to take decisions with regard to French aids to maintain farm incomes,[96] with regard to United Kingdom subsidies to users of fishing vessels,[97] and with regard to preferential tariffs charged on glasshouse growers for natural gas in the Netherlands.[98] So far as the notification of state aids is concerned, it is only the first sentence of art 88(3) of the Treaty which is applied to trade in agricultural products by art 4 of Regulation 26/62, and not the last sentence, which prohibits Member States from introducing the notified aid until the Commission has reached a decision and has been held to be directly effective as establishing proce-dural criteria which a national court can appraise in a line of cases beginning with Case 6/63 *Costa v ENEL*.[99]

Furthermore, much use is now made by the Commission of the principle laid down by the Court of Justice in Cases 15, 16/76 *France v Commission*[100] that the European Agricultural Guidance and Guarantee Fund may legitimately refuse to finance a Community aid provided under a common organization where a Member State supplements it with an illicit national aid. In that case, the French authorities added a supplementary national aid to the Community aid for the distillation of wines, and it was held that, as it was impossible to determine the quantity of wine which would have been distilled in France if there had been no national aid, the fund was not liable to reimburse France for any of the payments made.

On the other hand, it remains open to the Council, in the context of a common organization, to authorize a national aid. Thus Council Regulation 2799/98 estab-lishing agrimonetary arrangements for the euro,[101] provides for prices and amounts relating to the CAP to be fixed in euro and therefore eliminates any exchange risk for producers in the participating Member States. It nevertheless recognizes that producers in non-participant Member States are left to bear an exchange risk, and therefore authorizes those Member States to pay compensatory aid to farmers in cases of appreciable revaluation (as defined in the regulation) or where the exchange rate for certain aids or premiums is below that applicable previously.

Where, however, there is no common organization, there is no general applica-tion of the state aids rules to agricultural products, as has been expressly recognized by the Court of Justice in relation to the market in potatoes.[102] Particular difficulties

---

[96] Commission Decision 81/601 (OJ L220/37).
[97] Commission Decision 83/315 (OJ L169/38).
[98] Commission Decision 85/215 (OJ L97/49).				[99] [1964] ECR 585.
[100] [1979] ECR 321.				[101] OJ 1998 L349/1.
[102] Case 114/83 *Société d'Initiatives et de Coopération Agricoles v Commission* [1984] ECR 2589.

may therefore arise in so far as the free movement of goods rules do apply to agricultural products not subject to a common organization but the state aids rules do not. This was the background to the famous (or infamous) sheepmeat dispute with France, where France took the view that the United Kingdom system of deficiency payments constituted a state aid, yet the Court of Justice held that France could not prevent or restrict the import of sheepmeat which had benefited from the United Kingdom system.[103] A solution suggested by the Court was that nothing prevented the French authorities from adopting their own scheme of aids for the sheepmeat sector until a common organization of the market was established.

A more general solution was found in the continued use of art 38 of the EC Treaty, which provides that where an agricultural product is subject to a national market organization or equivalent rules in one Member State, which affect the competitive position of similar production in another Member State, a countervailing charge fixed by the Commission is to be applied by the other Member States to imports of the relevant product from that Member State, unless that state applies a countervailing charge on export. In effect this allows for countervailing charges to be imposed where national support measures give rise to low-priced (and presumably subsidized) exports. Whilst the development of common organizations has obviously limited the scope of this provision, it continued to be used after the end of the transitional period in a series of Commission regulations fixing countervailing charges on the import into Germany and the Benelux countries of ethyl alcohol of agricultural origin produced in France, although the Commission made it clear, as in the recitals to Commission Regulation 1407/78[104] in this series, that the real problem was the failure of the Council to legislate on the applicability of the state aids rules to this sector. This continued use of art 38 of the Treaty was upheld by the Court of Justice in the St Nikolaus Brennerei case,[105] where it was also held that art 38 could be invoked not only where a national organization continued lawfully to exist, but also where the national support measures might be incompatible with Community law. In that case, the imposition of countervailing charges to prevent distortion of competition could be coupled with enforcement proceedings against the Member State in question under art 226 of the Treaty.

Whilst at first sight art 38 might appear to authorize the imposition of charges equivalent to customs duties on imports from other Member States, it should be observed that these charges were not fixed unilaterally by the Member States but were fixed by the Commission to be applied by the Member States. It was clearly held in the sheepmeat case[106] that France had no power unilaterally to impose such charges on allegedly subsidized mutton and lamb exported from the United Kingdom to France. It may, however, be suggested that the real solution is to

---

[103] Case 232/78 Commission v France [1979] ECR 2729.

[104] OJ 1978 L170/24 (repealed by Commission Regulation 841/80 (OJ 1980 L90/30)).

[105] Case 337/82 St Nikolaus Brennerei und Likörfabrik, Gustav Kniepf-Melde GmbH v Hauptzollamt Krefeld [1984] ECR 1051.

[106] Case 232/78 Commission v France [1979] ECR 2729.

extend the state aids rules (which do allow for social and regional considerations) to agricultural products in general; in any event it may be doubted whether the Commission would regard the continued use of art 38 after the end of 1992 as being compatible with the concept of an area without internal frontiers in which there is free movement of goods under art 14(2) of the EC Treaty.

While Regulation 26 does not provide for the application of the substantive state aid rules to trade in agricultural products, the legislation establishing common organizations of agricultural markets usually provides for the enforcement of those rules in the sector covered by the specific organization, and Council Regulation 1257/1999[107] in principle applies the state aid rules to national measures to support rural development. The practical result is that the state aid rules can be invoked where there is a common organization, but not where the product is still subject to a national market organization—hence the need for the continued use of countervailing duties under art 38. Nevertheless, if the rules of a common organization are more severe than the general state aid rules, the former must prevail, as was held in Case 177/78 *Pigs and Bacon Commission v McCarren*,[108] where the payment of national export bonuses was found to breach the rules of the common organization of the market in pigmeat (thus avoiding the problem that the state aid rules cannot usually be invoked by individuals before national courts).

Status of special agricultural rules

Whilst art 32(2) of the EC Treaty, providing that the rules for the establishment of the common market are to apply to agricultural products 'save as otherwise provided in arts 33 to 38', may generally be regarded as authorizing derogations from the normal Treaty rules in favour of agricultural products, such as those resulting from art 36 with regard to the competition rules, it has also been interpreted as meaning that the general rules of the Treaty must give way to any stricter rules laid down in specific agricultural legislation. This first clearly appeared in Case 83/78 *Pigs Marketing Board v Redmond*,[109] which concerned the marketing system operated by the Northern Ireland Pigs Marketing Board, where the United Kingdom argued that the board was a 'state monopoly' within the meaning of art 31 of the EC Treaty, and that by virtue of art 44 of the Act of Accession (1972) it would not require to be adjusted in accordance with that provision until 31 December 1977 (the facts giving rise to the action having occurred on 12 January 1977). The Court of Justice, however, pointed out that the production and marketing of pigs was governed by a common organization of the market, by then contained in Council Regulation 2759/75,[110] which applied in the United Kingdom from 1 February 1973 by virtue of art 60(1) of the Act of Accession

---

[107] OJ 1999 L160/80.   [108] [1979] ECR 2161.   [109] [1978] ECR 2347.
[110] OJ 1975 L282/1.

(1972), and held quite simply that the provisions of the Treaty relating to the common agricultural policy have precedence, by virtue of art 32(2) of the EC Treaty, over the other rules relating to the establishment of the common market, in case of any discrepancy, so that the longer period of grace allowed to state monopolies was not relevant. The rules of the common organization were interpreted as requiring every producer to have access to an open market regulated solely by the instruments provided for by that organization, with the result that any national provisions which prevented producers from buying and selling freely within the state in which they were established were incompatible with the principles of the common organization.

This principle of the precedence of agricultural legislation was repeated in Case 177/78 *Pigs and Bacon Commission v McCarren*,[111] which concerned a levy raised by the Irish Pigs and Bacon Commission and used, among other things, to finance an 'export bonus'. The same point about state monopolies arose, but also in that case an issue arose as to the provision in the regulation establishing the common organization which provided for the application of arts 87 to 89 of the treaty on state aids 'save as otherwise provided in this regulation'. It was held that the application of the general state aid rules (which permit certain aids, and are not substantively directly effective so as to be enforceable by individuals before national courts) was subordinate to the provisions governing the common organization. Regulation 2759/75 on the common organization of the market in pigmeat, and the provisions on the free movement of goods held to be an integral part of it, did not appear expressly to prohibit the payment of bonuses. The Court of Justice nonetheless found that according to the idea on which the regulation dealing with the common organization of the market in pigmeat was based, the products referred to in it were in fact required to move freely within the Community at the price level resulting from the operation of the machinery for the common organization of the market. Neither Member States nor agencies on which they had conferred powers were entitled to create advantages for the marketing of national products as against those of other Member States by means of financial machinery such as the grant of bonuses. Hence, irrespective of the general state aids rules, national export subsidies may not be paid where there is a common organization of the market.

Legal requirement for common organizations and policies

It has already been observed that in the absence of a common organization, agricultural products, whether or not covered by a national organization of the market, become subject to the general rules of the common market with regard to

---

[111] [1979] ECR 2161.

importation, exportation, and movement within the Community.[112] Perhaps of greater practical importance, however, is the legal vacuum which may be created in so far as Member States are unable to take protective measures. Thus, in Case 68/76 *Commission v France*,[113] which involved French restrictions on the export of potatoes, France claimed that, in the absence of a common organization, Member States could, under arts 33 to 38 of the EC Treaty, still take measures of a short-term nature derogating from the basic Treaty rules on free movement. The Court of Justice held, however, that after the end of the transitional period arts 33 to 38 could not justify a unilateral derogation from (in this case) art 29 forbidding measures having equivalent effect to quantitative restrictions on exports, even if no common organization had been introduced. It added that far from there being a lacuna for Member States to fill, by reason of the transfer of power to the Community, and the reason for that transfer, problems such as (in this case) the potato shortage should from the end of the transitional period be settled by Community measures taken in the interest of all producers and consumers in the Community.

A similar view was expressed in the sheepmeat case,[114] where the Court, whilst recognizing the difficulties involved, reaffirmed that after the expiry of the transitional period, those matters and sectors 'specifically assigned to the Community' are the responsibility of the Community, so that a decision to adopt any necessary special measures could no longer be made unilaterally by the Member States concerned. It added that the fact that this had not been done did not justify the maintenance by a Member State of a national organization of the market features of which were incompatible with the Treaty requirements relating to the free movement of goods.

This inability of a Member-State to act unilaterally except in accordance with the general Treaty rules was emphasized once more in Case 288/83 *Commission v Ireland*,[115] where it was held that the Irish government could not prevent the import of Cyprus potatoes in free circulation in the United Kingdom. However, the strongest statement of the inability of a Member State to act in the absence of a common organization or policy occurred in the context of fisheries. Under art 102 of the Act of Accession (1972) a common policy on fisheries conservation measures should have been adopted by the end of 1978, but the common policy was not in fact adopted until January 1983. The position after the end of 1978 came before the Court of Justice in Case 804/79 *Commission v United Kingdom*,[116] where the United Kingdom argued that, even after the expiry of the period laid down in art 102, Member States retained residual powers and duties until the Community had fully exercised its powers, but the Court firmly held that 'Member States are . . . no longer entitled to exercise any power of their own in the matter of conservation measures in the waters under their jurisdiction', at

---

[112] Case 288/83 *Commission v Ireland* [1985] ECR 1761.
[113] [1977] ECR 515.   [114] Case 232/78 *Commission v France* [1979] ECR 2729.
[115] [1985] ECR 1761.   [116] [1981] ECR 1045.

least with regard to resources to which the fishermen of the other Member States have an equal right of access (which left the question open with regard to exclusive zones). Furthermore, although the Council had not taken the relevant conservation measures, 'the transfer to the Community of powers in this matter being total and definitive, such a failure to act could not in any case restore to the Member States the power and freedom to act unilaterally in this field', thus repeating the view the Court had taken ten years earlier with regard to the supply provisions of the Euratom Treaty.[117] In the result, it was stated that in principle conservation measures must remain as they were at the end of 1978, subject to amendment to take account of biological and technological developments, but that Member States had no power to lay down new conservation policies. With regard to such amendments, or the introduction of necessary interim conservation measures, the Member States may only act as trustees of the common interest so that they become under a duty not only to undertake detailed consultations with the Council and to seek its approval in good faith, but also not to lay down national conservation measures in spite of objections, reservations, or conditions which might be formulated by the Commission.

This approach may perhaps be explained by the fact that the Court of Justice has derived an exclusive external competence from the Community's internal competence with regard to fisheries,[118] and the internal and external aspects of fisheries policy are so interlinked that the exclusivity of the one must be reflected in the other. Be that as it may, the effective result is that where there is a legal requirement for a common organization or policy, there is also a practical need for such an organization or policy, at least where protective or interventionist measures are regarded as desirable.[119]

Protection of health

Measures taken to protect the health of humans, animals, and plants are self-evidently likely to be encountered in trade in agricultural products, and as a matter of law they represent an area where the general Treaty rules may be particularly relevant to trade in agricultural products. It should however be said at the outset that national measures to protect health both under art 30 of the EC Treaty and under the case-law concept of the protection of mandatory requirements may only be justified where the matter at issue is not governed by provisions of Community law[120] or where the national measures are authorized by provisions of Community law. More particularly, a Member State may not invoke its own legislation where

---

[117] Case 7/71 *Commission v France* [1971] ECR 1003.
[118] Cases 3, 4, 6/76 *Officier van Justitie v Kramer* [1976] ECR 1279; see also *Opinion 1/94* [1994] ECR I-5267.
[119] The issue of exclusive Community competence is considered at greater length in Chapter 7.
[120] See Case 25/88 *Wurmser* [1989] ECR 1105 at 1128.

EC directives expressly require a Member State to allow the marketing of goods which comply with the provisions of those directives,[121] and national legislation will not be justified if the Community legislation is intended to regulate the matter at issue in a comprehensive manner. This was clearly shown in Case 28/84 *Commission v Germany*,[122] where a series of animal foodstuffs directives were found to create a comprehensive system with regard to the composition and preparation of animal foodstuffs, so that Germany could not lay down its own rules on minimum and maximum levels of certain ingredients. Similarly, where Community law sets up a comprehensive system of health controls on export, as in trade in fresh poultrymeat, the importing Member State may no longer impose systematic checks on importation under its own law.[123] Thus in the 2001 outbreak of foot-and-mouth disease in the UK, the UK measures were largely taken within the framework of Council Directive 85/511 on Community measures for the control of foot-and-mouth disease[124] and subject to specific Commission decisions[125] taken under powers conferred by some twelve different directives concerned with animal and public health.[126] There is however one respect in which the enactment of comprehensive Community legislation no longer appears totally to exclude national legislation. Following amendments made by the Treaty of Amsterdam, to the extent that health measures adopted under the common agricultural policy may be regarded as measures of 'harmonization', art 95 of the EC Treaty envisages situations where Member States may be allowed to maintain national provisions or even introduce new national provisions despite the adoption of Community measures. Under art 95(4), if, after the adoption by the Council or by the Commission of a harmonization measure, a Member State deems it necessary to *maintain* national provisions on grounds of major needs referred to in art 30,[127] or relating to the protection of the environment or the working environment, it is required to notify the Commission of these provisions as well as the grounds for maintaining them. Furthermore, under art 95(5), if, after the adoption by the Council or by the Commission of a harmonization measure, a Member State deems it necessary to *introduce* national provisions based on new scientific evidence relating to the protection of the environment or the working environment on grounds of a problem specific to that Member State arising after the adoption of the harmonization

---

[121] Case 148/78 *Ratti* [1979] ECR 1629, which concerned directives on the labelling of paints and varnishes.

[122] [1985] ECR 3097.

[123] Case 190/87 *Moormann* [1988] ECR 4689, Case 186/88 *Commission v Germany* [1989] ECR 3997.

[124] OJ 1985 L315/11.

[125] Commission Decision 2001/172 (OJ 2001 L62/22) amended and consolidated in Commission Decision 2001/356 (OJ 2001 L125/46).

[126] According to the list contained in the recitals to Commission Decision 2001/356 (OJ 2001 L125/46).

[127] For a discussion of this phrase see N Green, T Hartley, and J Usher, *Legal Foundations of the Single European Market* (1991) at 85–86.

measure, it is again required to notify the Commission of the envisaged provisions as well as the grounds for introducing them. In both cases, the Commission is required within six months of the notifications to approve or reject the national provisions involved after having verified whether or not they are a means of arbitrary discrimination or a disguised restriction on trade between Member States and whether or not they constitute an obstacle to the functioning of the internal market, although in the absence of a decision by the Commission within this period the national provisions are deemed to have been approved, unless the Commission notifies the Member State concerned that the period should be extended for a further period of up to six months, when justified by the complexity of the matter and in the absence of danger for human health. It is also provided in art 95(7) and (8) that when a Member State is authorized to maintain or introduce national provisions derogating from a harmonization measure, the Commission must immediately examine whether to propose an adaptation to that measure, and that when a Member State raises a specific problem on public health in a field which has been the subject of prior harmonization measures, it must bring it to the attention of the Commission which must immediately examine whether to propose appropriate measures to the Council.

The art 95 derogations clearly might justify the maintenance of national provisions relating to health which would be justifiable as restrictions on the free movement of goods. However, new national measures can only be justified under the very narrow criteria laid down in art 95(5): new scientific evidence relating to the protection of the environment or the working environment on grounds of a problem specific to that Member State arising after the adoption of the harmonization measure. In any event, in both cases, the national measures in principle require the authorization of the Commission, which appears to confirm that it is a matter of Community rather than national competence.

In so far as Community health measures have been taken, they are not necessarily coterminous with the development of common organizations. Historically, they took the form of separate Council directives issued under the dual authority of art 37 of the EC Treaty, relating to the common agricultural policy, and art 94, which is the general provision relating to the approximation of laws. Ironically, however, some of the early Community health legislation did relate to products which even now are still not yet subject to common organizations, such as Council Directives 69/464 and 69/465,[128] respectively concerned with the control of potato wart disease and the control of potato cyst eelworm. However, from the 1980s until the entry into force of the current text of art 152 of the EC Treaty on the protection of human health, Community health legislation relating to agricultural products, such as Council Directive 85/649[129] prohibiting the use in livestock farming of certain substances having a hormonal action, was adopted under

---

[128] JO 1969 L323/1, 3 (sp edn 1969 (II), pp 561, 563).
[129] OJ 1985 L382/228.

art 37 of the Treaty alone. This practice was tested in two actions brought by the United Kingdom against the Council with regard to the legal base for the directive on the use of hormones in beef, and a directive on the minimum standards for keeping battery hens, in Cases 68/86 and 131/86 *United Kingdom v Council*.[130] The European Court held that agricultural legislation could not ignore requirements of general interest such as consumer protection or the protection of the health and life of both humans and animals, so the fact that it pursued those requirements did not take it outside the scope of art 37 if it regulated the production and marketing of agricultural products. This approach was continued more recently in Case C-269/97 *Commission and European Parliament v Council*,[131] where the Commission and Parliament argued that Council Regulation 820/97[132] on the identification and registration of bovine animals and the labelling of beef and beef products, introduced as a reaction to the BSE crisis, should have been adopted as an internal market measure under art 95 (which involves co-decision with the Parliament) rather than under art 37 (which only involves consultation of the Parliament). The Court held that it was entirely appropriate to take account of public health considerations in the context of art 37, particularly in the light of the introduction of the then art 129, the predecessor of the current art 152, which required that health protection measures should form a constituent part of the Community's other policies.

Art 152 as amended by the Treaty of Amsterdam allows the adoption of measures, 'by way of derogation from art.37', in the veterinary and phytosanitary fields which have as their direct objective the protection of public health. It is therefore of some interest to observe that the successor regulation to Council Regulation 820/97,[133] EP and Council Regulation 1760/2000 on the identification and registration of bovine animals and the labelling of beef and beef products[134] was adopted (by co-decision) on the joint legal base of art 37 and art 152. It seems that this will be the pattern for the future so far as measures intended to protect human health are concerned. Indeed EP and Council Regulation 999/2001 on transmissible spongiform encephalopathies adopted in 2001,[135] following more than sixty Commission decisions on BSE from 1989 onwards based on safeguard clauses for emergency measures in various directives on animal and public health,[136] was adopted under art 152(4)(b) alone. The same legal base was also used for EP and Council Directive 2001/10[137] amending Council Directive 91/68[138] as regards scrapie, whereas the original 1991 directive had been based on art 37 of the EC Treaty.

Be that as it may, the use of art 37 does enable a wide range of matters to be taken into consideration. In its series of judgments with regard to the prohibition of hormones in beef, the European Court stated that 'in view of the divergent

[130] [1988] ECR 855 and 905 . [131] 4 April 2000. [132] OJ 1997 L117/1.
[133] Ibid [134] OJ 2000 L204/1. [135] OJ 2001 L147/1.
[136] See Commission Press Release IP/01/641 (3 May 2001).
[137] OJ 2001 L147/41. [138] OJ 1991 L46/19.

appraisals which had been made, traders were not entitled to expect that a prohibition on administering the substances in question to animals could be based on
scientific data alone'.[139] It was further held that the requirement of what was then
Council Directive 81/602 on the prohibition of certain substances having a
hormonal action[140] that the Commission should take account of scientific developments did not pre-empt 'the conclusions which may be drawn therefrom by
the Council in the exercise of its discretion'.[141] This may be contrasted with the
insistence by the WTO Appellate Body[142] on the production of scientific evidence
when these measures were challenged as being in breach of the Uruguay Round
Agreement on the Application of Sanitary and Phytosanitary Measures.[143]

It has generally been accepted by the Court of Justice that such Community
measures are not a hindrance to intra-Community trade but are intended to
achieve the gradual abolition of measures adopted unilaterally by the Member
States which might be regarded as justified under the general Treaty rules despite
their restrictive effect on trade between Member States.[144] It has been held that
the Community measures themselves must have due regard to freedom of trade
within the Community,[145] but the Court has accepted that it was justifiable for
Council Directive 77/93[146] on protective measures against the introduction into
the Member States of harmful organisms of plants or plant products, which in
principle required inspection to be carried out by the exporting Member State
and allowed only sampling in the importing Member State, to define sampling as
inspections carried out on up to one-third of the consignments introduced from
a given Member State.[147]

On the other hand, it is clear that Community legislation may restrict exports
from one Member State to the rest of the Community in order to protect the rest
of the Community from a risk arising in that Member State. This may be illustrated
by Commission Decision 96/239[148] on emergency measures to protect against BSE,
which prohibited all exports of bovine animals, beef, veal, or derived products from
the UK. The prohibition extended not only to exports to other Member States,
but also to all other exports, so as to prevent deflection of trade. The validity of this
prohibition was upheld in Case C-180/96R *UK v Commission*.[149] A similar prohibition on export may be found for example in Commission Decision 2001/356 on
protection measures with regard to foot-and-mouth disease in the UK.[150]

[139] Case C-331/88 *R v SoS for Health ex p Fedesa* [1990] ECR I-4023 at para 10.
[140] OJ 1981 L222/32.
[141] Case C-331/88 *R v SoS for Health ex p Fedesa* [1990] ECR I-4023 at para 10.
[142] WT/DS26/AB/R and WT/DS48/AB/R.
[143] A highly perceptive analysis of this difference of approach may be found in J Scott, 'On Kith
and Kine (and Crustaceans): Trade and the Environment in the EU and WTO' in J Weiler (ed), *The
EU, the WTO and the NAFTA: Towards a Common Law of International Trade* (2000) 125–167.
[144] Case 37/83 *Rewe Zentral AG v Direktor der Landwirtschaftskammer Rheinland* [1984] ECR 1229.
[145] Case 37/83 (n 142 above), at 1248, 1249, and at 600.
[146] OJ 1977 L26/20.
[147] Case 37/83 (n 142 above), at 1249 and at 600, 601.   [148] OJ 1996 L78/47.
[149] [1996] ECR 1–3903.   [150] OJ 2001 L125/46.

Where the holding of inspections is governed by Community law, it would appear that Member States cannot claim that parallel inspections under national law may be justifiable under the general rules of the EC Treaty,[151] but it has been held that where directives regulated the composition and preparation of animal foodstuffs, but did not regulate health inspections of these products, Member States could still justify national health inspections under the general Treaty rules.[152] Under these rules, total or partial restrictions on the import or export of goods, and inspections carried out by reason of import or export, are in principle prohibited as measures equivalent to quantitative restrictions on imports and exports under arts 28 and 29 of the Treaty,[153] but they may be justified under art 30 if they are intended to protect the health and life of humans, animals, or plants, provided they do not constitute a means of arbitrary discrimination or a disguised restriction on trade between Member States.

Before turning to a detailed consideration of art 30, however, attention should be drawn to its relationship to the 'mandatory requirements' recognized by the Court in its judgment in Case 120/78 *Rewe v Bundesmonopolverwaltung für Branntwein*.[154] The Court there stated that, while a national trading rule applying equally to domestic and imported products (in this case, relating to the alcoholic strength of 'cassis de Dijon') could well have the effect of preventing the sale within a Member State of goods legitimately marketed in another Member State, 'obstacles to movement within the Community resulting from disparities between the national laws relating to the marketing of the products in question must be accepted in so far as those provisions may be recognised as being necessary in order to satisfy mandatory requirements relating in particular to the effectiveness of fiscal supervision, the protection of public health, the fairness of commercial transactions and the defence of the consumer'. However, a national trading rule constituting such an obstacle which is not necessary to satisfy a mandatory requirement may be categorized as a measure equivalent to a quantitative restriction on imports prohibited by art 28 of the EC Treaty. Hence, there is a potential overlap between this case law and art 30: under the *Cassis de Dijon* doctrine, a measure applying equally to domestic and imported products which is necessary for the protection of health will not constitute a measure equivalent to a quantitative restriction; on the other hand, the justification under art 30 is only triggered if the measure is prima facie equivalent to a quantitative restriction; yet, for a measure relating to imports to be justified under art 30 it has long been held that effective measures for the same purpose must be taken with regard to domestic production.[155]

However, although protection of health was considered in the *Cassis de Dijon* case itself, it would appear to be the current practice of the Court to consider

---

[151] This is by analogy with Case 148/78 *Pubblico Ministero v Ratti* [1979] ECR 1629.
[152] Case 73/84 *Denkavit Futtermittel GmbH v Land Nordhein-Westfalen* [1985] ECR 1019.
[153] See eg Case 4/75 *Rewe-Zentralfinanz v Landwirtschaftskammer Bonn* [1975] ECR 843.
[154] [1979] ECR 649.
[155] Case 4/75 *Rewe-Zentralfinanz v Landwirtschaftskammer Bonn* [1975] ECR 843.

whether measures are justified on health grounds in the light of art 30, even if those measures are equally applicable to domestic products as well as to imports. Hence, in Case 97/83 *Melkunie*[156] which was concerned with Dutch legislation relating to the presence of active coliform bacteria and active micro-organisms in milk products, the Fifth Chamber held that this 'equally applicable' legislation was prima facie a measure having equivalent effect to a quantitative restriction, in so far as it prohibited the marketing of goods lawfully produced and marketed in the exporting Member State, but that it was justified under art 30.

In the context of differing national views of what is needed to protect health, it would, in fact, appear to be the Court's practice to accept the more restrictive approach where there is shown to be scientific disagreement as to the safe levels of bacteria, additives,[157] or pesticides.[158] A similar approach to the assessment of risk where there is scientific disagreement has been taken with regard to the Community's own health legislation. Thus the validity of the prohibition of all exports of bovine animals, beef, veal, or derived products from the UK imposed by Commission Decision 96/239[159] on emergency measures to protect against BSE was upheld in Case C-180/96R *UK v Commission*[160] despite evidence that there was not scientific agreement as to the risk.

To fall within the protection of art 30 of the EC Treaty, and thus not offend against the prohibitions on quantitative restrictions, a national measure must constitute a 'seriously considered health policy', which was held, in Case 40/82 *Commission v United Kingdom*,[161] not to be the case with regard to the British policy adopted in 1981 imposing a prohibition on imports into Great Britain of poultrymeat and eggs from all other Member States except Denmark and Ireland. The expressed aim of this prohibition was to enable Newcastle disease (of which the last outbreak in Great Britain had been in 1978, and the last outbreak in France in 1976) to be combated by a slaughter policy, and the import restrictions were intended to ensure that imports could only be accepted from Member States (namely Denmark and Ireland) which were totally free from Newcastle disease, which prohibited the use of vaccine, and which imposed compulsory slaughter requirements in the event of an outbreak of the disease. The Court of Justice doubted that this was a seriously considered health policy, because it was introduced in a matter of days, whereas the previous change to a policy of vaccination in 1964 had been preceded by elaborate reports and studies, it followed domestic pressure to restrict the growing imports of French poultry products, it was timed to exclude French turkeys from the 1981 Christmas market, and the prohibition on French imports was not lifted when the French changed their policy so as to accord with the three conditions stated by the British authorities. Furthermore, to

---

[156] [1984] ECR 2367.   [157] Case 53/80 *Kaasfabriek Eyssen* [1981] ECR 409.
[158] Case 54/85 *Mirepoix* [1986] ECR 1067.
[159] OJ 1996 L78/47.   [160] [1996] ECR 1-3903.
[161] [1982] ECR 2793. It was this judgment which led to the action for damages in *Bourgoin SA v Ministry of Agriculture, Fisheries and Food* [1986] QB 716.

avoid being categorized as arbitrary discrimination, measures with regard to imports must be matched by effective measures taken with regard to domestic products.[162]

Assuming that it does fall within a seriously considered health policy, in order to be justified under art 30 of the EC Treaty a national measure must be reasonable, or proportionate to the objective it pursues. Hence, in the poultrymeat case,[163] it was held that a total prohibition on imports could only be justified if the United Kingdom could show that it was the only possibility open to it, and the Court of Justice took the view that less stringent measures could have been used. A total ban may, however, be permissible in the case of prohibited additives, as in the Dutch rules prohibiting the addition of nisin to processed cheese for sale on the Dutch market, which were at issue in the *Kaasfabriek Eyssen* case.[164] The proportionality rule was particularly considered in Case 124/81 *Commission v United Kingdom*[165] where it was held that the functions served by the United Kingdom requirement that an import licence be obtained to import UHT milk could equally well be met by declarations by importers, and that the functions served by the United Kingdom requirement that imported UHT milk be retreated (which was effectively a prohibition on imports) could equally well be met by a requirement that importers produce certificates issued by the competent authorities of the exporting Member States coupled with controls by means of samples. This matter has subsequently been regulated by a directive on health and animal health problems affecting intra-Community trade in heat-treated milk.[166]

In general the Court of Justice has taken the view, however, that for a Member State both to require a certificate from the exporting Member State and to carry out itself systematic inspection of the imported goods goes beyond what may be justified under art 30 of the Treaty.[167] In the *United Foods* case[168] it was held that although a Member State could still carry out health inspections of fish, it was a disguised restriction on trade to require twenty-four hours' notice to be given before imported fish could be inspected, given that fresh fish was a highly perishable commodity.

Where a health inspection is justified under art 30 of the EC Treaty, or it is required by Community law, the further problem arises as to whether the Member State may charge for carrying it out. In trade between Member States, the Court of Justice has consistently held that unless a national charge falls within the general scope of internal taxation or constitutes payment for a service to the particular importer or exporter (rather than a service in the general interest[169]), it will be prohibited as a charge equivalent to a customs duty under art 25 of the Treaty.

---

[162] See eg Case 4/75 *Rewe-Zentralfinanz v Landwirtschaftskammer Bonn* [1975] ECR 843.
[163] Case 40/82 *Commission v United Kingdom* [1982] ECR 2793.
[164] Case 53/80 *Officier van Justitie v Koninklijke Kaasfabriek Eyssen BV* [1981] ECR 409.
[165] [1983] ECR 203.
[166] Council Directive 85/397 (OJ 1985 L226/13).
[167] Case 251/78 *Denkavit Futtermittel GmbH v Minister für Ernährung* [1979] ECR 3369.
[168] Case 132/80 *United Foods BV v Belgium* [1981] ECR 995.
[169] This was held with regard to quality controls in Case 63/74 *W Cadsky SpA v Istituto nazionale per il Commercio Estero* [1975] ECR 281.

This was confirmed in a case in relation to Danish inspections of groundnuts and groundnut products which were agreed to be justified under art 30.[170] On the other hand, charges may be levied where inspections are carried out by national authorities pursuant to requirements of Community law. The Court was faced with this problem in the *Bauhuis* case,[171] a reference for a preliminary ruling from a Dutch court in proceedings brought by a cattle dealer to recover fees paid for the veterinary public health inspections of certain animals carried out by the Netherlands authorities before the export of those animals. Basically the question at issue was whether these fees constituted charges having equivalent effect to customs duties on exports. It would appear that certain of the fees were paid on the inspection of bovine animals and swine required by an Council directive on animal health problems affecting intra-Community trade in bovine animals and swine.[172] On the other hand, some of the fees related to inspections other than those laid down by the directive or on animals other than those referred to in the directive, and carried out solely under national law. The Court dealt with these two situations separately.

With regard to the inspections carried out under the directive, the Court pointed out that the directive harmonized the animal health measures in force in the Member States by making it obligatory for them to standardize domestic provisions in this field in accordance with the requirements of the directive. The harmonization or approximation required by the directive would appear mainly to have consisted in imposing upon Member States exporting cattle the obligation to ensure compliance with certain veterinary and public health measures intended, among other things, to guarantee that the exported animals are not a source of contagious disease. Of course to comply with the directive, a Member State usually had to introduce legislation of its own, but the Court pointed out that the measures in question were not prescribed by each Member State in order to protect some interest of its own but by the Council in the general interest of the Community; and so the Court deduced that they could not therefore be regarded as unilateral measures which hinder trade but rather as operations intended to promote the free movement of goods, in particular by rendering ineffective the obstacles to this free movement which might be created by the measures for veterinary and public health inspections adopted pursuant to art 30 of the Treaty. The Court concluded that fees charged for inspections required by Community law which are uniform and are required to be carried out before dispatch within the exporting country do not constitute charges having an effect equivalent to customs duties on exports provided they do not exceed the actual cost of the inspection for which they were charged. Indeed the Court went so far as to say that the reasons for the prohibition of any obstacle to intra-Community trade, whether such an obstacle takes the form

---

[170] Case 158/82 *Commission v Denmark* [1983] ECR 3573.
[171] Case 46/76 *Bauhuis v Netherlands* [1977] ECR 5.
[172] Council Directive 64/432 (OJ 1964, p 1977 (sp edn 1963–1964, p 164)).

of charges having an effect equivalent to customs duties or of measures having effect equivalent to quantitative restrictions, do not apply to this case. This approach has been maintained in the post-1992 single internal market.[173]

A Community system of charges was introduced by Council Directive 85/73 on the financing of veterinary inspections and controls required by specific Community legislation.[174] Under this directive, Member States are required to ensure that a Community fee is collected to cover the cost occasioned by inspections of and controls on slaughter, cutting and storage, imports of meat, and fishery products (Annex A), live animals, and products of animal origin (Annexes B and C). These fees are in general of a flat-rate nature (ie per animal or per tonne of the relevant product) and are now set in euro.[175] However, while there is an obligation to collect these Community fees, under art 5(2) of the directive, Member States are authorized to charge an amount exceeding the levels of the Community fees provided that the total fees do not exceed the actual cost of inspection. In effect therefore, the overall parameter set by the previous case law remains relevant, and it has been held in Case C-374/97 *Feyrer v Landkreis Rottal-Inn*[176] that, because of this possibility, a trader cannot claim a directly effective right to pay the fees set out in the directive.

A similar approach has been taken in the case law with regard to fees payable for inspections under international agreements. In Case 89/76 *Commission v Netherlands*[177] the Court applied the same criteria to hold that fees (not exceeding the actual cost) could be charged for phytosanitary inspections carried out under the 1951 International Plant Protection Convention,[178] to which all the Member States were party, since these inspections were not unilateral measures but were intended to assist the free movement of goods.

On the other hand, with regard to the charges for the inspections carried out under Dutch law alone, the Court said that the reasons which render lawful the collection of appropriate duties for the carrying out of uniform Community inspections of general application cannot be applied to situations which continue to consist of obstacles set up unilaterally, even if the domestic inspections are measures for the promotion of exports. The Court therefore concluded that fees charged by the exporting state for inspections carried out by the authorities of that state which are not required by Community regulation or directive, but which have been prescribed for the purpose of checking whether the conditions to which the Member State of destination has made the importation subject have been complied with, constitute charges having an effect equivalent to customs duties.[179]

[173] See eg Case C-109/98 *CRT France International* [1999] ECR I-2237 at para 19.

[174] Consolidated text printed as an annex to Council Directive 96/43 (OJ 1996 L162/1).

[175] Transitional measures were provided in Commission Regulation 807/1999 (OJ 1999 L102/68).

[176] [1999] ECR I-5153.

[177] [1977] ECR 1355.

[178] International Plant Protection Convention (Rome, 6 December 1951; TS 16 (1954); Cmd 9077).

[179] An approach followed more recently in Case C-109/98 *CRT France International* [1999] ECR I-2237 at para 19.

Different considerations have to be borne in mind where inspections are carried out at the external frontier of the Community on products imported directly from non-Member States. Regulations establishing common organizations of the market generally prohibit charges having an equivalent effect to customs duties in trade with third countries, such as Council Regulation 805/68, the original legislation on the common organization of the market in beef and veal[180] which was at issue in the *Marimex* case,[181] and which contained a proviso 'save as otherwise provided in this regulation or where derogation therefrom is decided by the Council'.[182] However, in Case 70/77 *Simmenthal SpA v Amministrazione delle Finanze dello Stato*,[183] following the opinion of Advocate General Warner, the Court of Justice held that the prohibition had a different aim and a different basis in internal and external Community trade. In internal trade it is intended to secure the free movement of goods, but in external trade the prohibition must be considered in the light of the requirements of the common commercial policy and the Common Customs Tariff, notably that imports from third countries should be subject to uniform treatment. In particular, the Court held that the principle laid down in the *Bauhuis* case[184] does not apply to trade with third countries. Although the Court did not say so in as many words, there is, of course, no Community policy in favour of the free movement of goods into the Community from third countries: indeed the prohibition here is not so much on charges having equivalent effect to customs duties as such but on their imposition by Member States individually in such a manner as to upset the uniform external protection of the Community. The Court in fact held that the Council and Commission may create exceptions or derogations from the prohibition on such charges, provided that the ensuing charges have a uniform effect in all Member States in trade with third countries.

The question whether the *Bauhuis* principle applied arose because of the enactment of Council Directive 72/462[185] on health and veterinary inspection problems upon importation of bovine animals and swine and fresh meat from third countries. This required Member States to carry out certain health inspections on animals and meat, and to charge for such inspections. The charging provisions are drafted in a similar way and, if art 23(4) might be taken as an example, provide that 'all expenditure incurred pursuant to this article shall be chargeable to the consignor, the consignee or their agents, without repayment by the state'. The question of its effect did not finally prove relevant since the Court held that the charges it required to be imposed must be related to inspections carried out under the terms of the directive. It was, however, found that the Community measures

---

[180] Council Regulation 805/68 (JO 1968 L148/24 (sp edn 1968 (I), p 187)), art 20(2).

[181] Case 84/71 *Marimex SpA v Italian Ministry for Finance* [1972] ECR 89.

[182] A similar provision continues in force under art 35(2) of the current Council Regulation 1254/1999 on the common organization of the market in beef and veal (OJ 1999 L160/21).

[183] [1978] ECR 1453.

[184] Case 46/76 *Bauhuis v Netherlands* [1977] ECR 5.

[185] JO 1972 L302/28 (sp edn 1972 (31 December) (3), p 7).

required to implement the directive had not in fact been taken, with the result that it was not possible to carry out the inspections under the directive, and the directive could not justify the levying of any charges. This defect was subsequently rectified by the enactment of Council Directive 85/73[186] on the financing of health inspection and controls of fresh meat and poultrymeat. In the interim, legislation such as art 9 of Council Directive 64/433[187] and art 11 of Council Directive 72/461[188] on health problems affecting intra-Community trade in fresh meat provided that, in the absence of Community provisions relating to imports from third countries, national provisions relating to such imports should not be more favourable than those governing intra-Community trade. In the event, the Court had to accept in the *Simmenthal* case that in such a case a Member State must hold and charge for inspections where such inspections would be held and could be charged for in internal Community trade, and in Case 30/79 *Land Berlin v Wigei*[189] it even accepted that such charges could exceed those levied on inspections of Community products, provided they were not manifestly disproportionate. Although this may avoid reverse discrimination against Community products, it hardly aids the preservation of the uniformity of the Community's external stance, although the Court asserted in Case 1/83 *IFG Intercontinentale Fleischhandelsgesellschaft mbH & Co KG v Freistaat Bayern*[190] that there was no risk of diversion of trade if the charge for a health inspection did not exceed the cost of carrying it out.

In effect, this remains the solution under the revised text of Council Directive 85/73 on the financing of veterinary inspections and controls required by specific Community legislation.[191] As mentioned in the context of inspections in internal Community trade, this directive requires Member States to ensure that a Community fee is collected to cover the cost occasioned by inspections of and controls on, inter alia, imports from third countries of meat. These fees are in general of a flat-rate nature (ie per animal or per tonne of the relevant product). However, while there is an obligation to collect these Community fees, under art 5(2) of the directive, Member States are authorized to charge an amount exceeding the levels of the Community fees provided that the total fees do not exceed the actual cost of inspection.

---

[186] OJ 1985 L32/14. [187] JO 1964 p. 2012 (sp edn 1963–1964, p 185).
[188] JO 1972 L302/24 (sp edn 1972 (31 December) (3), p 3).
[189] [1980] ECR 151. [190] [1984] ECR 349.
[191] Consolidated text printed as an annex to Council Directive 96/43 (OJ 1996 L162/1).

2

Aims, objectives, and principles of the common agricultural policy

Aims and objectives

Article 33 of the EC Treaty sets out five express objectives of the common agricultural policy and three further matters of which account should be taken. The five express objectives are:

1. to increase agricultural productivity by promoting technical progress and by ensuring the rational development of agricultural production and the optimum utilization of the factors of production, in particular labour;
2. to ensure a fair standard of living for the agricultural community, in particular by increasing the individual earnings of persons engaged in agriculture;
3. to stabilize markets;
4. to ensure the availability of supplies; and
5. to ensure that supplies reach consumers at reasonable prices.

As will be self-evident, in economic and political reality these objectives are not easy to reconcile, and the Court of Justice has in fact recognized that the Community institutions may allow any one of these objectives 'temporary priority in order to satisfy the demands of the economic factors or conditions in view of which their decisions are made'.[1]

In practice most common organizations were originally based on a common price system for key products, although the twin pressures of the need to reduce surplus production led in the 1990s to reduction in guaranteed prices for the products, and a greater emphasis on direct payments to producers. In general the Court of Justice has treated these mechanisms as being intended to give certain guarantees of income to agricultural producers, thus fulfilling the second objective of art 33(1) of the EC Treaty, rather than for the benefit of those further down the distributive chain. An illustration of this is Case 2/75 *Einfuhr- und Vorratsstelle für Getreide und Futtermittel v Mackprang*,[2] which was a reference for a preliminary ruling as to the

---

[1] Case 5/73 *Balkan-Import-Export GmbH v Hauptzollamt Berlin-Packhof* [1973] ECR 1091.
[2] [1975] ECR 607.

validity of a Commission decision of 8 May 1969[3] authorizing Germany to limit its intervention purchases of certain cereals to those harvested in Germany. The background to this was that the French franc had suffered a fall in its forward rate in the spring of 1969 and it became profitable to buy cereals in France and resell them in Germany to the intervention agency there, since the intervention prices expressed in French francs and German marks remained unaltered, despite their real value having changed, a problem, incidentally, which the current financial mechanisms are intended to prevent. The case arose from the refusal of the German intervention agency to accept from a cereal merchant certain French cereals which were in transit to Germany on 8 May 1969. The Court of Justice held that the intervention system was set up with a view to guaranteeing to producers a market for their cereals at reasonable prices where there are no markets available providing normal profit margins. The Court accepted, however, that it was necessary to avoid any inducement to transport the goods with the sole purpose of obtaining more favourable intervention-conditions, and in fact held that the decision was valid, pointing out that in any event it could not harm producers of cereals because an offer to intervention at the marketing centres of the Member State where the cereals were at the time remained perfectly possible.

In Cases 67–85/75 *Lesieur Cotelle et Associés SA v Commission*[4] the Court even held that a subsidy granted for oilseeds, harvested and processed within the Community, under Council Regulation 136/66[5] was intended as a guarantee for growers of the seeds. The applicants were in fact oil millers and not seed growers. The Court said that in so far as the regulation is intended to give guarantees, the latter relate to colza seed farmers and not processors, as appears from art 24 of the regulation, according to which the derived intervention price guaranteed that producers would be able to sell their produce at a price which, allowing for market fluctuations, was as close as possible to the target price.[6] The subsidies granted to seed processors were not intended to guarantee the processors a fixed payment for their processing but to enable them to buy Community seed at prices close to the target price. The Court concluded that the oil millers could not claim any guarantee under the regulation. However, in the *Oilseeds* dispute with the United States[7] a GATT panel took a different view from the European Court as to the legal nature of the subsidies. The GATT panel took the view that a payment not made directly to the producers is not paid 'exclusively' to them within the terms of art III:8(b) of GATT, and found that the EC Regulations did not in fact ensure that payments to producers were based on the prices processors actually had to pay when purchasing Community oilseeds.

---

[3] Commission Decision 69/138 (JO 1969 L112/1).

[4] [1976] ECR 391.

[5] JO 1966, p 3025 (sp edn 1965–1966, p 221).

[6] As to intervention prices and target prices, see Chapter 4 below.

[7] 25 January 1990, see P Pescatore, W Davey, and A Lowenfeld, *Handbook of GATT Dispute Settlement* (1991) 525.

However, it is only Community agricultural producers who are intended to benefit, so in the period before German reunification, the EC Treaty Protocol on German Internal Trade did not enable agricultural producers of the German Democratic Republic to benefit from refunds payable under the common agricultural policy.[8]

The first of the five objectives of the common agricultural policy is the aim of increasing productivity. Undoubtedly output did grow to an extent where persistent surpluses have been created, although there may be room for argument as to how far this is attributable to scientific progress and how far it is attributable to common policy. From the legal point of view, the type of legislation giving effect to this objective was exemplified in Council Directives 72/159, 72/160, and 72/161,[9] respectively concerned with the modernization of farms, the encouragement of the cessation of farming and the reallocation of agricultural areas, and the provision of land-economic guidance for persons engaged in agriculture. They were replaced in 1985 by Council Regulation 797/85[10] on improving the efficiency of agricultural structures, the successor regulations to which were in turn replaced in 1999 by Council Regulation 1257/1999[11] on support for rural development from the European Agricultural Guidance and Guarantee Fund. It must be said, however, that measures prohibiting production have been upheld: faced with a table wine surplus, the Court of Justice upheld the validity of legislation prohibiting the planting of new vines, holding such a restriction justified in the general Community interest.[12]

The aim of achieving a fair standard of living for the agricultural community explains why the prices under common organizations of the market were set at a level above world prices. However, the same price guarantees were usually available both to small peasant farmers and to agricultural producers operating on an industrial scale, and differences in efficiency appear to have led to an increased divergence in agricultural incomes. Fundamental legal problems have therefore arisen as to (1) whether prices may be reduced, and (2) whether producers could be offered income support rather than price support.

With regard to the first problem, the Treaty obligation is to 'increase' individual earnings, and until 1985 no actual reduction in common prices was made,[13] although some common prices were increased by less than the rate of inflation. A preferred method was to maintain common prices but to impose a levy which would effectively reduce the guaranteed prices for certain producers, or on the happening of certain events. The milk co-responsibility levy introduced by Council Regulation 1079/77,[14] which had the effect of reducing prices for most milk producers, was

[8] Case 14/74 Norddeutsches Vieh- und Fleischkontor GmbH v Hauptzollamt-Ausfuhrerstattung Hamburg-Jonas [1974] ECR 899.
[9] JO 1972 L96/1, 9, 15 (sp edn 1972 (II), pp 324, 332, 339).
[10] OJ 1985 L93/1.
[11] OJ 1999 L160/80.
[12] Case 44/79 Hauer v Land Rheinland-Pfalz [1979] ECR 3727.
[13] See Commission Regulation 2124/85 (OJ 1985 L198/31).
[14] OJ 1977 L131/6.

upheld by the Court of Justice as a measure to stabilize markets,[15] and Council Regulations 856/84 and 857/84[16] introduced an 'additional levy' on quantities of milk delivered beyond a 'guarantee threshold' (that is, a limit beyond which the guaranteed price system will not operate). This levy was set at a level which exceeded the guaranteed support price, and thus constituted a penalty. This system was continued for a further period of seven years from 1 April 1993 by Regulation 3950/92,[17] and has been continued for a further eight years from 1 April 2000 by Regulation 1256/1999.[18] Indeed, the common organization of the market in sugar has, since the version introduced by Council Regulation 1785/81,[19] imposed a levy even on production within the basic quotas therein set out to meet the cost of disposing of such of that production as is surplus to current requirements.[20]

Under the policy of stabilizers agreed in 1988, a combination of co-responsibility levy and guarantee threshold was used in other sectors, including cereals. However, it was repealed for that market following the introduction of lower (and reducing) guarantee prices by Council Regulation 1766/92,[21] a policy continued in Council Regulation 1253/1999.[22] There has instead been a move towards producer support, currently set out in Council Regulation 1251/1999[23] on a support system for producers of certain arable crops. This sets up a system of area payments for EC producers of arable crops. In general it is linked to an obligation to set aside 10 per cent of the relevant area, but for 'small' producers (those with an area less than that needed to produce 92 tonnes of cereals) there is no set-aside obligation. A linkage between these aspects may be seen from the fact that Council Regulation 1253/1999[24] continues the reduction in intervention prices for the 2000–2001 and 2001–2002 marketing years, and anticipates a final reduction in 2002–2003. Conversely, Council Regulation 1251/1999[25] increases area payments for some arable crops for 2000–2001 and 2001–2002, and anticipates further increases related to the final reduction in the intervention price.

The aim of stabilizing markets must in reality be read with the aim of assuring the availability of supplies. The underlying assumption of the common agricultural policy appears to be that supplies can only be made continuously available if there is over-production, since crops and animals cannot be persuaded to grow exactly to numbers or quantities required by the planners' predictions. Hence there has to be some system to ensure that agricultural producers do not lose out as a result of what might be termed 'desirable' over-production and then reduce their production the following years creating shortages. With regard to products of which the Community can produce the bulk of its requirements, the common organizations seek to avoid the cycle of glut and shortage through a system of guaranteed prices

[15] Case 138/78 *Stölting v Hauptzollamt Hamburg-Jonas* [1979] ECR 713.
[16] OJ 1984 L90/10, 13.   [17] OJ 1992 L405/1.   [18] OJ 1999 L160/73.
[19] OJ 1981 L177/4.
[20] Currently set out in Council Regulation 1260/2001 (OJ 2001 L178/1).
[21] OJ 1992 L181/1.   [22] OJ 1999 L160/18.   [23] OJ 1999 L160/1.
[24] OJ 1999 L160/18.   [25] OJ 1999 L160/1.

and guaranteed disposal for goods which cannot be sold on the open market. However, in so far as this guaranteed price system prevents over-production from reducing market prices, an undesirable over-production has developed, resulting in remedies such as the milk co-responsibility levy. The common organization of the market in sugar, introduced by Council Regulation 1009/67 and currently re-enacted in Council Regulation 1260/2001[27] has on the other hand always imposed production quotas, and under Regulation 1260/2001 the quota system is continued until the 2005–2006 marketing year. In Case 250/84 *Eridania Zuccherifici Nazionali SpA v Cassa Conguaglio Zucchero*[28] the Court of Justice held it justifiable to base the quotas on actual production, so that the Italian quota could be less than Italian consumption. From the economic point of view, however, the Court of Auditors published a Special Report in 1991 suggesting that this system based on historical production had both promoted inefficiency and left the Community with serious over-production.[29] It has nevertheless been continued in force.

Even in the cereals market, Council Regulation 1451/82[30] introduced the principle of a 'guarantee threshold' under which over-production might lead to a reduction in the intervention price, and, in the milk market, Council Regulation 856/84[31] introduced the principle that deliveries beyond the guarantee threshold would lead to the imposition of an additional levy. However, the guarantee threshold for cereals was repealed by Council Regulation 1579/86,[32] which introduced a general co-responsibility levy. However, reflecting the new emphasis on reducing surplus production, Regulation 1760/87[33] introduced aids for the 'set-aside' of arable land and for the 'extensification' of production (ie a reduction of at least 20 per cent in the output of certain surplus products from the farm concerned), which has evolved into the scheme of Regulation 1251/1999[34] on a support system for producers of certain arable crops, which in principle requires a set-aside of 10 per cent of the relevant land.

Little Community agricultural legislation appears to have been aimed specifically to ensure reasonable prices for consumers, apart from legislation designed to remove surpluses, such as 'Christmas butter' allowances. More generally, consumers may benefit from the application of export levies when world prices are higher than Community prices.

The three factors which art 33(2) of the EC Treaty requires to be taken into account in working out the common agricultural policy and the special methods for its application are:

1. the particular nature of agricultural activity, which results from the social structure of agriculture and from structural and natural disparities between the various agricultural regions;

[26] OJ 308, 18 December 1967, p 1 (sp edn 1967, p 304).
[27] OJ 2001 L178/1.   [28] [1986] ECR 117.
[29] Special Report 4/91, OJ 1991 C290/1 at 44.
[30] OJ 1982 L164/1.   [31] OJ 1984 L90/10.   [32] OJ 1986 L139/29.
[33] OJ 1987 L167/1.   [34] OJ 1999 L160/1.

2.   the need to effect the appropriate adjustments by degrees; and
3.   the fact that in the Member States agriculture constitutes a sector closely
     linked with the economy as a whole.

With regard to the first of these factors, many common organizations have, by
their very nature, a regional impact, although it was only after the accession of
the United Kingdom, Ireland, and Denmark that Council Directive 75/268[35] on
mountain and hill farming, and farming in less-favoured areas, was adopted.
However, both regional interests and links with the economy as a whole can be
seen in the current Council Regulation 1257/1999 on support for rural development,[36] which in turn is linked to Council Regulation 1260/1999 laying down
general provisions on the structural funds.[37] More generally, with regard to the
extent to which agricultural legislation as such should reflect regional considerations, the judgment of the Court in Case 250/84 Eridania[38] is of considerable
importance. In upholding the validity of sugar quotas allocated to Italy on the
basis of historic production rather than consumption, the Court stated expressly
that regional specialization was a permissible objective of a common organization
of the market. Hence, there would appear to be little difference in status between
these 'factors to be taken into account' and the objectives of the common agricultural policy strictly so called.

General principles derived from the Treaty[39]

The traditional view of the Commission was that the common agricultural policy
was based on the single market, Community preference, and financial solidarity.[40]
The concept of the agricultural single market will be considered in the context of
the structures of common organizations[41] and the principle of financial solidarity
will be considered in the context of the financial mechanisms of common organizations.[42] Community preference, whatever its domestic political attractions, was
mentioned expressly in the EC Treaty only in the original art 44(2), a provision
which allowed Member States to introduce a non-discriminatory system of
minimum prices during the transitional period. That article referred to 'the development of a natural preference between Member States', and in Case 5/67 W Beus
GmbH & Co v Hauptzollamt München[43] the Court of Justice held it to be one of
the principles of the Treaty, effectively generalizing this very specific illustration of
the principle. The price structure of most common organizations has inexorably

---

[35] OJ 1975 L128/1: see now arts 13–21 of Council Regulation 1257/1999 on support for rural
development (OJ 1999 L 160/80).
[36] OJ 1999 L160/80.   [37] OJ 1999 L161/1.
[38] Case 250/84 Eridania Zuccherifici Nazionali SpA v Cassa Conguaglio Zucchero [1986] ECR 117.
[39] See JA Usher, General Principles of EC Law (1998) chapter 2.
[40] See eg Commission, The Agricultural Policy of the European Community (3rd edn, 1982) 14, 15.
[41] See Chapter 4 below.   [42] See Chapter 5 below.   [43] [1968] ECR 83.

led to Community preference. A particular illustration of the principle may, however, be found in Case 55/75 *Balkan-Import-Export GmbH v Hauptzollamt Berlin-Packhof*,[44] where an importer complained that monetary compensatory amounts, designed to compensate for the difference between real rates of exchange and agricultural rates of exchange where there was a risk of disturbances in trade in agricultural products, were imposed on imports of Bulgarian cheese into Germany but not on imports of similar Italian cheese. It was held that, with regard to the cheese coming from Italy, the general principle of Community preference justified a different assessment of the possibilities of disturbance according to whether the products involved came from another Member State or from a third country. However, the former arts 44, 45, and 47 of the EC Treaty were repealed on the entry into force of the Treaty of Amsterdam in May 1999. While the concept of Community preference is often referred to as one of the fundamentals of the CAP, it is interesting to speculate whether the general principle can survive the repeal of the Treaty provision from which it was derived. It may nevertheless be suggested that as a general principle of Community law, it has an existence separate from that of the former art 44(2).

Be that as it may, a difference of emphasis may be perceived in the Commission's 1998 Report on the Agricultural Situation in the EU, where it declared that it sought to develop 'a competitive agricultural sector able to compete on world markets without having recourse to subsidies that are increasingly less acceptable internationally'.[45]

Perhaps the most important legal principle laid down expressly by the EC Treaty in relation to agricultural common organizations is the requirement in art 34(2) that common organizations 'shall exclude any discrimination between producers or consumers within the Community'. As interpreted by the European Court in Case 5/73 *Balkan v HZA Berlin-Packhof*[46] this refers to discrimination as between producers or as between consumers, the relationship between the two groups being the concern of art 33 of the EC Treaty, stating the objectives of the common agricultural policy. Discussion of the precise scope of this provision, and in particular of the question whether it produces direct effects, has been overtaken by the fact that the Court of Justice has held that it is 'merely a specific enunciation of the general principle of equality which is one of the fundamental principles of Community law',[47] a principle which is hence a touchstone against which the validity of any Community act may be assessed. On the other hand, there are a number of decisions holding that, in the particular circumstances, differences in treatment do not amount to discrimination, or are objectively justified. Examples

---

[44] [1976] ECR 19.

[45] *The Agricultural Situation in the EU: 1998 Report* (2000) para 54.

[46] [1973] ECR 1091.

[47] Cases 117/76 and 16/77 *Albert Ruckdeschel & Co v Hauptzollamt Hamburg-St Annen* [1977] ECR 1753 at 1769, Cases 124/76 and 20/77 *Moulins et Huileries de Pont-à-Mousson SA v Office National Interprofessionnel des Céréales* [1977] ECR 1795 at 1811.

which might be given are Case 8/78 *Milac GmbH v Hauptzollamt Freiburg*[48] where the Court found that, on the material before it, the applicant had not shown what constituted the discrimination alleged to result from provisions applying a corrective amount to imports into Germany and the Benelux countries from other Member States of skimmed milk powder but not to imports of whole milk powder, and Case 2/77 *Hoffmann's Stärkefabriken AG v Hauptzollamt Bielefeld*,[49] where the Court held that there were objective grounds for the difference between the treatment accorded potato starch producers and that accorded maize starch producers by regulations reducing the production refund on maize starch and potato starch but allowing special transitional measures with regard to potato starch alone.

The fine dividing line between a valid and an invalid difference in treatment imposed upon another sub-group of starch producers, the manufacturers of isoglucose, is illustrated in Cases 103, 145/77 *Royal Scholten-Honig (Holdings) Ltd v Intervention Board for Agricultural Produce*,[50] in which isoglucose manufacturers challenged the validity of Council regulations respectively freezing and eventually eliminating production refunds on maize starch (and other agricultural starches) used for the manufacture of isoglucose, and introducing a system of production levies on the manufacture of isoglucose. With regard to the regulation freezing and eliminating the production refund,[51] the Court repeated that art 34(2) of the EC Treaty was a specific enunciation of the principle of equality, which 'requires that similar situations shall not be treated differently unless the differentiation is objectively justified'. In the light of this, the Court went on to consider whether the situation of isoglucose was comparable to that of other products of the starch industry—and it is perhaps in itself interesting to note that it was the products rather than the producers which the Court considered. It was found that there was no competition between starch and isoglucose, or between isoglucose and other products derived from starch, except possibly glucose, and that even there the two products had different applications so that they could not be in a comparable competitive situation. On the other hand, it was stated that as isoglucose was at least partially interchangeable with sugar, the maintenance of the production refund in favour of manufacturers of isoglucose might have constituted discrimination against manufacturers of sugar. From this, although it had referred initially to the general principle of equality, the Court concluded that the regulation did not infringe the rule of non-discrimination between Community producers.

In relation to the regulation introducing a production levy on isoglucose,[52] the Court considered whether isoglucose and sugar were in comparable situations. It pointed out that the Council had recognized in the recitals to the regulation that isoglucose was a direct substitute for liquid sugar, and, in the recitals to a regulation

---

[48] [1978] ECR 1721.   [49] [1977] ECR 1375.   [50] [1978] ECR 2037.
[51] Council Regulation 1862/76 (OJ 1976 L206/3).
[52] Council Regulation 1111/77 (OJ 1977 L134/4).

amending that regulation, that 'any Community decision on one of those products necessarily affects the other'. Having found that isoglucose and sugar were in effect in a comparable position, the Court went on to state that isoglucose manufacturers and sugar manufacturers were nevertheless treated differently as regards the imposition of the production levy, in that it only affected sugar produced outside the basic quota but within the maximum one, whereas it applied to the whole of isoglucose production. It was also noted that sugar manufacturers benefited from the intervention system, whereas isoglucose manufacturers did not. The final question, however, was whether this difference in treatment could be objectively justified. On behalf of the Council and Commission, it was argued that, since the price of isoglucose tended to follow the intervention price of sugar, the high intervention price of sugar (stated to be 15 per cent higher than the price which would have been fixed by normal criteria) gave a notional 15 per cent advantage to isoglucose, which roughly corresponded to the 5 units of account maximum levy. The Court rejected this argument, stating that a similar advantage, if it existed, could be enjoyed by a sugar manufacturer with a favourably situated modern factory. It was further argued that the levy roughly corresponded to the charges borne by sugar manufacturers on the whole of their production, if that produced outside the quotas was taken into account. The Court rejected this argument also, pointing out that sugar manufacturers paid beet growers a reduced price for beet used for sugar produced outside the basic quota, and that sugar manufacturers could limit their charges simply by limiting their production (in effect keeping to their quotas), whereas a limit on production by an isoglucose manufacturer would be without effect as regards the rate of levy per unit weight. The Court held, although this time it had commenced simply by a reference to art 34(3) of the Treaty, that the provisions of the regulation establishing the production levy system for isoglucose offended against the general principle of equality of which the prohibition on discrimination set out in art 34(2) was a specific expression.

The *Isoglucose* cases[53] show very clearly the methodology of the Court of Justice when dealing with an alleged breach of the principle of equality. The first step is to see whether the products or producers between which or whom there is said to be discrimination are in fact in a comparable situation, which in the present cases appears to have been synonymous with a competing position. If they are not, as was the case with isoglucose and other starch products, that is the end of the matter. If they are in a comparable situation, the next step is to see if there is a difference in treatment between them. If there is a difference in treatment, the third and final step is to see whether it is objectively justified—and the approach of the Court in the *Isoglucose* cases appears to have been that it was for the Community institutions to show that the difference was objectively justified rather than for the producers affected to show that it was not justified.

---

[53] Cases 103, 145/77 *Royal Scholten-Honig (Holdings) Ltd v Intervention Board for Agricultural Produce* [1978] ECR 2037.

Another clear example of discrimination may be found in Case C-309/89 *Codorniu v Council*.[54] The action concerned a provision in a Council regulation[55] which reserved the word 'crémant' for certain quality sparkling wines produced in specified regions of France and Luxembourg. According to the recitals, the aim was to protect traditional descriptions used in France and Luxembourg. The applicant was a Spanish company manufacturing quality sparkling wines produced in specified regions, and it had since 1924 designated one of its wines 'Gran Cremant de Codorniu', a graphic trademark of which it was the holder. The regulation prevented it using the term 'crémant' in relation to Spanish wines and thus from using its trademark, so the applicant sought its annulment. It was held on the substance that the reservation of the word 'crémant' to France and Luxembourg treated comparable situations differently and could not be justified on objective criteria, so that the provision constituted discrimination contrary to arts 12 and 34(2) of the EC Treaty.

Although, at first sight, art 34(2) and the underlying general principle may seem only to govern the validity of Community legislation, the European Court has held in Cases 201 and 202/85 *Klensch v Luxembourg Secretary of State for Agriculture*[56] that it applies to any measure taken in the context of a common organization of an agricultural market, whether that measure is taken by the Community authorities or the national authorities. Hence, in that case, the exercise by the Luxembourg government of its discretion under the milk quota system to choose the reference year from which quotas would be calculated was held to be subject to the principle of non-discrimination.

Furthermore, the general principle of equality of treatment is applied not just to producers and consumers in the Community but also, for example, to importers, as in Case 165/84 *Krohn*[57] where it was held that the principle was breached by legislation which did not allow importers of manioc from Thailand to cancel their licences, following the introduction of a quota regime, but did allow such licences to be cancelled by those importing manioc from any other country. This was reaffirmed with regard to the market in bananas (which are largely imported into the Community from third countries) in Case C-280/93 *Germany v Council*.[58] It was there stated that 'the common organisation of the market for the banana sector covers operators who are neither producers nor consumers. However, because of the general nature of the principle of non-discrimination, the prohibition of discrimination also applies to other categories of economic operators who are subject to the common organisation of a market.' The Court then went on to dismiss the plea of breach of the principle on the grounds that the situations of the different economic operators were not comparable due to the different market systems operated by the Member States prior to the adoption of the regulation at

---

[54] [1994] ECR I-1853.
[55] Council Regulation 2045/89 (OJ 1989 L202/12).
[56] [1986] ECR 3477.   [57] [1985] ECR 3997.   [58] [1994] ECR I-4973.

issue, and the differences in treatment introduced by the regulation were essentially inherent in the objective of integrating previously compartmentalized markets.

General principles derived from the laws of the Member States

It is in the field of agriculture that the Court of Justice has developed and applied many of the general principles of Community law which may be regarded as being derived from the laws of the Member States.[59] Thus it was in an agricultural dispute that Advocate General Dutheillet de Lamothe in his opinion in the *Internationale Handelsgesellschaft* case[60] defined the principle of proportionality[61] as being that 'citizens may only have imposed on them, for the purposes of the public interest, obligations which are strictly necessary for those purposes to be attained'. It was there held by the Court of Justice that the system of deposits required for export licences under the common organization of the market in cereals did not breach the principle of proportionality. An example of a breach of the principle of proportionality is to be found in the *Bela-Mühle, Granaria*, and *Olmühle* cases,[62] a series of references for preliminary rulings, where the Court held that a Council regulation effectively requiring manufacturers of animal foodstuffs to incorporate intervention skimmed milk powder into their products at a price three times that of the soya husks for which it was substituted imposed an obligation which was disproportionate, and not necessary to attain the objective of reducing stocks of milk powder, and was discriminatory within the meaning of art 34(2) of the EC Treaty. Not surprisingly, it held the regulation to be invalid.

Similarly, in Case 181/84 *R v Intervention Board for Agricultural Produce, ex p E D and F Man (Sugar) Ltd*[63] it was held that where the objective of a deposit was to ensure that sugar was exported, it was a breach of the principle of proportionality to require the forfeiture of the whole deposit when the exporter was late (by a few hours) in applying for the formal export licence, when there was still enough time to carry out the export transaction. The basis of this decision was a distinction between the primary obligation to carry out the export transaction and the secondary obligation to apply for an export licence within a specific time, the Court taking the view that to penalize failure to comply with the secondary

---

[59] See JA Usher, *General Principles of EC Law* (1998) chapter 1.

[60] Case 11/70 *Internationale Handelsgesellschaft mbH v Einfuhr- und Vorratsstelle für Getreide und Futtermittel* [1970] ECR 1125.

[61] See T Tridimas, *General Principles of EC Law* (1999) chapter 3, JA Usher, *General Principles of EC Law* (1998) chapter 3.

[62] Case 114/76 *Bela-Mühle Josef Bergmann KG v Grows-Farm GmbH & Co KG* [1977] ECR 1211, Case 116/76 *Granaria BV v Hoofdproduktschap voor Akkerbouwprodukten* [1977] ECR 1247, Joined Cases 119, 120/76 *Olmühle Hamburg AG v Hauptzollamt Hamburg-Waltershof* [1977] ECR 1269.

[63] [1985] ECR 2889.

obligation as severely as failure to comply with the primary obligation would breach the principle of proportionality. The distinction between primary and secondary obligations would appear to underlie the judgment in Case 122/78 *Buitoni*[64] and a further gloss was put on it in Case 21/85 *Maas v Bundesanstalt für Landwirtschaftliche Marktordnung*[65] where a deposit paid under the food aid legislation had been forfeited because the exporter loaded the goods into ships a few days late and because the ships used were older than the fifteen years specified in the legislation. The Court held the obligation to load the goods within a fixed time limit was a primary obligation, but that in the context of sea transport a delay of a few days did not necessarily breach that obligation, and, since the goods, in fact, arrived at their destination on time, the loss of the deposit could not be justified. With regard to the use of ships less than fifteen years old, which was held not to be a primary obligation, particularly since it was not required under other similar legislation, it was decided that this requirement should be interpreted as including ships equated with ships less than fifteen years old for insurance purposes, and that even if the ships used did not fall within the requirement as so interpreted, it was disproportionate to require the whole deposit to be forfeited.

This may, however, be contrasted with the decision in Case 9/85 *Nordbutter*[66] in the context of legislation granting a subsidy on skimmed milk used for feeding animals other than calves. This required a quarterly declaration of the number of calves on the holding, and under Commission Regulation 188/83,[67] the subsidy was reduced by 10 per cent if the declaration was up to ten days late, and was lost totally thereafter. It was held by the Court that since this expressly allowed for minor infringements of the deadline it did not breach the principle of proportionality. Similarly, in the *Man* case[68] it was held that where the objective of a deposit was to ensure that sugar was exported, it was a breach of the principle of proportionality to require the forfeiture of the whole deposit when the exporter was late (by a few hours) in applying for the formal export licence, when there was still enough time to carry out the export transaction.

On the other hand, highly technical rules laid down for the payment of, for example, denaturing premiums may well be strictly applied. Case 272/81 *Société RU-MI v Fonds d'Orientation et de Régularisation des Marchés Agricoles*[69] involved a highly specific formula for the denaturing of skimmed milk powder so as to ensure that it could not be used as a feed for young calves, the intention being that it could, however, be used as feed for pigs and poultry. The Court of Justice took the view that it was not disproportionate to withhold the whole of the special aid for denaturing if the formula was not strictly followed, because of the risk that the product might thereby be diverted from its intended use. However, Council Regulation 1300/84[70] introduced a legislative application of the principle of proportionality in

---

[64] [1979] ECR 677. [65] [1986] ECR 3537. [66] [1986] ECR 2831.
[67] OJ 1983 L25/14. [68] [1985] ECR 2889. [69] [1982] ECR 4167.
[70] OJ 1984 L125/3.

the context of premiums for the non-marketing of milk and the conversion of dairy herds, so that a reduced premium could be paid where there were minor breaches of the rules, rather than the premium being entirely lost.

Another general principle which may make the exercise of legislative and administrative discretion in the context of the common agricultural policy subject to severe constraints is the principle of the protection of legitimate expectations.[71] A striking (and expensive) example relates to the milk quota scheme. A series of actions were brought by dairy producers who had agreed to give up dairy production for a period of five years under an earlier Community scheme and had not produced any milk during the year (1983 in their case) taken as the base year for calculating the milk quotas when the milk quota system was introduced. They had therefore not been granted any milk quota when the quota system was introduced in 1984 by Council Regulation 857/84. This meant in practical terms that they could not return to milk production when the five-year period expired. However, the Court held this legislation unlawful[72] as constituting a breach of the general principle of the protection of legitimate expectation. While it accepted that producer who had voluntarily ceased production for a certain period could not expect not to be subject to rules of market or structural policy adopted in the interim, nevertheless a producer who had been encouraged by a Community measure to suspend marketing for a limited period might legitimately expect not to be subject to restrictions which affect him only because he took advantage of the Community provisions. In particular the Court held that they could not have foreseen that they would be totally excluded from the market.

Following these judgments, the producers concerned were subsequently granted a quota based on 60 per cent of their production during the year before they began to take part in the 'outgoers' scheme by Council Regulation 764/89, and this also was held to be unlawful by the Court as a breach of the general principle of the protection of legitimate expectation.[73] This time, while accepting that it was legitimate to ensure that the outgoers did not gain an undue advantage by comparison with the producers who continued to deliver, it was found that the reduction applied to the outgoers was more than double the highest reduction suffered by producers who continued to deliver, so that again it was a restriction which affected the outgoers only because they took advantage of the Community provisions.

However, there is only a limit on the exercise of discretion where there is a legitimate expectation, and it has long been established that economic operators may not have a legitimate expectation that a situation which may be modified at the discretion of the Community institution will be maintained.[74]

---

[71] See T Tridimas, *General Principles of EC Law* (1999) chapter 5, JA Usher, *General Principles of EC Law* (1998) chapter 4.

[72] Case 120/86 *Mulder* [1988] ECR 2321, Case 170/86 *Deetzen* [1988] ECR 2355.

[73] Case C-189/89 *Spagl* [1990] ECR I-4539, Case C-217/89 *Pastätter* [1990] ECR I-4585.

[74] See eg Case C-350/88 *Delacre & Others v Commission* [1990] ECR I-395.

A further problem as to whose conduct or representations may give rise to legitimate expectations arises from the fact that most Community law is administered at the national level by national authorities and officials. At the least, it is clear that the conduct of a national authority which acts in breach of Community law, and has been declared by the Commission to be acting in breach of Community law, cannot give rise to a legitimate expectation. In Case C-24/95 *Land Rheinland-Pfalz v Alcan Deutschland*[75] it was held that the action of a regional government, which paid out a state aid without notifying the Commission under art 88(3) of the EC Treaty, leading to a formal decision by the Commission holding the aid unlawful, could not create a legitimate expectation on the part of the recipient that the aid was legitimate. The recipient could not therefore resist a demand for repayment of the aid, even though the regional government waited so long before commencing proceedings for its recovery that the action would have been barred on grounds of legal certainty in German administrative law.

On the other hand, there are situations where Community law itself declares national authorities to be the competent authorities, and indeed specific provisions which protect legitimate expectations in this context. An example is Council Regulation 1697/79 on post-clearance recovery of import or export duties.[76] Art 5(2) of that regulation provides for waiver of post-clearance recovery where the initial non-collection of the duty is due to an error by the competent authorities, the person liable has acted in good faith, and where that person has complied with all the legislative provisions in force with regard to the customs declaration. It has been held that 'competent authorities' in this context include 'any authority which, acting within the scope of its powers, furnishes information relevant to the recovery of customs duties and which may thus cause the person liable to entertain legitimate expectations'.[77] It has further been accepted that the competent authorities may, in an appropriate context, be the customs authorities of a country to which the EC Treaty does not apply, such as the Faeroese authorities in Cases C-153 and 204/94 *R v Commissioners of Customs and Excise ex p Faroe Seafood*.[78] It was there held that under the Commission regulation defining 'originating products' for the application of the customs procedure for certain products coming from the Faeroe Islands, it was for the Faeroe Islands authorities to issue EUR.1 certificates if the goods could be regarded as originating there. The Court therefore concluded that the Faeroese authorities were entrusted by the Community with the task of furnishing information relevant to the recovery of customs duties 'and may therefore arouse legitimate expectations in the person liable'.[79] This would be the case where the exporter had declared the goods to be of Faeroese origin in reliance on the actual knowledge by the Faeroese authorities of all the facts necessary for applying the customs rules in question. It would not, of course,

---

[75] [1997] ECR I-1591 at 1621.   [76] OJ 1979 L197/1.
[77] Case C-348/89 *Mecanarte* [1991] ECR I-3277 at para 22.
[78] [1996] ECR I-2465.   [79] Ibid at 2541.

be the case where those authorities had been misled by incorrect declarations on the part of the exporter, an illustration again of the fact that nobody can claim to rely on a situation caused by their own breach of Community law.

Property rights

A particular aspect of the general principles of Community law which has arisen in the context of the common agricultural policy is that of the recognition and creation of property rights under EC agricultural legislation. The essentials of the recognition of property rights as a general principle of Community law are to be found in Case 44/79 *Hauer v Land Rheinland-Pfalz*.[80] The background was that Mrs Hauer, in 1975, applied to the *Land* authorities for permission to start growing vines on her property in Bad Durkheim, such permission having a few days earlier been granted to the owners of some neighbouring land. Under the relevant German legislation, vines could only be cultivated on land recognized as being suitable therefor, and the *Land* authorities turned down her application in January 1976 on the ground that her property was not suitable. Mrs Hauer put in a formal complaint objecting to the decision in her case, later that same month, and her complaint was rejected in October 1976, this time not only on the ground that her land was not suitable, but also on the ground that Council Regulation 1162/76 on measures designed to adjust vine-growing potential to market requirements,[81] which had been enacted in the meantime, prohibited all new planting of vine varieties classed as wine grape varieties, and also prohibited the grant of authorization for such new plantings.

The specific questions referred to the European Court related, however, to the interpretation of the regulation rather than to its validity. The first asked whether the prohibition on new plantings of vines applied where permission to grow vines had been requested before the entry into force of the regulation, and the second asked whether it applied generally, ie irrespective of whether the land in question was regarded as suitable for cultivating vines, within the meaning of the German legislation.

The Court was able to deal relatively briefly with these two questions, finding that the prohibitions in the regulation did indeed apply where permission to plant vines had been sought before its entry into force, and that they applied irrespective of the nature of the land in question. This, however, brought the Court to the real crux of the matter. In its order for reference, the German court had indicated that if the regulation was so interpreted, it might not be applicable in Germany on the grounds that it was not compatible with arts 12 and 14 of the German Basic Law, concerning rights of property and the right to carry on a business activity. The Court in fact took this as an invitation for it to assess its validity in terms of

---

[80] [1979] ECR 3727.   [81] OJ 1976 L135/32.

principles of Community law. So doing, it turned first to the question of rights of property in the Community system, taking as its starting point art 1 of the First Protocol to the Human Rights Convention, which it described as reflecting the concepts common to the constitutions of the Member States.[82] It noted that while this provision recognized that 'every natural or legal person is entitled to the peaceful enjoyment of his possessions', it nonetheless preserved the 'right of a State to enforce such laws as it deems necessary to control the use of property in accordance with the general interest'. Nonetheless, although it took the view that the regulation amounted to a control on use of property, the Court felt that the rule in the Convention did not enable it to give a sufficiently precise answer to the problem and so it considered also the rules applied in the various Member States. This it did not merely in general terms, but by reference to specific provisions of, in this case, the German, Italian, and Irish constitutions. The conclusion the Court drew from its analysis was that property ownership is subject to inherent obligations, to social requirements, and the requirements of the common good. It further noted that all the wine-producing countries of the Community imposed restrictions on the planting of vines, selection of varieties, and methods of cultivation, and that nowhere were these restrictions regarded as necessarily infringing property rights.

On the basis that Regulation 1162/76 was an example of this type of restriction, the Court then considered whether the prohibitions introduced were appropriate to the aims pursued by the Community viticultural legislation which were to establish a lasting balance in the wine market, and to improve the quality of wine put on the market. In this context Regulation 1162/76 was a temporary measure aimed at preventing any increase in the over-production which already existed. It was thus held not to be an undue restriction on the exercise of property rights, being justified by the aims the Community was pursuing in the general interest. In this, the Court agreed both with the Opinion of AG Capotorti and indeed with the observations put in by the German government.

The Court then turned to the question whether the regulation constituted a breach of the right to the free pursuit of business activity. In this context, it was pointed out that the regulation did not prevent anyone from cultivating existing vineyards, and in so far as the prohibition on new planting affected the freedom to carry on the activity of viticulture it was the natural consequence of the limitations on property rights, and was justified for the same reasons.

AG Capotorti did discuss whether compensation should have been payable for such a limitation of property rights, but concluded that this would only be the case where the measure amounted to expropriation, which he did not consider to be the situation here.[83] By way of contrast, the common organization of the

---

[82] In Case 36/75 *Rutili* [1975] ECR 1219 the Court had described the Community rules limiting the powers of Member States with regard to the movements of migrant workers as being specific manifestation of the principle embodied in arts 8 to 11 of the convention.

[83] [1979] ECR at 3762.

market in wine does provide for the payment of a premium where a producer undertakes the permanent abandonment of vine growing on a particular area.[84]

Limits on the substance of property rights were indicated in Case C-280/93 *Germany v Council*[85] where Germany argued that the introduction of the common organization of the market in bananas deprived traders who traditionally marketed third country bananas of their market shares and therefore breached their property rights. The Court however asserted that no economic operator could claim a right to property in a market share which he held at a time before the establishment of a common organization of a market, since such a market share constituted only a momentary economic position exposed to the risks of changing circumstances.

Questions of the creation of property rights have arisen in particular in those markets where the Community has imposed production quotas. It has been observed that 'it is impossible to ignore the vigorous trade in quota which has developed in some Member States',[86] which may be contrasted with the view of the Court of Auditors that this trade in quotas prevented the system being fully effective to reduce over-production.[87] The fundamental question is the extent to which a measure intended to reduce production may be regarded, as a matter of Community law, as giving rise to property rights which should be protected.

The system of milk quotas is entirely a creature of European Community law. It was introduced by Council legislation in 1984,[88] which, with the aim of reducing the excessive output of milk and milk products, provided for the imposition of a punitive levy on producers or purchasers exceeding defined reference quantities, with the proviso that the levy on the purchaser was to be passed on to the producer. The question of property rights arose from the fact that the existence of milk quota depends upon a combination of a producer and a holding.

The initial allocation of quota in April 1984 depended on deliveries or direct sales by the producer during the relevant reference year. However, whilst the initial allocation depended on the activities of the producer, subsequent transfer was defined in the Community legislation in terms of the holding. Art 7, para 1 of Council Regulation 857/84 provided that where a holding was sold, leased, or transferred by inheritance, all or part of the corresponding reference quantity should be transferred to the purchaser, tenant, or heir according to procedures to be determined. There were a limited number of exceptions, but it may be observed that the Council regulations themselves were silent about reversion to the landlord at the expiry of a lease, and about compensation for a departing tenant who did not intend to continue milk production. However, the Commission implementing Regulation

---

[84] Council Regulation 1493/1999 (OJ 1999 L179/1) art 8.

[85] [1994] ECR I-4973.

[86] M Cardwell, *Milk Quotas* (1996) at 91.

[87] Court of Auditors, Special Report 4/93 on the implementation of the quota system intended to control milk production (OJ 1994 C12/1).

[88] Council Regulation 857/84, now repealed and replaced by Council Regulation 3950/92, as amended. See Chapter 4 below.

1371/84 referred in its art 5(3) to other cases of transfer which had 'comparable legal effects' so far as producers were concerned.[89]

The questions of reversion, compensation, and property rights arose in Case 5/88 *Wachauf v Bundesamt für Ernährung und Fortwirtschaft*.[90] In its judgment in that case, the European Court expressly accepted that the reversion of a holding at the expiry of a lease did give rise to 'comparable legal effects' to the types of transfer listed in the regulation, so that in principle the quota would go with the holding. It further held that, at least where the allocation of the quota was the result of the tenant's own labours, it would be a breach of the tenant's fundamental rights to deprive him of the fruits of his labour without compensation. However, the Court concluded that the Community legislation in fact left the Member States enough discretion to ensure that the tenant was able either to keep all or part of his quota or to receive compensation if he gave it up. It should be observed that the Court also held, presumably because the dispute arose in the context of a national outgoers' scheme, that the part of the quota for which the tenant received compensation could not be transferred to the landlord, but should be treated as being released.

It has subsequently become clear that the Court's use of the phrase 'fruits of his labour' in *Wachauf* is both precise and important. The Court was not recognizing that quota as such was a property right but that in that particular case, where the holding had not been let as a dairy unit, and it was the tenant who had acquired and introduced the dairy cows and the technical facilities required for milk production, the quota represented the fruits of the tenant's labour. This follows from the decision in Case C-2/92 *R v MAFF ex p Bostock*,[91] which involved the termination of a lease of a holding which had been let as a dairy farm in England before the provisions of the Agriculture Act 1986, dealing with the consequences of the termination of a lease of a holding which had been let as a dairy farm, entered into force. The quota therefore reverted with the holding to the landlord with no express provision as to compensation, and the tenant argued that this was a breach of the general principle of respect for property in Community law. While the Court did reaffirm that the requirements flowing from the protection of fundamental rights in the Community legal order are also binding on Member States when they implement Community rules,[92] it did not accept the tenant's argument that protection of the right of property required the Member State to make provision for compensation to be paid to the outgoing tenant by the landlord or to confer on the tenant a direct right to claim compensation from the landlord. After emphasizing that *Wachauf* was concerned with the protection of the fruits of the tenant's labours, the Court held that the right to

---

[89] For the current legislation, see Chapter 4 below.
[90] [1989] ECR 2609.   [91] [1994] ECR I-35.
[92] For a discussion of this issue in the context of *Wachauf* see T Tridimas, *The General Principles of EC Law* (1999) 226–227.

property safeguarded by the Community legal order does not include the right to dispose, for profit, of an advantage such as reference quantities allocated in the context of the common organization of a market, which does not derive from the assets or occupational activity of the person concerned.[93]

A similar view was taken with regard to the introduction of a system of premium rights (production quotas) attributed to the producers of sheepmeat, goatmeat, or beef and veal in Case C-38/94 *R v Minister for Agriculture, Fisheries and Food, ex p Country Landowner's Association*.[94] Here the premium rights could be transferred by the producer with the holding or, subject to surrendering a proportion of the rights transferred to the national reserve, without transferring the holding. The landowners claimed that Member States should be required to introduce a compensation mechanism for the loss suffered by the owners of agricultural land in particular where the premium right was transferred by producers who did not own the land on which they farmed. The landowners argued that the allocation of freely transferable quotas to tenant producers would have the effect of reducing the capital value of the land. This point was accepted by MAFF but they refuted the existence of any obligation upon them to compensate the landowners for this loss. The Court reaffirmed its jurisprudence in the *Bostock* case, declaring that no general principle of law upheld by the Community legal order, in particular, the principle of protection of the right to property, required that such compensation be paid. On the other hand, it stated that it was for each Member State to assess the need for such measures having regard in particular to the national arrangements for implementing the rules in question and the national rules governing the relationship between landlord and tenant.

Finally, in Case C-63/93 *Duff & Others v Minister for Agriculture and Food, Ireland & the Attorney General*,[95] where it was alleged inter alia that the failure to grant additional milk quota to producers who had adopted development plans under Community law infringed their property rights, the Court held that the rules in question did not affect the *substance* of the right to property as the rules were aimed at the general Community interest and allowed the producers to continue to produce milk at the level of their production prior to the entry into force of the new rules.[96]

Use of general principles

Perhaps the most frequent use of these general principles in relation to Community agricultural legislation is as a guide to interpretation, so as to ensure the validity of that legislation, rather than as a criterion for determining the validity

---

[93] See also Case C-44/89 *Von Deetzen v Hauptzollamt Hamburg-Jonas (Von Deetzen II)* [1991] ECR I-5119 at para 27.
[94] [1995] ECR I-3875.   [95] [1996] ECR I-569.   [96] Ibid, at para 30.

of that legislation. The general principle of legal certainty was so used in the *Deuka* cases.[97] In the first of these the Court of Justice was asked whether a Commission regulation was invalid in so far as it provided that an increased denaturing premium should be discontinued even in respect of wheat purchased by the denaturer before the regulation came into force. Having found that a denaturing undertaking may well arrange its programme on the basis of an entire crop year, for the sake of legal certainty the Court held that the regulation had to be applied in such a way that there might still benefit from the system those quantities of goods purchased before the coming into force of the regulation, provided the request (for a premium) was made to the intervention agency before the expiry of the time limit arising from the regulation. Interpreted in this way, the regulation was held to be valid. In the second *Deuka* case, similar questions arose concerning the validity of regulations respectively reducing and abolishing the relevant denaturing premium, and a similar answer was given: the Court stated that where there had been a commitment to denaturing before the expiry of the periods stipulated in the regulations, it was right to apply, in the interests of legal certainty, for the computation of the amount of the denaturing premium, the provisions in force at the time the application was lodged, even if the technical mixing was not done until a subsequent date. On the other hand, there are numerous examples mentioned above where it was not possible to interpret the Community legislation so as to comply with the general principles, and the legislation was therefore declared invalid.[98]

Just as the general principles derived from the Treaty are held to be binding upon Member States when acting in the context of Community law,[99] so also are those general principles derived from the laws of the Member States. This is, perhaps, most clearly illustrated by the attitude of the European Court to claims that a restriction on the import of agricultural products is justified on health grounds under art 30 of the Treaty,[100] where it has consistently been emphasized that the restriction must be proportionate to the objective it pursues, as in the cases involving United Kingdom restrictions on imports of poultrymeat[101] and UHT milk.[102]

It may also be observed that it was in the context of a common organization of the market the Court of Justice developed, in Case 5/71 *Aktien-Zuckerfabrik Schöppenstedt v Council*,[103] the theory that the Community could incur non-contractual liability in relation to harm caused even by legislation involving measures of economic policy where it constitutes a sufficiently serious violation of a superior rule of law for the protection of the individual, so that, for example, legislation breaching a general principle of Community law such as the principle of the

---

[97] Case 78/74 *Deuka v Einfuhr- und Vorratsstelle für Getreide und Futtermittel* [1975] ECR 421, Case 5/75 *Deuka v Einfuhr- und Vorratsstelle für Getreide und Futtermittel* [1975] ECR 759.

[98] See eg Case 181/84 *ED and F Man* [1985] ECR 2889, Case 120/86 *Mulder* [1988] ECR 2321.

[99] Cases 201 and 202/85 *Klensch v Luxembourg Secretary of State for Agriculture* [1986] ECR 3477.

[100] See Chapter 1 above.

[101] Case 40/82 *Commission v UK* [1982] ECR 2793.

[102] Case 124/81 *Commission v UK* [1983] ECR 203.   [103] [1971] ECR 975.

protection of legitimate expectation could give rise to a liability in damages, as was held in Case 74/74 *CNTA v Commission*.[104] Whilst the simple fact that such a principle has been breached may not in itself be a sufficiently 'serious' violation,[105] it was a breach of the general principle of equality of treatment by a regulation abolishing production refunds on quellmehl whilst retaining them for pre-gelatinized starch which gave rise to the first actual award of damages in the *Ireks-Arkady* case.[106]

An example of the dividing line between conduct which will and will not give rise to liability may be found in Cases C-104/89 and C-37/90 *Mulder v Council and Commission*.[107] These were actions brought by dairy producers who, as mentioned above, had agreed to give up dairy production for a period of five years under an earlier Community scheme and had not produced any milk during the year (1983 in their case) taken as the base year for calculating the milk quotas, and had therefore not been granted any milk quota when the quota system was introduced in 1984 by Council Regulation 857/84. However, following judgments of the Court holding this legislation unlawful,[108] they had subsequently been granted a quota based on 60 per cent of their production during the year before they began to take part in the 'outgoers' scheme by Council Regulation 764/89, and this also was held to be unlawful by the Court.[109] In both instances, the legislation was held to breach the general principle of the protection of legitimate expectations, but in the action for damages it was held that only the initial legislation granting no quota at all gave rise to liability on the part of the Community institutions.

The explanation given by the Court is that in taking no account at all of the situation of the producers concerned, the Community institutions had manifestly and gravely disregarded the limits on the exercise of their powers, and this failure fell outside the normal inherent economic risks of the sector concerned. On the other hand the legislation which gave the outgoers a quota based on 60 per cent of their previous production did take account of their situation (even if it breached the principle of the protection of legitimate expectations), and it represented a choice of economic policy which reflected the need not to upset the fragile balance achieved on the milk market and the need to balance the interests of the outgoers with those of other producers. In the Court's view, the Council had thus taken account of a higher public interest and had not manifestly and gravely disregarded the limits on the exercise of its powers.

It may be submitted that in determining whether a breach of a superior rule is sufficiently serious, this judgment places rather more emphasis on the institution's

---

[104] [1975] ECR 533.
[105] Cases 83, 94/76 and 4, 15, 40/77 *Bayerische HNL v Council and Commission* [1978] ECR 1209.
[106] Case 238/78 *Ireks-Arkady v Council and Commission* [1979] ECR 2955.
[107] [1992] ECR I-3061.
[108] Case 120/86 *Mulder* [1988] ECR 2321, Case 170/86 *Deetzen* [1988] ECR 2355.
[109] Case C-189/89 *Spagl* [1990] ECR I-4539, Case C-217/89 *Pastätter* [1990] ECR I-4585.

conduct than on the severity of the harm suffered by the applicant; it may respectfully be doubted whether a loss of 40 per cent of production is a normal trading risk.

Techniques of interpretation

Whilst the general principles discussed above may serve as aids to interpretation—and the Court has developed a further general principle that where a provision of Community secondary legislation may be interpreted either in a way which conflicts with underlying principles of Community law or in a way which accords with those principles, preference should be given to the latter interpretation[110]—it is also in the field of agricultural law that the techniques of interpretation characteristic of the European Court have been particularly developed. In the United Kingdom, the European Court is perhaps most typically associated with a 'purposive' style of interpretation;[111] that is, that legislation is interpreted in the light of what, in its context, appears to be its purpose. It was on this basis, for example, that the Court refused to give a single meaning for 'agricultural holding'[112] and it is also on this basis that the Court has interpreted the legal mechanisms common to common organizations.[113]

Without entering into too detailed an analysis of the development of this technique, it would appear, at least in part, to be linked to the fact that all the official Community languages are equally authentic, as was recognized by the Court itself in Case 61/72 *Mij PPW International v Hoofdproduktschap voor Akkerbouwprodukten*,[114] where the obligations of national authorities with regard to the dispatch of 'advance fixing certificates' were at issue. The Court there stated that 'No argument can be drawn either from any linguistic divergences between the various language versions, or from the multiplicity of the verbs used in one or other of those versions, as the meaning of the provisions in question must be determined with respect to their *objective*' (emphasis added). Looking at the objectives of the system of advance fixing certificates, the Court noted that they were only issued on payment of a deposit by the trader, and that payment of, in this case, export refunds depended on the presentation of a certificate by the trader. From this, it held that the national authorities had a duty to ensure that such certificates actually reached applicants for them, and that this obligation was not fulfilled by sending them by ordinary post when they failed to reach the addressee.

---

[110] Case 218/82 *Commission v Council* [1983] ECR 4063.
[111] See the judgment of Lord Denning MR in *Buchanan v Babco* [1977] 1 All ER 518, 522.
[112] Case 85/77 *Santa Anna v INPS* [1978] ECR 527, 540.
[113] eg Case 113/75 *Frecassetti v Italian Finance Administration* [1976] ECR 983 and Case 6/77 *Schouten v Hoofdprodukt schap voor Akkerbouwprodukten* [1977] ECR 1291, on the old system of import levies.
[114] [1973] ECR 301.

A rather more esoteric example of the same impetus to purposive interpretation came to light in Case 100/84 *Commission v UK*.[115] It involved a joint fishing operation by British and Polish trawlers in the Baltic sea some 40 to 80 miles off the Polish coast. The British trawlers cast empty nets into the sea which were taken over by Polish trawlers. The Polish trawlers then trawled the nets, but did not take them on board. After the trawl was completed, the ends of the nets were passed to the British trawlers by the Polish trawlers, and the fish were landed onto the British trawlers. The question at issue was whether the fish were to be treated as being British in origin, in which case no CCT duty was payable (the view of the UK government), or as being Polish in origin, in which case CCT duty was payable (the view of the Commission). Under the EC legislation, fish were to be treated as wholly obtained in one country if they were 'taken from the sea' by vessels registered in that country and flying its flag.[116] After considering the different language versions of that provision, which it held not to be decisive one way or the other, the Court looked to its purpose and general scheme, concluding that the origin of the fish should depend on the flag or registration of the vessel which catches them, and that the vessel which locates the fish and separates them from the sea by netting them performs the essential part of that operation. Hence, the fish were of Polish origin.

Similarly, resort may be had to the purposive approach to apply Community law in a situation not precisely envisaged by the draftsmen, or where the terminology in any language may be capable of more than one interpretation. Hence, in Case 109/84 *Von Menges*[117] in the context of a dairy conversion scheme designed to encourage farmers to leave milk production, it was held that a farmer who replaced his herd of dairy cows with a herd of sheep which he used for producing sheep's milk could not benefit from the scheme, since although his sheep's milk did not fall within the common organization of the market in milk it competed with products falling within that organization, so that his activity was not helping to reduce the surplus of dairy production, which was the aim of the scheme.

However, the Court looks only to the purpose of the published version of the legislation and not to an underlying political purpose if that is not apparent. In Case 69/84 *Padovani*,[118] the Court, therefore, took at face value legislation which reduced the import levy on cereals imported by sea into Italy, purporting to take account of high port charges and unloading costs in Italy: in that case it held that the reduced levy was only payable if the cereals were not only declared to the Italian authorities but also physically unloaded in an Italian port, so that the full levy was payable where the cereals were trans-shipped to the Netherlands. On the other hand, it has been suggested[119] that the reduced levy really served the purpose of reducing prices on the Italian market.

---

[115] [1985] ECR 1169.

[116] Council Regulation 802/68 (JO 1968 L148/1) art 4(2)(f). Now consolidated in Council Regulation 2913/92 on the Community Customs Code (OJ 1992 L302/1).

[117] [1985] ECR 1289.   [118] [1985] ECR 1859.

[119] See eg E Neville-Rolfe, *The Politics of Agriculture in the European Community* (1984) 230.

Linked with its purposive approach is a cautious willingness by the Court to apply legislation by analogy to situations not falling within its precise terms. The attitude of the Court may, however, most clearly be illustrated by a pair of cases in which it refused to apply legislation by analogy. The *Neumann*[120] and *Ludwig*[121] cases, which were both referred to the European Court by the Bundes-verwaltungsgericht, raised the question of the application by analogy of provisions of Council Directive 72/462 on health and veterinary inspection problems upon importation of bovine animals and swine and fresh meat from third countries,[122] requiring Member States to carry out health inspections on certain types of meat imported from third countries and to charge for such inspections. In the *Neumann* case, the respondent had imported game, notably venison and wild boar, from third countries into the Federal Republic of Germany in 1975. In the *Ludwig* case the appellant had imported tins of beef goulash from Hungary in 1974. In each case the meat was inspected by the local authorities, and in each case a charge was made for such inspection, and the Bundesverwaltungsgericht was satisfied in each case that these charges were prohibited as charges having equivalent effect to customs duties.

Both importers appealed to their local administrative courts against the imposi-tion of charges. In the *Neumann* case, the Verwaltungsgericht of Frankfurt allowed the appeal, but in the *Ludwig* case, the Verwaltungsgericht of Hamburg held that Council Directive 72/462 should be extended by analogy to importations of tinned meat from third countries, and that it authorized the imposition of charges for the inspection of such meat. The Bundesverwaltungsgericht indicated in the order for reference that it agreed with the Frankfurt court, but that since the Hamburg court had expressed a contrary view, there was sufficient doubt in the matter to justify a reference to the European Court, and in both cases it asked specifically whether the relevant provisions of the directive were applicable by analogy 'with the result that the Member States are entitled or obliged to carry out health inspections and may impose charges for such inspections'.

In fact, before judgment was delivered in these cases, the Court decided in Case 70/77 *Simmenthal v Italian Finance Administration*,[123] that the relevant provisions of the directive could not be applied by Member States because the necessary Community implementing legislation had not been enacted. Hence, the directive could not have justified the charges in question whether they fell within its scope expressly or by analogy. Nonetheless, both AG Warner and the Court did consider the question whether it was possible to apply the directive by analogy. In the single Opinion he delivered in the two cases, AG Warner analysed the earlier case law on interpretation by analogy,[124] and concluded that the authorities established a general rule and an exception, the general rule being that 'the application of a provision of

---

[120] Case 137/77 *City of Frankfurt v Neumann* [1978] ECR 1623.
[121] Case 138/77 *Ludwig v City of Hamburg* [1978] ECR 1645.
[122] JO 1972 L302/28.   [123] [1978] ECR 1453.   [124] [1978] ECR at 1641–1642.

Community legislation may not be extended to a case that is outside the express scope of that provision', and the exception being that 'where legislation contains an obvious lacuna, which must needs be filled, resort may be had to an analogy in order to fill it'. He then considered the scope of the directive, which in its art 1(1) was stated to apply to imports of 'domestic bovine animals and swine for breeding, production or slaughter' and 'fresh meat of domestic animals of the following species: bovine animals, swine, sheep and goats and solipeds'. Fresh meat was defined in art 2(o) as 'meat which has not undergone any preserving process; however, chilled and frozen meat shall be considered to be fresh'. In the light of these provisions, AG Warner stated as his opinion that game and tinned beef had been deliberately excluded from the scope of the directive, and that their omission could not be regarded as a lacuna that might be filled by judicial decision.

The Court reached the same result, but from a somewhat different angle, basing itself on the fact, which it had emphasized in the decision in *Simmenthal*, that the prohibition on charges having equivalent effect to customs duties on imports from third countries is intended to protect the Community's uniform external stance *vis-à-vis* third countries. The Court pointed out that the directive was intended not to strengthen the protection of public health and safety, but to establish uniform systems of inspection so as to prevent competition being distorted and trade being diverted. It stated that the imposition of charges under the directive was linked to the establishment of a uniform Community system of inspections corresponding to the needs of the Common Customs Tariff, and that to allow Member States uni-laterally to impose charges could go against this aim; hence, provisions allowing charges to be imposed could not be extended beyond their specific scope. The Court added that the directive was not an illustration of a general principle of Community law under which charges could be imposed for any inspection carried out at the external frontiers of the Community, but an example of the derogations from the basic prohibition on the imposition by Member States of charges having equivalent effect to customs duties on goods imported from third countries.

On the other hand, in its contemporaneous judgment in Case 6/78 *Union Française des Céréales v HZA Hamburg-Jonas*,[125] the Court held that a 'force majeure' clause[126] in the basic regulation governing export refunds could be read into a regulation governing accession compensatory amounts, since accession compen-satory amounts served the same purpose as export refunds in trade with new Member States.

Similarly, analogy may be used to remedy a breach of a basic principle, so that when, in Case 165/84 *Krohn*[127] it was held to be a breach of the principle of equality of treatment not to allow importers of manioc from Thailand to cancel their licences when importers from other third countries could do so, the Court

[125] [1978] ECR 1675.
[126] See B Loyant, 'La force majeure et l'organisation des marchés agricoles' (1980) Revue trimestrielle de droit européen 256.
[127] [1985] ECR 3997.

held that the parallel legislation governing imports from countries other than Thailand should be applied by analogy to imports from Thailand. Application of legislation by analogy has also been used to prevent a breach of a general principle: in Cases 201 and 202/85 *Klensch v Luxembourg Secretary of State for Agriculture*,[128] it was decided that where Council Regulation 857/84[129] did not provide expressly for the reallocation of the milk quota of a farmer who left dairy farming of his own volition, the rules which would have applied if he had left dairy farming under the special outgoers' scheme should apply by analogy, so that his quota should go to the national reserve. To allocate his quota to the purchaser to which he had made his deliveries, as the Luxembourg government had done, would, in the Court's view, breach the principle of non-discrimination with regard to other producers, and would tie that producer to the one purchaser if he wanted to re-enter the market.

[128] [1986] ECR 3477.   [129] OJ 1984 L90/13.

3

Agricultural support: the international context

Background

Agriculture is an area where the trade of developed countries appears to be conducted on a highly artificial basis reflecting the system of support used in their internal markets. The reality is that agricultural trade is an area where developed countries have not been willing to allow free reign to market forces. Using OECD figures[1] which compare agricultural support in terms of producer subsidy equivalent, whether it takes the form of price support or the form of a subsidy as such, the average level of support in the OECD member countries in 1999 was the equivalent of a producer subsidy of 40 per cent—which makes the Community figure of 49 per cent seem not far out of line. It is perhaps ironic to observe that in the period 1986–1988, before the Uruguay Round negotiations which led to the entry into force of the Agreement on Agriculture, the OECD average had similarly been 40 per cent, and EU average had been lower than its current level at 44 per cent. The 1999 figure for the United States was 24 per cent (25 per cent in 1986–1988), somewhat lower but hardly insignificant, but for Japan it was 65 per cent (67 per cent) and for Switzerland 73 per cent (73 per cent). In terms of support for each producer, the Community figure of $17,000 per farmer was somewhat lower than the OECD average of $20,000 per farmer and lower than the United States figure of $21,000 per farmer, a difference which presumably reflects the difference in size of production units as between the Community and the United States.

This situation has been achieved through a combination of domestic support (whether of products or of producers), import protection, and assistance to exports, and against this background, agricultural trade has always received special treatment in the GATT context. Indeed, in the very early days of GATT, in 1951, the United States amended its domestic agricultural legislation to enable quotas and licence fees to be imposed on imports of agricultural products which threatened to disturb domestic price support programmes, and in order to be able to apply this legislation, the United States sought and eventually obtained (in 1955) a waiver

---

[1] OECD, *Agricultural Policies in OECD Countries: Monitoring and Evaluation 2000* (2000).

from its GATT obligations, arguing that the nature of its domestic agricultural support programmes meant that imports were attracted in such exceptional quantities that the domestic programmes were being adversely affected.[2] It may be suggested that this waiver set the tone for future regulation of agricultural trade.

Be that as it may, it will be seen that domestic support for agricultural products and producers, protection against imports of agricultural products, and assistance for exports of agricultural products are not in themselves prohibited under GATT rules; neither indeed are they prohibited under the Uruguay Round Agreement on Agriculture. Rather, the Uruguay Round Agreement on Agriculture requires their reduction in line with the commitments undertaken by the participant states. However, it also regards some forms of support as less likely to cause distortion of trade than others, and allows these forms of support to be excluded from the commitments to reduce support; it may be suggested that this helps to explain how states which on the face of have complied with their Uruguay Round obligations are still providing agricultural support at levels similar to those which prevailed before the Uruguay Round.

Domestic support

While common organizations of EC agricultural markets will be considered in the next chapter, the archetypical illustration of domestic support for agricultural production in the EC may be found in the market in cereals, which has been fundamentally changed during the 1990s. At the heart of the original version were a target price and an intervention price. The target price indicated the level of price it was hoped Community producers would receive, and as a matter of law was fixed for Duisburg in West Germany as being the centre of the area with the greatest deficit of cereals in the Community (even though the same nominal prices apply throughout the whole Community). The intervention price on the other hand has traditionally represented the price at which national authorities, such as the United Kingdom Intervention Board for Agricultural Produce, are legally required to purchase products subject to the price system which are offered to them, and was fixed for Ormes in France, as being the production area having the greatest surplus of cereals in the Community. The relevance of fixing a geographical location for the target and intervention prices was that the difference between those prices included an element to allow for the costs of transport between Ormes and Duisburg. Under the 1992 reforms, the target and intervention prices ceased to have geographical links, and were fixed by Council Regulation 1766/92[3] so as to be reduced by fixed amounts over a three-year period, starting from a

---

[2] R Hudec, *The GATT Legal System and World Trade Diplomacy* (2nd edn, 1990) 181 ff, J McMahon, *European Trade Policy in Agricultural Products* (1988) 41.
[3] OJ 1992 L181/21.

lower level than that previously applied; the target price, following implementation of the Uruguay Round Agreement on Agriculture, was abolished in 1995 by Council Regulation 1528/95.[4] Council Regulation 1253/1999[5] continues the reduction in intervention prices for the 2000–2001 and 2001–2002 marketing years, and anticipates a final reduction in 2002–2003. Conversely, Council Regulation 1251/1999[6] increases area payments for some arable crops for 2000–2001 and 2001–2002, and anticipates further increases related to the final reduction in the intervention price.

Such price machinery has not been unique to the European Community. The illustration may be taken of the American concept of the 'parity price' based on the idea that there should be the same relationship between prices paid by farmers and prices received by farmers as existed in the years from 1909 to 1914, which were deemed to be 'normal' years;[7] costs could therefore be used to calculate prices on a formula derived from the situation in those base years. Also, the Americans used so-called 'non-recourse' loans. Under this scheme, government loans were available to farmers against the security of eligible crops. If prices fell below the level assumed in the loan, the farmer would fail to repay the loan and the government would take possession of the crop, but would have no remedy against the farmer for the money outstanding because of the 'non-recourse' nature of the loan. In other words, the government would buy the crops at the loan price. On the other hand, if the market price rose above the loan rate, the farmer would repay the loan and keep the profit. The practical effect would appear to have been very similar to the Community intervention system.

Leaving on one side the question of the support as such, two major trade problems are caused by support systems involving producer subsidies. From the point of view of external suppliers selling into the Community, such a system of subsidies may mean that domestic producers can sell at a world price lower than their costs, if the subsidy makes up the difference, so that external suppliers obtain no price advantage. This point was at issue in the *Oilseeds* dispute between the United States and the Community. In the oilseeds market, the Community had made GATT concessions leading to low rates of duty, and, although a target- and intervention-price structure was provided for these seeds under Council Regulation 136/66,[8] the basic method of ensuring that Community prices were paid was that whenever the target price was higher than the world-market price a subsidy was granted for such seeds harvested and processed within the Community, this subsidy being equal to the difference between the target price and the world-market price. In the *Oilseeds* dispute a GATT panel[9] held the EC oilseeds subsidy scheme to constitute

---

[4] OJ 1995 L148/3.   [5] OJ 1999 L160/18.   [6] OJ 1999 L160/1.

[7] For an account of US support mechanisms, see K Meyer, D Pedersen, N Thorson, and J Davidson, *Agricultural Law, Cases and Materials* (1984), chapter 1B 'Economic Regulation of Agriculture' at 26–35.

[8] JO 1966, p 3025.

[9] 25 January 1990, see P Pescatore, W Davey, and A Lowenfeld, *Handbook of GATT Dispute Settlement* (1991) 525.

an impairment of the tariff concessions in favour of the United States, on the basis that 'the United States could not reasonably have anticipated the introduction of subsidy schemes which protect producers completely from the movement of prices for imports and thereby prevent the tariff concessions from having any impact on the competitive relationship between domestic and imported oilseeds'.

The other and perhaps better recognized problem which arises from producer subsidies is that of subsidized exports—even where no export subsidy as such is granted. This is perhaps best illustrated by what has happened in the Community where there has been no common organization. By virtue of art 36 of the Treaty, competition rules apply in agriculture only to the extent the Council determines, and in the context of the state aids rules (which are treated by the Treaty as competition rules), the implementing Council Regulation 26/62 does not apply the substantive Treaty rules to agricultural products. Art 4 of the regulation merely provides for the application of the provisions requiring the review of existing systems of aid by the Commission and requiring the notification of new aids. Hence, as discussed in Chapter 1, the application of the substantive state aids rules to trade in agricultural products depends on the terms of the regulations establishing common organizations of the market for the products in question. Where, however, there is no common organization, there is no general application of the state aids rules to agricultural products, as was expressly recognized by the European Court in relation to the market in potatoes in Case 114/83 *Société d'Initiatives v Commission*.[10] Particular difficulties may therefore arise in so far as the free movement of goods rules do apply to agricultural products not subject to a common organization but the state aids rules do not. This was the background to the famous (or infamous) sheepmeat dispute between the UK and France, where France took the view that the UK system of deficiency payments constituted a state aid, yet the Court held that France could not prevent or restrict the import of sheepmeat which had benefited from the UK system,[11] with the result that the French system of intervention to support the price of domestic sheepmeat could be totally undermined by cheaper imports from the UK. A solution suggested by the Court was that nothing prevented the French authorities from adopting their own scheme of aids for the sheepmeat sector until a common organization of the market was established.

Turning to support as such, the principle laid down in art III of GATT is that 'the contracting parties recognize that internal taxes and other internal charges, and laws, regulations and requirements affecting the internal sale, offering for sale, purchase, transportation, distribution or use of products, and internal quantitative regulations requiring the mixture, processing or use of products in specified amounts or proportions, should not be applied to imported or domestic products so as to afford protection to domestic production'. However, under art III:8(b), 'the

[10] [1984] ECR 2589.
[11] Case 232/78 *Commission v France* [1979] ECR 2729.

provisions of this Article shall not prevent the payment of subsidies exclusively to domestic producers, including payments to domestic producers derived from the proceeds of internal taxes or charges applied consistently with the provisions of this Article and subsidies effected through governmental purchases of domestic products'. It is therefore expressly provided that direct payments may be made to domestic producers without having to be offered to other producers, and that subsidies may be offered to domestic products through governmental purchases (ie intervention, in Community jargon).

However, in order to benefit from this exemption, producer subsidies must be paid to producers, as was pointed out in the *Oilseeds* dispute with the United States[12] where, as has already been mentioned, a panel found the EC subsidy scheme to have prevented the United States from obtaining full advantage from its tariff concessions since it prevented those concessions from having any impact on the competitive relationship between domestic and imported oilseeds. However, the panel also took a different view from the European Court as to the legal nature of the subsidies. In Cases 67–85/75 *Lesieur Cotelle and Others v Commission*,[13] the Court had held that the subsidy granted for oilseeds harvested and processed within the Community, under Council Regulation 136/66,[14] was intended as a guarantee for growers of the seeds. The applicants in that case were, in fact, oil millers and not seed growers. The Court said that in so far as Regulation 136/66 was intended to give guarantees, the latter related to colzaseed farmers and not processors, as appeared from art 24 of the regulation, according to which the derived intervention price guaranteed that producers would be able to sell their produce at a price which, allowing for market fluctuations, was as close as possible to the target price. The subsidies granted to seed processors were not intended to guarantee the latter a fixed payment for their processing, but to enable them to buy Community seed at prices close to the target price. The Court concluded that the oil millers could not claim any guarantee under Regulation 136/66. However, the GATT panel took the view that a payment not made directly to the producers is not paid 'exclusively' to them within the terms of art III:8(b), and found that the EC regulation did not in fact ensure that payments to producers were based on the prices processors actually had to pay when purchasing Community oilseeds.

Under art 3 of the Uruguay Round Agreement on Agriculture, 'a Member shall not provide support in favour of domestic producers in excess of the commitment levels specified in Section I of Part IV of its Schedule', and in the case of the EC domestic support is required to be reduced, by a global 20 per cent, but taken from a 1986–1988 base, although under art 6(5) and Annex II payments under production-limiting programmes (eg set-aside) and decoupled income

---

[12] 25 January 1990, see P Pescatore, W Davey, and A Lowenfeld, *Handbook of GATT Dispute Settlement* (1991) 525.
[13] [1976] ECR 391.   [14] JO 1966, p 3025.

support do not need to be reduced. Art 6 of the Agreement on Agriculture provides that the domestic support reduction commitments of each Member contained in Part IV of its Schedule 'shall apply to all of its domestic support measures in favour of agricultural producers with the exception of domestic measures which are not subject to reduction in terms of the criteria set out in this Article and in Annex 2 to this Agreement'.

Under art 6(5) on the other hand, direct payments under production-limiting programmes are not subject to the commitment to reduce domestic support if such payments are based on fixed area and yields; or such payments are made on 85 per cent or less of the base level of production; or livestock payments are made on a fixed number of head. In this context, it may be observed that, by way of example, the area payments under art 4 of Council Regulation 1251/1999[15] on a support system for producers of certain arable crops are calculated by multiplying the basic amount per tonne by the average cereal yield determined in the regionalization plan for the region concerned, and are in principle subject to an obligation to set aside a proportion of the area down to arable crops (currently, under art 6 of the Regulation, 10 per cent, but at the time the Uruguay Round negotiations were completed the basic set-aside rate was 15 per cent under art 7 of Council Regulation 1765/92[16]). Area payments are also envisaged in the beef sector under Council Regulation 1254/99,[17] and from 2005 in the dairy sector under Council Regulation 1255/99.[18] With regard to livestock payments are made on a fixed number of head; perhaps the most obvious example is the ewe headage payment under Council Regulation 2647/98 on the common organization of the market in sheepmeat:[19] here there is an overall maximum guaranteed level fixed at 63,400,000 head of ewes.[20]

Art 6(5)(b) of the agreement states expressly that the exemption from the reduction commitment for direct payments meeting the above criteria shall be reflected by the exclusion of the value of those direct payments in a Member's calculation of its total level of domestic support.

Annex 2 sets out in greater detail the domestic support measures which are not subject to the reduction commitments. The basic rule set out in the first paragraph is that domestic support policies for which exemption from the reduction commitments is claimed 'shall meet the fundamental requirement that they have no, or at most minimal, trade distortion effects or effects on production'. It is therefore provided that all policies for which exemption is claimed must conform to the following basic criteria:

- the support in question shall be provided through a publicly funded government programme (including government revenue forgone) not involving transfers from consumers; and

[15] OJ 1999 L160/1. [16] OJ 1992 L181/12.
[17] OJ 1999 L160/21; see Annex IV. [18] OJ 1999 L160/48.
[19] OJ 1998 L312/1. [20] Art 13(1).

- the support in question shall not have the effect of providing price support to producers.

With regard to direct payments to producers, paragraph 5 states that support provided through direct payments (or revenue forgone, including payments in kind) to producers for which exemption from reduction commitments is claimed must meet the basic criteria set out in paragraph 1, plus specific criteria applying to individual types of direct payment as set out in paragraphs 6 to 13. Where exemption from reduction is claimed for any existing or new type of direct payment other than those specified in paragraphs 6 to 13, it is required to conform to criteria (ii) to (v) of paragraph 6 in addition to the general criteria set out in paragraph 1.

Paragraph 6 deals with 'decoupled income support', ie payments which, while they may be calculated from production during a base year, do not depend on current production. It is provided that:

(i) Eligibility for such payments shall be determined by clearly defined criteria such as income, status as a producer or landowner, factor use, or production level in a defined and fixed base period.
(ii) The amount of such payments in any given year shall not be related to, or based on, the type or volume of production (including livestock units) undertaken by the producer in any year after the base period.
(iii) The amount of such payments in any given year shall not be related to, or based on, the prices, domestic or international, applying to any production undertaken in any year after the base period.
(iv) The amount of such payments in any given year shall not be related to, or based on, the factors of production employed in any year after the base period.
(v) No production shall be required in order to receive such payments.

It may be suggested that the EC area payments discussed above meet these criteria.

Paragraph 7 deals with government financial participation in income insurance and income safety-net programmes, providing that:

(i) Eligibility for such payments shall be determined by an income loss, taking into account only income derived from agriculture, which exceeds 30 per cent of average gross income or the equivalent in net income terms (excluding any payments from the same or similar schemes) in the preceding three-year period or a three-year average based on the preceding five-year period, excluding the highest and the lowest entry. Any producer meeting this condition shall be eligible to receive the payments.
(ii) The amount of such payments shall compensate for less than 70 per cent of the producer's income loss in the year the producer becomes eligible to receive this assistance.
(iii) The amount of any such payments shall relate solely to income; it shall not relate to the type or volume of production (including livestock units) undertaken by

the producer; or to the prices, domestic or international, applying to such production; or to the factors of production employed.

(iv) Where a producer receives in the same year payments under this paragraph and under paragraph 8 below (relief from natural disasters), the total of such payments shall be less than 100 per cent of the producer's total loss.

Under paragraph 8, payments (made either directly or by way of government financial participation in crop insurance schemes) for relief from natural disasters do not count in the calculation of domestic support, provided that eligibility for such payments arises only following a formal recognition by government authorities that a natural or like disaster (including disease outbreaks, pest infestations, nuclear accidents, and war on the territory of the Member concerned) has occurred or is occurring; and shall be determined by a production loss which exceeds 30 per cent of the average of production in the preceding three-year period or a three-year average based on the preceding five-year period, excluding the highest and the lowest entry. Thus compensation for the slaughter of herds during a foot-and-mouth disease outbreak would not count as domestic support. It is further made clear that payments made following a disaster are to be applied only in respect of losses of income, livestock (including payments in connection with the veterinary treatment of animals), land, or other production factors due to the natural disaster in question, and that payments should compensate for not more than the total cost of replacing such losses and shall not require or specify the type or quantity of future production, and should not exceed the level required to prevent or alleviate further loss. Where a producer receives in the same year payments under this paragraph and under paragraph 7 (income insurance and income safety-net programmes), the total of such payments must be less than 100 per cent of the producer's total loss.

Exemption is also granted under paragraph 9 for structural adjustment assistance provided through producer retirement programmes, such as arts 10–12 of Council Regulation 1257/1999 on support for rural development from the EAGGF.[21] It is provided that eligibility for such payments must be determined by reference to clearly defined criteria in programmes designed to facilitate the retirement of persons engaged in marketable agricultural production, or their movement to non-agricultural activities, and that payments must be conditional upon the total and permanent retirement of the recipients from marketable agricultural production.

Also excluded from the calculation of total domestic support, by virtue of paragraph 10, is 'structural adjustment assistance provided through resource retirement programmes', ie such measures as set-aside, grubbing-up, and outgoers' schemes. Eligibility for such payments must be determined by reference to clearly defined criteria in programmes designed to remove land or other resources, including livestock, from marketable agricultural production, and payments must be conditional

[21] OJ 1999 L160/80.

upon the retirement of land from marketable agricultural production for a minimum of three years, and in the case of livestock on its slaughter or definitive permanent disposal. Payments must not require or specify any alternative use for such land or other resources which involves the production of marketable agricultural products, and they must not be related to either the type or quantity of production or to the prices, domestic or international, applying to production undertaken using the land or other resources remaining in production.

Structural adjustment assistance provided through investment aids is also excluded from the basic calculation by virtue of paragraph 11. Under this provision, eligibility for such payments must be determined by reference to clearly defined criteria in government programmes designed to assist the financial or physical restructuring of a producer's operations in response to objectively demonstrated structural disadvantages, such as support for less-favoured areas under chapter V of Council Regulation 1257/1999 on support for rural development from the EAGGF.[22] Eligibility for such programmes may also be based on a clearly defined government programme for the reprivatization of agricultural land, a matter of some importance in the Central and Eastern European countries which have applied to join the EU. The amount of such payments in any given year must not be related to, or based on, the type or volume of production (including livestock units) undertaken by the producer in any year after the base period, and it must not be related to, or based on, the prices, domestic or international, applying to any production undertaken in any year after the base period. The payments must be given only for the period of time necessary for the realization of the investment in respect of which they are provided, and they must not mandate or in any way designate the agricultural products to be produced by the recipients except to require them *not* to produce a particular product. Finally, the payments must be limited to the amount required to compensate for the structural disadvantage.

Payments under environmental programmes are also excluded from the calculation, which would appear to cover support for agri-environment production methods and commitments under arts 22–24 of Council Regulation 1257/1999 on support for rural development from the EAGGF.[23] Paragraph 12 requires that eligibility for such payments shall be determined as part of a clearly defined government environmental or conservation programme and be dependent on the fulfilment of specific conditions under the government programme, including conditions related to production methods or inputs, though the amount of payment must be limited to the extra costs or loss of income involved in complying with the government programme.

Payments under regional assistance programmes are similarly excluded from the calculation. Under paragraph 13, eligibility for such payments must be limited to producers in disadvantaged regions, and each such region must be a clearly designated contiguous geographical area with a definable economic and administrative

---

[22] OJ 1999 L160/80.   [23] Ibid.

identity, considered as disadvantaged on the basis of neutral and objective criteria clearly spelt out in law or regulation and indicating that the region's difficulties arise out of more than temporary circumstances. In the EC context, under Council Regulation 1258/1999 on the financing of the common agricultural policy,[24] in principle the Guidance Section finances only rural development measures falling within Objective 1 programmes and the rural development Community initiative. Under Regulation 1260/1999[25] on the Structural Funds, Objective 1 is defined as covering those areas where GDP per capita in terms of purchasing power is less that 75 per cent of the Community average,[26] and it is provided that 69.7 per cent of the €195 billion allocated to the Structural Funds for 2000–2006 should go on Objective 1 projects.[27]

It is further provided that the amount of such payments in any given year must not be related to, or based on, the type or volume of production (including livestock units) undertaken by the producer in any year after the base period other than to reduce that production, nor must it be related to, or based on, the prices, domestic or international, applying to any production undertaken in any year after the base period. Such payments must be available only to producers in eligible regions, but they must be generally available to all producers within such regions. Where the payments are related to production factors, they must be made at a degressive rate above a threshold level of the factor concerned. Finally, the payments must be limited to the extra costs or loss of income involved in undertaking agricultural production in the prescribed area.

Looked at from an EC perspective, the Agreement on Agriculture has encouraged the move which had already begun away from a system of product support (intervention) to a system involving an element of producer support (eg area payments and set-aside). Such a move also automatically has the effect both of reducing the amount of internal support which is taken into account for WTO purposes, and reducing the level of export support which is required. As mentioned earlier in this chapter, Council Regulation 1253/1999[28] continues the reduction in intervention prices for the 2000–2001 and 2001–2002 marketing years, and anticipates a final reduction in 2002–2003. Conversely, Council Regulation 1251/1999[29] increases area payments for some arable crops for 2000–2001 and 2001–2002, and anticipates further increases related to the final reduction in the intervention price.

Import charges and market access

In the traditional EC system of support exemplified in the earlier version of the common organization of the market in cereals based on target and intervention prices fixed respectively for Duisburg and Ormes, geography also played a role in

---

[24] OJ 1999 L160/103. [25] OJ 1999 L161/1. [26] Art 3.
[27] Art 7. [28] OJ 1999 L160/18. [29] OJ 1999 L160/1.

the external aspects of the price structure: in order to ensure that the price structure was not upset by lower-priced imports, a threshold price was fixed, notionally for the port of Rotterdam, representing the minimum price at which the relevant goods may enter the Community. This threshold price was calculated not from the intervention price but from the higher target price (thus ensuring that the intervention price was not likely to be undercut), and the difference between the target price and the threshold price again included an element to allow for the cost of transport between Rotterdam and Duisburg. Like the target and intervention prices, under the 1992 version of the common organization the threshold price ceased to have a geographical link, and was fixed by Council Regulation 1766/92 so as to be reduced by fixed amounts over a three-year period.

If (as was usually the case) the world price, calculated on a CIF basis for Rotterdam, was lower than the threshold price, the difference had to be covered by an import levy. The legal nature of import levies gave rise to some contention. As far as the external protection afforded by the levies is concerned, the EC was insistent that they must, in their objectives, be distinguished from customs duties. The European Court pointed out in Case 17/67 *Neumann v Hauptzollamt Hof*[30] that, whatever similarities import levies may have to customs duty, a levy was a charge regulating external trade connected with a common price policy and not a customs duty as such.

With regard to such import restrictions, it could be argued that there was no express provision of GATT prohibiting variable levies unless the products concerned benefited from tariff bindings,[31] although others have argued that they may fall within the concept of quantitative restrictions under art XI.[32] The variable import levy does not appear to have been challenged directly except where the Community, in first introducing common organizations, tried to negotiate the withdrawal of concessions previously offered by Member States in relation to the products at issue. This was the case with regard to the introduction of the common organization of the market in poultrymeat, giving rise to a 'chicken war' with the United States,[33] which was settled not by contesting the basic issues but by a panel reaching a compromise on the value of import restrictions to be applied by the USA in response to the EC variable levy on poultry imports.

In any event, while art XI:1 of GATT lays down that in principle imports and exports should be subject to no prohibitions or restrictions other than duties, taxes, or other charges, whether made effective through quotas, import or export licences, or other measures, art XI:2 permits import restrictions on any agricultural or fisheries product, imported in any form, necessary to the enforcement of governmental measures which operate:

---

[30] [1967] ECR 441.

[31] I Garcia Bercero, 'Trade Laws, GATT, and the Management of Trade Disputes between the US and the EEC' (1985) Yearbook of European Law 149 at 165.

[32] E McGovern, *International Trade Regulation: GATT, the United States and the European Community* (1982) 342.

[33] R Hudec, *The GATT Legal System and World Trade Diplomacy* (2nd edn, 1990) 238–240.

(i)   to restrict the quantities of the like domestic product permitted to be marketed or produced, or, if there is no substantial domestic production of the like product, of a domestic product for which the imported product can be directly substituted; or

(ii) to remove a temporary surplus of the like domestic product, or, if there is no substantial domestic production of the like product, of a domestic product for which the imported product can be directly substituted, by making the surplus available to certain groups of domestic consumers free of charge or at prices below the current market level; or

(iii) to restrict the quantities permitted to be produced of any animal product the production of which is directly dependent, wholly or mainly, on the imported commodity, if the domestic production of that commodity is relatively negligible.

These restrictions however must not be such as 'will reduce the total of imports relative to the total of domestic production, as compared with the proportion which might reasonably be expected to rule between the two in the absence of restrictions'. In effect, therefore, import restrictions may be justified if linked to the regulation of the internal market—and there are in fact currently production limits of one sort or another on many of the major EC common organizations, in the form of quotas and guarantee thresholds.

On the other hand, EC import restrictions have been held to breach art XI. In the case of tomato concentrates,[34] the Community imposed a minimum import price below which imports were prohibited, and a compulsory deposit would be lost if imports took place below that price. It was found that the forfeiture was a restriction within the meaning of art XI and that the system of support for tomatoes did not constitute a governmental measure restricting domestic production under art XI:2(c).

The fundamental aim of the Agreement on Agriculture with regard to import restrictions is to convert permitted restrictions into customs duties, in the name of greater transparency, subject to commitments that they should be reduced. Under art 4(2) Members shall not maintain, resort to, or revert to any measures of the kind which have been required to be converted into ordinary customs duties, except as otherwise provided for in art 5, which allows for safeguard measures where either the volume of imports exceeds a trigger level or the price of imports falls below a trigger level, and Annex 5, which deals with cases of special treatment. A footnote to art 4(2) then performs the rather important task of defining the measures which are required to be converted into ordinary customs duties: 'These measures include quantitative import restrictions, variable import levies, minimum import prices, discretionary import licensing, non-tariff measures maintained through state trading enterprises, voluntary export restraints and similar border measures other than ordinary customs duties, whether or not the measures

[34] BISD 25th Supp 68.

are maintained under country-specific derogations from the provisions of the GATT 1947, but not measures maintained under balance-of-payments provisions or under other general, non-agriculture-specific provisions of the GATT 1994 or of the other Multilateral Trade Agreements in Annex 1A to the WTO.'

In the context of the EC, this meant that import levies were required to be converted into tariffs, and in the EC's case reduced by an average of 36 per cent from a 1986–1988 base. The EC's obligations to convert levies to tariffs and to reduce support under the Uruguay Round Agreement were effected under Council Regulation 3290/94,[35] though in the cereals market the customs duties appear to be of a flat-rate nature. However, the influence of the old levy has not disappeared completely, to reflect the fact that while the old levy diminished as world prices rose, a customs duty would in principle be added to the high world price: while the customs duty under normal conditions sets the limit on the import duties payable, under art 10(2) of Regulation 1766/92 as amended by Regulation 3290/94, for many products what is actually payable is an import duty equal to the relevant intervention price increased by 55 per cent, minus the CIF import price, provided it does not exceed the CCT duty. The practical effect therefore is to reduce the import duties to a lower level than the customs duty when the world price for the products in question rises. Nevertheless, as a consequence of the change to customs duties, there was no longer a need for a threshold price, and the target price therefore no longer served any practical purpose, and was abolished by Council Regulation 1528/95.[36]

Outside the matters covered by the Agreement on Agriculture, the impact on the evolution of an EC common organization of an agricultural market of the basic GATT rules of most-favoured-nation treatment under art I, and non-discrimination with regard to quotas, in particular tariff quotas, under art XIII is very clearly shown in the banana sector. The common organization of the market in bananas was introduced only in 1993, in Council Regulation 404/93.[37] The timing of its intro-duction may be related to the completion of the single internal market by the end of 1992 under art 14 of the EC Treaty, in that the UK and France had quota regimes giving preference to imports from their former colonies, and had previously been authorized not to grant Community treatment to bananas from other countries in free circulation in other Member States. At the domestic level, the common orga-nization provided for limited financial support through producers' organizations, but only for a fixed level of production,[38] and it also provided for the payment of a premium to Community producers who cease to produce bananas.[39] However, the vast majority of bananas consumed in the EU are imported from third coun-tries, and it was with regard to these imports that the conflicts with WTO rules occurred. The regulation provided differential treatment for traditional imports from ACP countries[40] amounting to 857,700 tonnes, for non-traditional imports

---

[35] OJ 1994 L349/105.   [36] OJ 1995 L148/3.   [37] OJ 1993 L47/1.
[38] Art 12.   [39] Art 13.   [40] Listed in Annex I.

from ACP countries, and for imports from non-ACP third countries. The traditional ACP imports were free of duty, and a further tariff quota of 2 million tonnes was established, within which imports from non-ACP third countries paid a reduced tariff of €75 per tonne, and non-traditional imports from ACP countries were free of duty. The quota was raised in 1995 to 2.2 million tonnes, and a further 353,000 tonnes was added as a result of the 1995 enlargement of the EU. Outside this quota, imports were subject to the Common Customs Tariff duty, subject to a deduction of €100 per tonne for non-traditional imports from ACP countries.

Importation was subject to a licensing scheme,[41] and the quota was originally open as to 66.5 per cent to operators who marketed third country and/or non-traditional ACP bananas, as to 30 per cent to operators who marketed Community and/or traditional ACP bananas, and as to just 3 per cent to operators established in the Community who started marketing bananas other than Community and/or traditional ACP bananas from 1992. It was the allocation of 30 per cent of the quota licences to operators who marketed Community and/or traditional ACP bananas which was one of the factors which led the WTO Appellate Body[42] to hold that there was a breach of art II of the General Agreement on Trade in Services, requiring 'no less favourable treatment' for service providers from other participating states. Fairly clearly, the differential import system itself was difficult to reconcile with the most-favoured-nation principle laid down in art I of GATT[43] or the non-discriminatory administration of quotas required by art XIII, and the EC therefore negotiated a waiver at the time of the Uruguay Round, which was extended in 1996. However, it was held that this waiver was so drafted as to be appropriate only for the most-favoured-nation clause, and that it did not extend to art XIII, so that the EC was in breach of the requirement for non-discriminatory administration of quotas.

However, in the arbitration[44] on the level of suspension of concessions which could be imposed by the United States while the EU banana regime remained in breach of GATT and GATS,[45] the arbitrators suggested[46] that a WTO-consistent counterfactual would be a global tariff quota of 2.553 million tonnes subject to a duty of €75 per tonne, with unlimited access for ACP bananas at a zero tariff, with the ACP tariff preference being covered by a waiver. While the EC did not change the regime immediately along those lines, thereby suffering a US suspension of concessions of $191.4 million per year not to protect EC banana producers but to protect the perceived interests of banana producers in the ACP countries, in 2001 changes were made to the import aspects of the common organization, and agreement was reached with the USA and other complainants as to the shape of a longer-term policy.

---

[41] Art 17. [42] WT/DS27/AB/R.

[43] Indeed, art 168(2)(a)(ii) of the Fourth Lomé Convention required the Community to take the necessary measures to ensure more favourable treatment than that granted to third countries benefiting from the most-favoured-nation clause for the same products.

[44] Under art 22.6 of the Dispute Settlement Procedure (9 April 1999).

[45] WT/DS27/ARB. [46] Para XIII.174.

A transitional regime was introduced by Council Regulation 216/2001,[47] the recitals to which refer expressly to the recommendations of the dispute settlement body. So far as the services question is concerned, a new art 19 provides that the tariff quotas may be managed in accordance with 'the method based on taking account of traditional trade flows. . . . and/or other methods'. It would appear that the agreement with the USA was to use historic references,[48] but following further negotiations with Ecuador, 83 per cent of the quotas are to be managed this way and 17 per cent will be reserved for operators who do not have a suitable historic reference.[49] With regard to the quotas themselves, three bands of quota are envisaged, but under a new art 18, they are in principle open for imports of products originating in all third countries: quota A is for 2.2 million tonnes at a duty of €75 per tonne, quota B is for 353,000 tonnes at the same duty, and quota C is for 850,000 tonnes at a duty of €300. However, provision is made for a tariff preference of €300 per tonne for all imports from ACP countries, both inside and outside the quota, which would effectively allow duty-free access to ACP bananas under all three quotas.

However, under the agreement with the USA, 100,000 tonnes is to be moved from quota C to quota B, and the reduced quota C is then to be reserved exclusively for bananas of ACP origin[50]—which will require a waiver from art XIII of GATT, which the USA and Ecuador[51] have agreed to help to achieve. Longer term, it is proposed that a flat-tariff system will be introduced in 2006.[52]

Export subsidies

If (as was usually the case under the target- and intervention-price system) the world price was lower than the Community intervention price, and a Community producer wished to export into lower-priced world markets, there was (and still is[53]) power under the Community legislation to pay an export refund to cover the difference.

It would appear to be the system of export refunds that has given rise to the greatest number of complaints from the Community's trading partners. However, it has been suggested that export refunds, as the counterpart of the Community's variable import levies, were accepted in principle as compatible with GATT as a result of the Dillon Round negotiations.[54] In any event, art XVI of GATT merely requires Members to 'seek' to avoid the use of subsidies on the export of primary

---

[47] OJ 2001 L31/2.   [48] Commission MEMO/01/135 (11 April 2001).
[49] Commission IP/01/628 (2 May 2001).
[50] Commission MEMO/01/135 (11 April 2001).
[51] Commission IP/01/628 (2 May 2001).
[52] Commission MEMO/01/135 (11 April 2001).
[53] See Chapter 4 below.
[54] E Neville-Rolfe, *The Politics of Agriculture in the European Community* (1984) 26.

products; such subsidies are not as such a breach of GATT. If, however, a contracting party grants a subsidy which has the effect of *increasing* exports from its territory, it should not be applied so as to result in that party having 'more than an equitable share' of world export trade in that product, taking account of the shares held during a previous representative period. The concept of what was more than an equitable share was addressed in the Subsidies Code agreed in the Tokyo Round, art 10 of which defined it as including 'any case in which the effect of an export subsidy granted by a signatory is to displace the exports of another signatory bearing in mind developments in world markets'.

In this context, Australia and Brazil complained that Community export refunds on sugar had led to Community exporters having more than an equitable share of world export trade.[55] Although the panel found that the Community had increased its share of world markets, a link with Brazilian and Australian exports could not be shown, and it did not therefore conclude that the Community had taken a more than equitable share. It was found that the Community practice had helped depress world sugar prices, causing indirect harm to the complainants, but this could not be quantified. On the other hand, before the entry into force of the CAP, it was actually held in the case of French assistance to the export of wheat and wheat flour,[56] which involved differential bonuses and variable bonuses for exports, that the French share in the South-East Asian market had become inequitable, having risen from 0.7 per cent in 1954 to 46 per cent in 1958, to a large extent as the result of the subsidy arrangements.

Subsequently, the USA complained about EC subsidies on exports of wheat flour,[57] but the panel held that because of the artificial conditions of the market, a conclusion could not be reached on whether a more than equitable share of the market had been acquired. On the other hand, in the context of export refunds on pasta,[58] although the EC argued that they only related to the durum wheat contained in pasta, it was held that subsidies on processed goods did not benefit from the special treatment of primary agricultural products as such, making reference in particular to the Subsidies Code.

The Agreement on Agriculture requires the amount and range of such export subsidies to be reduced, but it does not require, or bring about, their elimination. Art 3(3) provides that 'subject to the provisions of paragraphs 2(b) and 4 of Article 9 of this Agreement, a Member shall not provide export subsidies listed in paragraph 1 of Article 9 in respect of the agricultural products or groups of products specified in ... its Schedule in excess of the budgetary outlay and quantity commitment levels specified therein and shall not provide such subsidies in respect of any agricultural product not specified in that Section of its Schedule'. In the

[55] BISD 26th Supp 290, 27th Supp 69, 29th Supp 82.
[56] BISD 7th Supp 46.
[57] 1983; see I Garcia Bercero, 'Trade Laws, GATT, and the Management of Trade Disputes between the US and the EEC' (1985) Yearbook of European Law 149 at 168.
[58] Ibid 168–169.

case of the EC, export refunds are to be reduced by an average of 36 per cent in amount and 21 per cent in volume from a 1986–1988 base. It may however be observed that the move away from a system of product support (intervention) to a system involving an element of producer support (eg area payments and set-aside) will automatically both reduce the amount of internal support which is taken into account for WTO purposes, as mentioned above, and reduce the level of export refunds which will be required. It has already been noted that Council Regulation 1253/1999[59] continues the reduction in intervention prices for the 2000–2001 and 2001–2002 marketing years, and anticipates a final reduction in 2002–2003. Conversely, Council Regulation 1251/1999 (OJ 1999 L160/1) increases area payments for some arable crops for 2000–2001 and 2001–2002, and anticipates further increases related to the final reduction in the intervention price.

A difference in emphasis can be seen in the provisions of the Agreement on Agriculture concerning export subsidies compared with the provisions on domestic support. While, in the case of domestic support, the agreement goes into great detail about the types of support that *do not* need to be reduced, in the case of export subsidies the Agreement goes into great detail about the financial assistance that *does* have to be reduced. The export subsidies subject to reduction commitments are defined in art 9(1) as including:

(a) The provision by governments or their agencies of direct subsidies, including payments-in-kind, to a firm, to an industry, to producers of an agricultural product, to a cooperative or other association of such producers, or to a marketing board, contingent on export performance.

(b) The sale or disposal for export by governments or their agencies of non-commercial stocks of agricultural products at a price lower than the comparable price charged for the like product to buyers in the domestic market.

(c) Payments on the export of an agricultural product that are financed by virtue of governmental action, whether or not a charge on the public account is involved, including payments that are financed from the proceeds of a levy imposed on the agricultural product concerned or on an agricultural product from which the exported product is derived.

(d) The provision of subsidies to reduce the costs of marketing exports of agricultural products (other than widely available export promotion and advisory services) including handling, upgrading and other processing costs, and the costs of international transport and freight.

(e) Internal transport and freight charges on export shipments, provided or mandated by governments, on terms more favourable than for domestic shipments.

(f) Subsidies on agricultural products contingent on their incorporation in exported products.

---

[59] OJ 1999 L160/18.

In the case of the EC, therefore, this definition includes not only export refunds as such, but also the sale for export of surplus intervention stocks at a price lower than the domestic price, and refunds on processed agricultural products.

Art 9(2) makes it clear that the export subsidy commitment levels represent for each year of the implementation period, in the case of budgetary outlay reduction commitments, the maximum level of expenditure for such subsidies that may be allocated or incurred in that year, and, in the case of export quantity reduction commitments, the maximum quantity of an agricultural product, or group of such products, in respect of which such export subsidies may be granted in that year. However, art 9(2)(b) allowed some movement from these figures provided the cumulative amounts of budgetary outlays did not exceed the cumulative amounts that would have resulted from full compliance with the relevant annual outlay commitment levels specified in the Member's Schedule by more than 3 per cent of the base period level of such budgetary outlays, and the cumulative quantities exported with the benefit of such export subsidies did not exceed the cumulative quantities that would have resulted from full compliance with the relevant annual quantity commitment levels specified in the Member's Schedule by more than 1.75 per cent of the base period quantities. This was subject to the overall proviso that the Member's budgetary outlays for export subsidies and the quantities benefiting from such subsidies, at the conclusion of the implementation period, should be no greater than 64 per cent and 79 per cent of the 1986–1990 base period levels, respectively. For developing country Members these percentages were 76 and 86 per cent, respectively.

Furthermore art 10 lays down measures intended to prevent the circumvention of export subsidy commitments. Under art 10(1), export subsidies not listed in art 9(1) of this agreement are not to be applied in a manner which results in, or which threatens to lead to, circumvention of export subsidy commitments; nor are non-commercial transactions to be used to circumvent such commitments, and under art 10(3) any Member which claims that any quantity exported in excess of a reduction commitment level is not subsidized must establish that no export subsidy, whether listed in art 9 or not, has been granted in respect of the quantity of exports in question. To this is added an undertaking in art 10(2) to work toward the development of internationally agreed disciplines to govern the provision of export credits, export credit guarantees, or insurance programmes and, after agreement on such disciplines, to provide export credits, export credit guarantees, or insurance programmes only in conformity therewith.

Art 10(4) envisages the possibility of food aid being used to circumvent the export subsidy commitments, and provides that Member donors of international food aid must ensure that the provision of international food aid is not tied directly or indirectly to commercial exports of agricultural products to recipient countries, that international food aid transactions, including bilateral food aid which is monetized, shall be carried out in accordance with the FAO 'Principles of Surplus Disposal and Consultative Obligations' including, where appropriate, the system of Usual Marketing Requirements (UMRs), and that such aid shall be provided to the extent possible in fully grant form or on terms no less concessional than those provided for in art IV of the Food Aid Convention 1986.

Finally, art 11 declares with regard to processed products that in no case may the per unit subsidy paid on an incorporated agricultural primary product exceed the per unit export subsidy that would be payable on exports of the primary product as such.

Status of WTO/GATT in EC law

It will be evident from this description of the Agreement on Agriculture that there has been a considerable interaction between the terms of that agreement and the development of the EC's modern common organizations of agricultural markets. This policy impact may be contrasted with the European Court's continued refusal to recognize provisions of GATT/WTO law as being capable of direct effect. Although before the Uruguay Round Agreement, to which the Community as such is a party, the Court had declared that the Community had replaced Member States in GATT,[60] that the provisions of GATT were binding on the Community, and that from the entry into force of the Common Customs Tariff on 1 July 1968 GATT was to be treated as a Community act for the purposes of interpretation,[61] it held that the general scheme of GATT, being characterized by flexibility and possibilities of derogation, was such that its provisions could not give rise to rights enforceable before national courts. Thus, as a matter of Community law, the provisions of GATT may not be invoked to challenge the validity of national legislation.[62] More intriguingly, the earliest judgment in the matter[63] held that provisions of GATT could not be invoked before a national court to challenge the validity of Community legislation unless they could be shown to be directly effective. While the concept of direct effect may hardly seem to be relevant in a direct action for the annulment of a Community act brought by a Member State which is itself party to GATT, it has been held in the context of such an action[64] that it is only if the Community intended to implement a particular obligation entered into within the framework of GATT, or if the Community act expressly refers to specific provisions of GATT,[65] that the Court can review the lawfulness of the Community act in question from the point of view of the GATT rules.

---

[60] Cases 21–24/72 *International Fruit Co NV v Produktschap voor Groenten en Fruit* [1972] ECR 1219, Case 38/75 *Douaneagent der NV Nederlandse Spoorwegen v Inspecteur der Invoerrechten en Accijnzen* [1975] ECR 1439, Cases 267–269/81 *Amministrazione delle Finanze dello Stato v SPI* [1983] ECR 801.

[61] See the cases cited in n 45 above.

[62] Cases 267–269/81 *Amministrazione delle Finanze dello Stato v SPI* [1983] ECR 801.

[63] Cases 21–24/72 *International Fruit Co NV v Produktschap voor Groenten en Fruit* [1972] ECR 1219.

[64] Case C-280/93 *Germany v Council* [1994] ECR I-4973.

[65] Case C-70/87 *Fediol* [1989] ECR 1781, Case C-69/89 *Nakajima v Council* [1991] ECR I-2069.

This approach has been maintained in the aftermath of the Uruguay Round Agreements.[66] Thus in Case C-307/99 *OGT Fruchthandelgesellschaft v HZA Hamburg-St Annen*,[67] it was held that the validity of the common organization of the market in bananas under an amended version of Council Regulation 404/93[68] could not be challenged by traders invoking arts I and XIII of GATT 1994, even though a WTO panel in a report dated 12 April 1999 had found that this amended version was in breach of those provisions. The Court repeated that the WTO Agreement and the agreements and understandings annexed to it 'are not in principle among the rules in the light of which the Court is to review the legality of measures adopted by the Community institutions', adding that Regulation 404/93, as amended, was not designed to ensure the implementation in the Community legal order of a particular obligation assumed in the context of GATT, and that it did not expressly refer to specific provisions of GATT.

To put the matter in context, however, mention might also be made of the US Uruguay Round Agreements Act 1994,[69] section 102(a)(1) of which provides that 'no provision of any of the Uruguay Round Agreements, nor the application of any such provision to any person or circumstance, that is inconsistent with any law of the United States shall have effect', and section 102(b)(2)(A) of which declares that 'no State law, or the application of such a State law, may be declared invalid as to any person or circumstance on the ground that the provision or application is inconsistent with any of the Uruguay Round Agreements' unless the action is brought by the US federal authorities against that state law. The use of the agreements as a criterion of validity at the behest of a trader therefore appears to be totally excluded in the US context.

Nevertheless, the policy importance of the Uruguay Round Agreements can hardly be overestimated.

---

[66] Case C-149/96 *Portugal v Council* [1999] ECR I-8395.
[67] 2 May 2001.   [68] OJ 1993 L47/1.   [69] Public Law 103–465.

4

Agricultural support: common organizations of agricultural markets

Cereals: the basic pattern of support

In order to attain the objectives set out in art 33 of the EC Treaty, a common organization of agricultural markets is required to be established under art 34, which provides for three alternative forms of common organization:

1. common rules on competition;
2. compulsory coordination of the various national market organizations;
3. a European market organization.

In practice it is the third of these that has usually been employed. The common organization may in particular include regulation of prices, aids for the production and marketing of the various products, storage and carry-over arrangements, and common machinery for stabilizing imports or exports.

The most developed of these common organizations create an integrated market with a single Community-wide price structure. However, despite the existence of the requisite legal framework, between 1971 and 1999 (when the euro was introduced) the practical realization of this ideal was hampered by floating exchange rates—and remains so hampered for those Member States which do not participate in the third stage of Economic and Monetary Union.[1] The common organization of the market in cereals has been of pivotal importance, since the common organizations of the markets in pigmeat, eggs, and poultrymeat[2] were treated as ancillary to it, prices being based on the cereal input of the products concerned. The common organization of the market in cereals may also be taken as the basic model of a fully developed Community market organization.

A transitional scheme was established under Council Regulation 19 of 4 April 1962.[3] This was replaced by a single market system in 1967, established under Council Regulation 120/67,[4] which indeed started the basis of the present form

---

[1] See Chapter 5 below.   [2] See below p 105.   [3] JO 1962, p 933.
[4] JO 1967, p 2269 (sp edn 1967, p 33).

of the organization. This suffered much amendment and it, and its subsisting amendments, were consolidated into Council Regulation 2727/75[5] which in turn was replaced by Council Regulation 1766/92.[6] This also has been much modified, in particular as a result of the WTO Uruguay Round negotiations and the Agenda 2000 programme.

The basic pattern of the common organization governing the market in cereals has been fundamentally changed during the 1990s. At the heart of the original version were a target price and an intervention price. The target price indicated the level of price it was hoped Community producers would receive, and as a matter of law was fixed for Duisburg in West Germany as being the centre of the area with the greatest deficit of cereals in the Community (even though the same nominal prices applied throughout the whole Community). The intervention price on the other hand has traditionally represented the price at which national authorities, such as the United Kingdom Intervention Board for Agricultural Produce, are legally required to purchase products subject to the price system which are offered to them, and was fixed for Ormes in France, as being the production area having the greatest surplus of cereals in the Community. Under the 1992 reforms, the target and intervention prices ceased to have geographical links, and were fixed by Council Regulation 1766/92[7] so as to be reduced by fixed amounts over a three-year period, starting from a lower level than that previously applied; this policy of progressive reduction has been maintained, and Council Regulation 1253/1999[8] anticipates a final reduction in 2002–2003. The target price on the other hand was abolished in 1995 by Council Regulation 1528/95,[9] following implementation of the Uruguay Round Agreement on Agriculture, which, by requiring import levies to be replaced by customs duties, deprived the target price of any practical function.

The relevance of fixing a geographical location for the target and intervention prices was that the difference between those prices included an element to allow for the costs of transport between Ormes and Duisburg. Geography also played a role in the external aspects of the price structure: in order to ensure that the price structure was not upset by lower-priced imports, a threshold price was fixed, notionally for the port of Rotterdam, representing the minimum price at which the relevant goods may enter the Community. This threshold price was calculated not from the intervention price but from the higher target price (thus ensuring that the intervention price was not likely to be undercut), and the difference between the target price and the threshold price again included an element to allow for the cost of transport between Rotterdam and Duisburg. Like the target and intervention prices, under the 1992 version of the common organization the threshold price ceased to have a geographical link, and was fixed by Council Regulation 1766/92 so as to be reduced by fixed amounts over a three-year period.

[5] OJ 1975 L281/1.   [6] OJ 1992 L181/21.   [7] OJ 1992 L181/21.
[8] OJ 1999 L160/18.   [9] OJ 1995 L148/3.

If (as was usually the case) the world price, calculated on a CIF basis for Rotterdam, was lower than the threshold price, the difference had to be covered by an *import levy*. In the converse situation, if a Community producer wished (or indeed wishes) to export into lower-priced world markets, there was, and remains, power under the Community legislation to pay an *export refund* to cover the difference.

Much of this system has been changed as a result of the Uruguay Round Agreement on Agriculture. As mentioned in the previous chapter, under art 6, domestic support (eg intervention purchasing) is required to be reduced, in the EC's case by a global 20 per cent, but taken from a 1986–1988 base, although under art 6(5) and Annex II payments under production-limiting programmes (eg set-aside) and decoupled income support do not need to be reduced. Under art 4, import levies are required to be converted into tariffs, and in the EC's case reduced by an average of 36 per cent from a 1986–1988 base, and under arts 3(3) and 9, export refunds are to be reduced, in the EC's case by an average of 36 per cent in amount and 21 per cent in volume from a 1986–1988 base. The EC's obligations to convert levies to tariffs and to reduce support under the Uruguay Round agreement were effected under Council Regulation 3290/94[10] though in the cereals market the customs duties appear to be of a flat-rate nature. However, the influence of the old levy has not disappeared completely: while the customs duty under normal conditions sets the limit on the import duties payable, under art 10(2) of Regulation 1766/92 as amended by Regulation 3290/94, for many products the import duty is equal to the relevant intervention price increased by 55 per cent, minus the CIF import price, provided it does not exceed the CCT duty. The practical effect therefore is to reduce the import duties to a lower level than the customs duty when the world price for the products in question rises. Nevertheless, as a consequence of the change to customs duties, there was no longer a threshold price to calculate, and the target price therefore no longer served any practical purpose, and was abolished by Council Regulation 1528/95.[11]

Since payments under production-limiting programmes (eg set-aside) and decoupled income support do not need to be reduced, the Uruguay Round Agreement has added further impetus to the development of support for agricultural producers rather than agricultural products. This is exemplified in Council Regulation 1251/1999[12] on a support system for producers of certain arable crops. This sets up a system of area payments for EC producers of arable crops. These area payments under art 4 of Council Regulation 1251/1999 are calculated by multiplying the basic amount per tonne by the average cereal yield determined in the regionalization plan for the region concerned, and are in principle subject to an obligation to set aside a proportion of the area down to arable crops. In general the payments are linked to an obligation to set aside 10 per cent of the relevant area, but for 'small' producers (those with an area less than that needed to produce 92 tonnes of cereals) there is no set-aside obligation. It may however be observed that

---

[10] OJ 1994 L349/105.   [11] OJ 1995 L148/3.   [12] OJ 1999 L160/1.

the move away from a system of product support (intervention) to a system involving an element of producer support (eg area payments and set-aside) has automatically both reduced the amount of internal support which is taken into account for
WTO purposes, and reduced the level of export refunds which are required.
Council Regulation 1253/1999[13] continues the reduction in intervention prices
for the 2000–2001 and 2001–2002 marketing years, and anticipates a final reduction in 2002–2003. Conversely, Council Regulation 1251/1999[14] increases area
payments for some arable crops for 2000–2001 and 2001–2002, and anticipates
further increases related to the final reduction in the intervention price.

The impact of the set-aside requirement may however be somewhat weakened
by the decision of the European Court in Case C-372/98 *R v MAFF ex p Cooke*.[15]
Under art 2 of the Commission Regulation[16] implementing what was then
Council Regulation 1765/92 establishing a support system for producers of certain
arable crops,[17] set-aside meant 'the leaving fallow of an area which has been cultivated in the previous year with a view to harvest'. Cooke had claimed set-aside
payments for an area including land which had been used to grow a temporary
grass which had been cut and used for silage. The UK Ministry of Agriculture
(MAFF) took the view that only land which had been used for one of the crops
whose production it was intended to reduce qualified for set-aside payments, and
refused payment. However, the Court took the view that there was no requirement that the land should have been sown with one of the arable crops listed in
the Council Regulation, and declared that any set-aside of cultivated land, regard-
less of the crop previously sown, 'contributes to the reduction of the area capable
of being given over to arable production'.

Be that as it may, in the context of organic production of agricultural products
under Council Regulation 2092/91,[18] an amendment[19] has been made to Council
Regulation 1251/1999[20] on a support system for producers of arable crops
providing that, on a holding all the production of which is managed in accordance with the requirements of the organic production regulation, land set aside
may be used for growing legume crops. The rationale for this is that growing
fodder legumes is an agronomic practice that restores the soil's fertility in a natural
way, and that growing such crops is important for developing organic production
of agricultural products.[21]

Target and threshold prices in the cereals scheme essentially served a function
of calculation and were not in themselves available to producers although it was
established that Member States could not legislate so as to deprive producers of
the opportunity of obtaining the target price.[22] The intervention price, on the

---

[13] OJ 1999 L160/18.   [14] OJ 1999 L160/1.   [15] 12 October 2000.
[16] Commission Regulation 762/94 (OJ 1994 L90/8).   [17] OJ 1992 L181/12.
[18] OJ 1991 L198/1.   [19] By Council Regulation 1038/2001 (OJ 2001 L145/16).
[20] OJ 1999 L160/1.
[21] See recital (3) to Council Regulation 1038/2001 (OJ 2001 L145/16).
[22] Case 31/74 *Galli* [1975] ECR 47.

other hand, which is the only element of the original price structure to survive, is the price guaranteed to the producer, albeit only to the producer.[23] However, it relates to goods delivered to the warehouse, before unloading.[24] The intervention agencies designated by the Member States are obliged to buy in cereals complying with quality and quantity requirements which are offered to them.[25] The intervention price was fixed by Council Regulation 1253/99[26] at 110.25 euro/tonne for the 2000/2001 marketing year, and at 101.31 euro/tonne for the 2001/2002 marketing year onwards, though a final reduction may be applied from 2002/2003 onwards in the light of market developments.[27] These reducing prices nevertheless remain subject to monthly increases during the course of each marketing year, fixed by Council Regulation 1666/2000[28] to range from 1 euro/tonne in November to 7 euro/tonne in June in 2000/2001, and from 0.93 euro/tonne in November to 6.51 euro/tonne in June from 2001/2002 onwards. This mechanism is intended to take some account of storage costs, but no increases are payable for the period July–October inclusive.

While import levies have disappeared, being replaced by customs duties, the Community has nevertheless maintained the system of export levies (now called export taxes) designed to prevent Community producers taking advantage of world prices when they are higher than Community prices. The relevant provisions[29] of Council Regulation 1766/92[30] are couched in general terms, allowing 'appropriate measures' to be taken when world prices reach the level of Community prices, threatening to disturb the Community market, but an example occurred in late 1995 and early 1996, when Commission Regulation 328/96[31] raised the export tax on common wheat (imposed by Regulation 2900/95) to 35 ECU per tonne.

As noted above, the EC's commitments under the Uruguay Round Agreement on Agriculture require export refunds to be reduced by an average of 36 per cent in amount and 21 per cent in volume from a 1986–1988 base, but there is no obligation to eliminate or replace them. The earlier case law with regard to the legal nature and consequences of export refunds therefore remains of interest. The Court of Justice held in Case 62/83 *Eximo Molkereierzeugnisse Handelsgesellschaft v Commission*[32] that a trader opting for advance fixing of an export refund cannot complain that he would have obtained a higher rate by claiming the refund at the time of export. In practice, differential export refunds may be encountered, calculated so as to take account of the particular characteristics of the market of importation. The Court has consistently held, as in Case 89/83 *Dimex Nahrungsmittel*[33]

---

[23] Case 2/75 *Einfuhr- und Vorratsstelle für Getreide und Futtermittel v Mackprang* [1975] ECR 607.
[24] Council Regulation 1766/92 (OJ 1992 L181/21) art 3(3) as amended by Council Regulation 1253/1999 (OJ 1999 L160/18).
[25] Council Regulation 1766/92 (OJ 1992 L181/21) art 4.
[26] OJ 1999 L160/18.
[27] Council Regulation 1766/92 (OJ 1992 L181/21) art 3(4) as amended by Council Regulation 1253/1999 (OJ 1999 L160/18).
[28] OJ 2000 L193/1.   [29] Art 16.   [30] OJ 1992 L181/21.
[31] OJ 1996 L47/1.   [32] [1984] ECR 2295.   [33] [1984] ECR 2815.

that such refunds, given their specific nature, are payable only on proof that the goods have been put into free circulation in the importing state. So far as the concept of export is concerned, particular problems may occur where the goods are trans-shipped within the Community. However, in Case 337/85 *Commission v Ireland*[34] it was held that, for the purpose of payment of export refunds, goods are exported from the first European Community port in which the customs export formalities are carried out, even if they are later trans-shipped in another European Community port.

As indicated in Chapter 3, it would appear to be the system of export refunds that has given rise to the greatest number of complaints from the Community's trading partners. However, apart from the reductions required by the Agreement on Agriculture, art XVI of GATT merely requires members to 'seek' to avoid the use of subsidies on the export of primary products. If, however, a contracting party grants a subsidy which has the effect of *increasing* exports from its territory, it should not be applied so as to result in that party having 'more than an equitable share' of world export trade in that product, taking account of the shares held during a previous representative period. Thus, Australia and Brazil complained that Community export refunds on sugar had led to Community exporters having more than an equitable share of world export trade.[35] Although the panel found that the Community had increased its share of world markets, a link with Brazilian and Australian exports could not be shown, and it did not therefore conclude that the Community had taken a more than equitable share. It was found that the Community practice had helped depress world sugar prices, causing indirect harm to the complainants, but this could not be quantified. On the other hand, before the entry into force of the CAP, it was actually held in the case of French assistance to the export of wheat and wheat flour,[36] which involved differential bonuses and variable bonuses for exports, that the French share in the South-East Asian market had become inequitable, having risen from 0.7 per cent in 1954 to 46 per cent in 1958, to a large extent as the result of the subsidy arrangements. Subsequently, the USA complained about EC subsidies on exports of wheat flour,[37] but the panel held that because of the artificial conditions of the market, a conclusion could not be reached on whether a more than equitable share of the market had been acquired. On the other hand, in the context of export refunds on pasta,[38] although the EC argued that they only related to the durum wheat contained in pasta, it was held that subsidies on processed goods did not benefit from the special treatment of agricultural products as such.

---

[34] [1987] ECR 4237.

[35] BISD 26th Supp 290, 27th Supp 69, 29th Supp 82.

[36] Ibid.

[37] See I Garcia Bercero, 'Trade Laws, GATT, and the Management of Trade Disputes between the US and the EEC' (1985) Yearbook of European Law 149 at 168.

[38] Ibid 168–169.

Licences and deposits

The system of import and export in the common organization of the market in cereals is inextricably interlinked with the issue of import and export licences and their concomitant system of deposits. Art 9 of Council Regulation 1766/92[39] requires all imports into the Community or exports therefrom to be subject to the issue of import or export licences, this issue being itself conditional upon the lodging of a deposit guaranteeing that importation or exportation will be effected during the period of validity of the licence. Although the licences are issued by the national authorities, they are Community licences and must be issued to any applicant irrespective of the place of his establishment in the Community; in the terms of art 9, they are valid throughout the Community. This system of import and export licences is widely used in other common organizations, and common detailed rules are contained in Commission Regulation 1291/2000.[40] The core of the system is to be found in art 8 of that regulation, providing that the licence comports both an authorization to carry out the transaction and an obligation to carry it out. The use of deposits to ensure that the obligation is performed is widely used in other common organizations, and the method has been adopted for transactions other than import and export. Common detailed rules for the application of the system of securities for agricultural products were consolidated in Commission Regulation 2220/85,[41] which has itself been much amended.

It is in this area that much of the case law on the principle of proportionality has arisen,[42] the validity of the licence and deposit system being upheld in Case 11/70 *Internationale Handelsgesellschaft v Einfuhr- und Vorratsstelle Getreide*[43] where the principle of proportionality was raised as a matter of German law, and the Court took account of it as a general principle of Community law. The system was there justified largely on the basis of the need for the Community and the Member States to have precise knowledge of intended transactions:

This knowledge, together with other available information on the state of the market, is essential to enable the competent authorities to make judicious use of the instruments of intervention, both ordinary and exceptional, which are at their disposal for guaranteeing the functioning of the system of prices instituted by the regulation, such as purchasing, storing and distributing, fixing denaturing premiums and export refunds, applying protective measures and choosing measures intended to avoid deflections of trade. This is all the more imperative in that the implementation of the common agricultural policy involves heavy financial responsibilities for the Community and the Member States.

It is necessary, therefore, for the competent authorities to have available not only statistical information on the state of the market but also precise forecasts on future imports and exports.

---

[39] OJ 1992 L181/21.   [40] OJ 2000 L152/1.   [41] OJ 1985 L205/5.
[42] See R Barents, 'The System of Deposits in Community Agricultural Law: Efficiency v Proportionality' (1985) EL Rev 239.
[43] [1970] ECR 1125.

In particular, deposits were needed because licences had to be issued to any applicant:

Since the Member States are obliged . . . to issue import and export licences to any applicant, a forecast would lose all significance if the licences did not involve the recipients in an undertaking to act on them. And the undertaking would be ineffectual if observance of it were not ensured by appropriate means.

The choice for that purpose by the Community legislature of the deposit cannot be criticized in view of the fact that that machinery is adapted to the voluntary nature of requests for licences and that it has the dual advantage over other possible systems of simplicity and efficacy.

The Court took the view that a mere declaration of transactions effected would not be adequate, and that a system of fines imposed after the event would pose administrative and legal complications, particularly since the traders involved would not necessarily be resident in the Member State seeking to enforce the obligation arising from the issue of the licence. It also strongly asserted that the system of deposits itself could not be equated with a penal sanction, since it was merely the guarantee that an undertaking voluntarily assumed would be carried out. However, where a trader is required to reconstitute a deposit because the transaction has not been carried out in time, it was held in Case 137/85 *Maizena*[44] that this was a sanction rather than a guarantee, the sanction being the counterpart of the anticipated release of the deposit.

With regard to the amount of the deposit, the Court held that account should be taken not so much of the deposit itself, which was repayable, but of the costs and charges involved in lodging it, finding that they did not, in that case, constitute an amount disproportionate to the total value of the goods in question and of the other trading costs. However, in its judgment given the same day in Case 26/70 *Einfuhr- und Vorratsstelle v Henck*[45] the Court did look at the size of the deposit: the case involved advance fixing of an export refund, and the deposit required was several times greater than that required where the refund was not fixed in advance. Nevertheless, the Court again held it to be justified:

It cannot be denied that as a principle it is necessary to fix the amount of the deposit required in the case of 'advance fixing' of the refund at a higher level than in the case of a transaction giving rise to the application of the refund applicable on the day of exportation. As the system of advance fixing was created in the interests of trade, it was necessary to provide at the same time, in the scheme of the regulation, for adequate guarantees to eliminate the possibility that machinery of the common organization of the markets might be upset by speculation made possible by the introduction of this option.

To that end, the deposit was fixed in such a manner as to take into account price trends and consequently the variation in refunds during the period of validity of the export licence. The amount of the deposit must be sufficient to take away from exporters any interest, as the prices on the external markets vary, in changing their export plans as they

[44] [1987] ECR 4587.   [45] [1970] ECR 1183.

are apparent from the licences applied for and issued. It appears therefore that the require-ment of a higher deposit in cases of advance fixing of the refund is a method necessary to guarantee compliance on the part of exporters with the obligation attached to the issue of the licence and thereby to ensure the accuracy of the forecasts of future market trends.

Taking into account the size of price fluctuations which can occur on the markets in question, this amount in no way appears excessive. Furthermore, determination of the amount of the deposit falls within the discretion of the authority having the power to adopt regulations in the matter.

With regard to the release of the security, art 31 of Commission Regulation 1291/2000[46] provides that the obligation or right arising from the licence is regarded as having been respectively fulfilled or excised when the customs formal-ities under art 24(1) of that regulation are completed, subject to the product being put into free circulation in the case of import. This reflects the Court's earlier case law which, for the purpose of determining whether the transaction had been completed within the time set by the licence, was prepared to take account of the time at which the goods were submitted to the customs authorities of the importing state, but would only do so if proof was adduced of the fact that the goods had later been put into free circulation.[47]

Regulation 1291/2000[48] does expressly exclude forfeiture of the deposit in certain cases of 'force majeure',[49] as more generally do arts 22 and 24 of Commission Regulation 2220/85.[50] In the *Internationale Handelsgesellschaft* case,[51] it was stated that this concept was not limited to absolute impossibility but must be understood in the sense of 'unusual circumstances, outside the control of the importer or exporter, the consequences of which, in spite of the exercise of all due care, could not have been avoided except at the cost of excessive sacrifice'. This could appear to have been slightly relaxed in a pair of judgments in 1974[52] where reference was made to 'abnormal circumstances, outside the control of the importer, and which have arisen in spite of the fact that the titular holder of the licence has taken all the precautions which could reasonably be expected of a prudent and dili-gent trader'. However, the application of the principle to a particular set of facts in a dispute between a trader and a national agency falls within the jurisdiction of the national court, as was made clear in Case 158/73 *Kampffmeyer v Einfuhr- und Vorratsstelle Getreide*[53] where it was claimed that loss of the import licence in the post constituted force majeure. The question, therefore, arose as to whether sending

---

[46] OJ 2000 L152/1.
[47] Case 186/73 *Norddeutsches Vieh- und Fleischkontor v Einfuhr- und Vorratsstelle Schlachtvieh* [1974] ECR 533, 543, Case 3/74 *Einfuhr- und Vorratsstelle Getreide v Pfutzenreuter* [1974] ECR 589, 597–598.
[48] OJ 2000 L152/1.
[49] eg art 32(1)(b)(i) in the case of exports.
[50] OJ 1985 L205/5.
[51] [1970] ECR 1125 at 1137 to 1138.
[52] Case 186/73 *Norddeutsches Vieh- und Fleischkontor v Einfuhr- und Vorratsstelle Schlachtvieh* [1974] ECR 533, 544, Case 3/74 *Einfuhr- und Vorratsstelle Getreide v Pfutzenreuter* [1974] ECR 589, 599.
[53] [1974] ECR 101.

the licence by ordinary post constituted the fulfilment of the duty of care owed by a reasonably diligent trader, and the European Court held that that was a matter of the application of the law rather than its interpretation, so that it was for the national court to decide whether the licence holder had acted as a prudent and diligent trader. However, the Court itself has held that to act in reliance upon an assurance of a national customs official that the period of validity of a licence could be extended does not in itself constitute force majeure.[54] Most importantly, it was held in Case 109/86 *Theodorakis*[55] that non-performance by the other contracting party does not constitute force majeure.

A legislative version of the distinction the Court has made in its case law on proportionality between primary and secondary obligations[56] is found in art 20 of Regulation 2220/85,[57] which distinguishes between primary, secondary, and subordinate requirements which a security is intended to guarantee, in so far as the relevant specific regulation has defined the primary requirement. In this context, secondary requirements are time limits for fulfilling a primary requirement, and subordinate requirements are any other requirement. Under this scheme, if a primary requirement is not fulfilled the security is forfeited in full,[58] if a secondary requirement is breached, but the primary requirement is fulfilled, 15 per cent of the sum secured is forfeited, plus a further percentage for each day by which the time limit is not met,[59] and if just a subordinate requirement is breached, just 15 per cent of the sum secured is forfeited.[60]

Other products: general issues

Other common organizations may use some or all of the techniques noted in the common organization of the market in cereals. A relatively complete combination of internal support and external protection is used for milk, beef and veal, sheep-meat, and sugar, but less comprehensive intervention systems are used for pigmeat, certain fruit and vegetables, and table wine, the last named more often being supported by storage and distillation aids. Other markets rely virtually entirely on external protection alone, notably eggs and poultry, wine other than table wine, and other fruit and vegetables. Lastly, there are some products such as peas and field beans, dried fodder, hops, flax and hemp, and silkworms for which flat-rate aids per hectare were granted. Such aids may however be seen as the genesis of the support system for producers of arable crops currently set out in Council Regulation 1251/1999,[61] discussed in the context of the cereals market above. This system crosses the traditional boundaries between common organizations, applying to cereals, oilseeds, protein crops, and flax.[62] The fundamental characteristics of the

---

[54] Case 125/87 *Corman* [1985] ECR 3039.
[55] [1987] ECR 4319.   [56] See Chapter 2 above.   [57] OJ 1985 L205/5.
[58] Art 22.   [59] Art 23.   [60] Art 24.
[61] OJ 1999 L160/1.   [62] As defined in Annex I of the regulation.

system are first that it involves payments on a per hectare basis decoupled from actual production,[63] the basic amount per tonne set out in the regulation being multiplied by the average cereal yield determined in the regionalization plan established by each Member State for the region concerned[64] and secondly that it involves the set-aside of 10 per cent of the area down to arable crops. This level of compulsory set-aside has been fixed for the marketing years from 2000/2001 to 2006/2007.[65] It does not however apply to producers who make a payment application for an area no bigger than the area which would be needed to produce 92 tonnes of cereals on the basis of the yields determined for their region.[66]

Certain of these common organizations which are of particular interest in the context of UK agriculture or which are of general legal importance will be considered briefly in the following paragraphs.

Milk

Under Council Regulation 1255/1999,[67] which replaced the original Regulation 804/68,[68] a target price is still set for milk as such[69] (given that it is relevant to the calculation of the levy payable when production quotas are exceeded), but intervention prices are set only for skimmed milk powder and butter;[70] that is, forms in which milk may be stored. Similarly, private storage aid may be granted for certain Italian cheeses.[71] However, for butter, intervention does not occur at the intervention price: art 6 of Regulation 1255/1999 provides rather that where the market price of butter in one or more Member States falls below 92 per cent of the intervention price for a representative period, buying-in shall be carried out by the intervention agencies in the Member State concerned under an open invitation to tender, although the buying-in price fixed by the Commission may not be less than 90 per cent of the intervention price. On the other hand, under art 7, skimmed milk powder may be bought in at the intervention price, but only between 12 March and 31 August in each year, and only within specific quantity limits.[72] Outside those limits buying-in is under an open standing invitation to tender. However, private storage aid may be paid for both butter and skimmed milk powder[73] as well as the specified Italian cheeses.[74] Conversely export refunds may be paid to enable Community milk products to be exported to the world market.[75]

While this traditional system of support continues, Regulation 1255/1999 also makes provision for direct payments to producers, as in the arable sector. Recital

[63] Art 2(2).   [64] Arts 3 and 4.   [65] Art 6(1).
[66] Art 6(7).   [67] OJ 1999 L160/48.
[68] OJ 1968 L148/13 (sp edn 1968 (II), p 176).
[69] Regulation 1255/1999 art 2.
[70] Ibid, art 4.   [71] Art 8.
[72] Fixed at 109,000 tonnes in art 7(2) of Regulation 1255/1999.
[73] Arts 6(3) and 7(3).   [74] Art 8.   [75] Art 31.

11 to the regulation links these payments to reduced market support in the milk sector, and it is also linked to the milk quota system discussed below. Under art 16 of the regulation, an annual dairy premium in envisaged as starting in 2005, payable per tonne of individual reference quantity (ie quota) eligible for premium and available on the holding. This premium is set to be paid at 5.75 euro/tonne in 2005, rising to 11.49 euro/tonne in 2006, and 17.24 euro/tonne in 2007. These sums are low, but it is envisaged that Member States may supplement them by premium supplements under art 18 and/or by area payments under art 19, provided they do not exceed the global amounts set out in Annex I to the Regulation. It is stated in recital 12 to the regulation that a Community-wide scheme with uniform payments would be 'too rigid', though it may be wondered whether a system reliant upon such national supplements can any longer be termed a 'common' organization. Under the scheme of premium supplements, the total of dairy premium plus premium supplement may not exceed 13.9 euro/tonne in 2005, 27.8 euro/tonne in 2006, and 41.7 euro/tonne in 2007. The area payments are granted per hectare of permanent pasture available to the producer during the calendar year concerned, provided no payments under the arable scheme are being claimed in relation to the same land, and provided the same land is not being used to comply with the stocking density requirements under the common organization of the market in beef and veal.[76] Unlike the premium supplements, there is no provision for the area payments to increase: the maximum area payment per hectare (including any payments under the beef and veal common organization) may not exceed 350 euro for the calendar year 2005 'and the subsequent calendar years'.

As well as these systems of support, various aids have from time to time been offered to promote the consumption of milk products, and a series of marketing measures is set out in arts 11 to 15 of Regulation 1255/1999.

It is in the milk market that surplus production has given rise to the most drastic remedies, albeit not in the form of a general reduction in the level of Community prices. Rather, a system of levies has been used, the first being a milk co-responsibility levy introduced by Council Regulation 1079/77,[77] which was upheld by the Court of Justice as a measure intended to stabilize markets,[78] even though it had the effect of reducing prices for most producers. This was coupled with a system of premiums for the non-marketing of milk and the conversion of dairy herds.[79]

This levy did not in itself achieve the desired reduction in production and in 1982, the year that the principle of a guarantee threshold was introduced into the cereals market, Council Regulation 1183/82[80] amended the basic Council Regulation 804/68[81] so as to introduce a guarantee threshold for milk and milk

---

[76] Council Regulation 1254/1999 (OJ 1999 L160/21 art 15(3)).
[77] OJ 1977 L131/6.
[78] Case 138/78 *Stölting v Hauptzollamt Hamburg-Jonas* [1979] ECR 713.
[79] Council Regulation 1078/77 (OJ 1977 L131/1).
[80] OJ 1982 L140/1.   [81] OJ 1968 L148/13 (sp edn 1968 (I), p 176).

products, derived from the 1981 production figures plus a margin of 0.5 per cent. However, the passing of this threshold triggered not a reduction in price but the introduction in 1984 of a production quota system linked to an 'additional levy' on deliveries and sales exceeding the quotas, fixed at such a level as to be virtually confiscatory and imposed for a period of five years from 1 May 1985. This period was extended to eight years by Regulation 1109/88[82] and the system was continued for another period of seven years from 1 April 1993 by Regulation 3950/92,[83] and has been continued for a further eight years from 1 April 2000 by Regulation 1256/1999.[84]

Quite apart from its substantive importance, the dairy produce quota system shows clearly the problems involved in controlling an 'administered market' at Community level, and its implementation in the United Kingdom gave rise to the creation of a new type of administrative tribunal, the Dairy Produce Quota Tribunals.[85] The Community rules were originally implemented in the United Kingdom by the Dairy Produce Quotas Regulations 1984, the current implementation being in the Dairy Produce Quotas Regulations 1997.[86]

Under the Community scheme, the levy is payable by the producer of cow's milk on milk or milk equivalent sold directly for consumption which exceeds the reference quantity for the twelve months in question,[87] and it is also (and more importantly) payable on quantities delivered by producers to a purchaser (ie an undertaking or grouping which purchases milk or other milk products from a producer to treat or process them or to sell them to one or more undertakings treating or processing milk or other milk products[88]) which exceed the reference quantity for that period. Such a purchaser is under a duty to recover the levy through the price paid by him or it to the producers.[89]

The reference quantities, or quotas, were in principle based on production in the 1981 calendar year plus a margin of 1 per cent, that is, the original 1982 guarantee threshold but with a further 0.5 per cent margin; however, for Ireland and Italy the 1983 figures were used. In the case of Ireland, this was stated to be because of the proportion of the gross national product involved. In the case of Italy it was because production in 1981 was the lowest for ten years and because Italian yields per cow are relatively low. However, the other Member States could also use suitably weighted 1982 or 1983 figures. In the United Kingdom, although the 1981 calendar year was chosen for direct sales quotas, the 1983 calendar year was chosen for wholesale quotas. The European Court has held that in exercising this choice the Member States remained subject to the general principle underlying

[82] OJ 1988 L110/27.   [83] OJ 1992 L405/1.   [84] OJ 1999 L160/73.
[85] Originally created by the Dairy Produce Quotas Regulations 1984, SI 1984/1047, Reg 6, Sch 5 (amended by SI 1984/1538 and SI 1984/1787), continued by the Dairy Produce Quotas Regulations 1997, SI 1997/733, Reg 34, Sch 6, but only for the purpose of completing the discharge of any functions exercisable under the previous regulations.
[86] See the Dairy Produce Quotas Regulations 1997, SI 1997/733.
[87] Council Regulation 3590/92 (OJ 1992 L405/1) art 1.
[88] Ibid, art 9(e).   [89] Art 2(2).

the common agricultural policy, notably art 34(2) of the EC Treaty prohibiting discrimination between producers, so that it was not open to the Luxembourg government to choose the year 1981 when, under local conditions of the market, that would have the effect of favouring one particular dairy at the expense of the others.[90] In the United Kingdom, the wholesale quotas were in general determined by reducing the 1983 figures by 9 per cent,[91] though other weightings were used for particular areas, such as Scottish area B (defined as Kintyre, south of Tarbet, and the islands of Arran, Bute, Coll, Gigha, Great Cumbrae, Little Cumbrae, and Orkney), where the figures were reduced by 5.8135 per cent, thus reflecting the provision of the original Commission regulation under which the weighting could take account of the trend of deliveries in a region in relation to the average in that Member State. This original special treatment may well explain why, under the current UK regulations, 'no person shall transfer quota on a transfer of a holding or part of a holding where the transfer would result in an increase or reduction in the total direct sales quota or total wholesale quota available for use by dairy enterprises located within a Scottish Islands area'.[92]

Purchaser quotas are simply the aggregate of the relevant wholesale quotas, and, therefore, may be correspondingly increased or reduced when the wholesale quotas are increased or reduced in accordance with the Community legislation. In 1986 the Council reduced the guaranteed total quantities by 3 per cent from the original base,[93] and further reductions were made in 1987 and 1988,[94] the latter continuing until the end of March 1993. However, Regulation 764/89[95] added an extra quantity to allow for quota to be allocated to those who had no production in the base year because they had taken advantage of an outgoers' scheme, following the European Court's finding that such producers had a legitimate expectation that they would be able to return to dairying after five years.[96] The 1992 regulation took as its starting point the quotas available on 31 March 1993,[97] and the 1999 Regulation took as its starting point the quotas available on 31 March 2000,[98] although it allows for subsequent marginal increases each year until 2008.

Though the quotas are allocated to producers, the legislation has from the outset enabled them to be transferred with the land. According to art 7(1) of Regulation 3950/92, as amended by Regulation 1256/1999, reference quantities available on

[90] Cases 201 and 202/85 *Klensch v Luxembourg Secretary of State for Agriculture* [1986] ECR 3477.

[91] Dairy Produce Quotas Regulations 1984 Sch 2, para 4(c).

[92] SI 1997/733, Reg 7(7); for the definition of Scottish Islands Area see Reg 2(1) as amended by SSI 2000/391.

[93] Council Regulation 1335/86 (OJ 1986 L119/19).

[94] Council Regulation 775/87 (OJ 1987 L78/5) and Council Regulation 1109/88 (OJ 1988 L110/27).

[95] OJ 1989 L84/2.

[96] Case 120/86 *Mulder* [1988] ECR 2321, Case 170/86 *Deetzen* [1988] ECR 2355.

[97] Council Regulation 3950/92 (OJ 1992 L405/1) art 4(1).

[98] Council Regulation 1256/1999 (OJ 1999 L160/73) art 1(5) amending art 4(1) of Council Regulation 3950/92.

a holding are to be transferred with the holding in the case of sale, lease, or transfer by inheritance, taking account of the areas used for dairy production and, where applicable, of any agreement between the parties. The same is to apply to other cases of transfers involving comparable legal effects. Whatever may have happened in the early days of the scheme, the UK implementation now makes it clear that quota may not be transferred on the grant of a licence to occupy land, or on the grant of a tenancy under which a holding (or a part of a holding) is occupied for a period of less than eight months in Scotland, ten months in England and Wales, and twelve months in Northern Ireland.[99] However, Regulation 1256/1999 evidences a certain hostility to some aspects of transfers using a lease, and added art 8a, under para (b) of which Member States are empowered not to apply these provisions.

Where land is transferred to public authorities, for use in the public interest or for non-agricultural purposes, Member States are required to ensure that the departing producer is in a position to continue milk production, if such is his intention. If land is transferred with a view to improving the environment, art 8(c) empowers the Member States to provide for the allocation of the quota relating to the holding concerned to the departing producer if he intends to continue milk production. In the case of rural leases due to expire without any possibility of renewal on similar terms, and comparable situations, Member States are required by art 7(2) to ensure that the quota on the holding is transferred to the producer taking it over, taking account of the legitimate interests of the parties.

It will be noted that the Council regulations themselves say nothing about reversion to the landlord as such at the expiry of a lease, and say nothing about compensation for a departing tenant who does not intend to continue milk production. In its judgment in Case 5/88 *Wachauf*,[100] the European Court held that, at least where the allocation of the quota was the result of the tenant's own labours, it would be a breach of the tenant's fundamental rights to deprive him of the fruits of his labour without compensation. However, the Court concluded that the Community legislation in fact left the Member States enough discretion to ensure that the tenant was able either to keep all or part of his quota or to receive compensation if he gave it up. It should be observed that the Court also held, presumably because the dispute arose in the context of a national outgoers' scheme, that the part of the quota for which the tenant received compensation could not be transferred to the landlord, but should be treated as being released. The United Kingdom scheme introduced by the Agriculture Act 1986[101] does provide a mechanism by which a tenant receives compensation for some of the quota, but it provides for the compensation to be paid by the landlord, to whom the quota is then transferred.

It has subsequently become clear that the Court's use of the phrase 'fruits of his labour' in *Wachauf* is both precise and important. The Court was not recognizing that quota as such was a property right but that in that particular case, where the

---

[99] SI 1997/773, Reg 7(5).   [100] [1989] ECR 2609.   [101] s 13 and Sch 1.

holding had not been let as a dairy unit, and it was the tenant who had acquired and introduced the dairy cows and the technical facilities required for milk production, the quota represented the fruits of the tenant's labour.

This follows from the decision in Case C-2/92 *R v MAFF ex p Bostock*,[102] which involved the termination of a lease of a holding which had been let as a dairy farm in England before the Agriculture Act 1986 entered into force. The quota therefore reverted with the holding to the landlord with no express provision as to compensation, and the tenant argued that this was a breach of the general principle of respect for property in Community law. While the Court did reaffirm that the requirements flowing from the protection of fundamental rights in the Community legal order are also binding on Member States when they implement Community rules, it did not accept the tenant's argument that protection of the right of property required the Member State to make provision for compensation to be paid to the outgoing tenant by the landlord or to confer on the tenant a direct right to claim compensation from the landlord. After emphasizing that *Wachauf* was concerned with the protection of the fruits of the tenant's labours, the Court held that the right to property safeguarded by the Community legal order does not include the right to dispose, for profit, of an advantage such as reference quantities allocated in the context of the common organization of a market, which does not derive from the assets or occupational activity of the person concerned.[103]

A similar view was taken with regard to the introduction of the system of premium rights (which are transferable like production quotas) attributed to the producers of sheepmeat, goatmeat, or beef and veal in Case C-38/94 *R v Minister for Agriculture, Fisheries and Food, ex p Country Landowners' Association*.[104] Here the premium rights could be transferred by the producer with the holding or, subject to surrendering a proportion of the rights transferred to the national reserve, without transferring the holding. The landowners claimed that Member States should be required to introduce a compensation mechanism for the loss suffered by the owners of agricultural land in particular where the premium right was transferred by producers who did not own the land on which they farmed. The landowners argued that the allocation of freely transferable quotas to tenant producers would have the effect of reducing the capital value of the land. This point was accepted by MAFF but they refuted the existence of any obligation upon them to compensate the landowners for this loss. The Court reaffirmed its jurisprudence in the *Bostock* case, declaring that no general principle of law upheld by the Community legal order, in particular, the principle of protection of the right to property, required that such compensation be paid. On the other hand, it stated that it was for each Member State to assess the need for such measures having regard

---

[102] [1994] ECR I-35.

[103] See also Case C-44/89 *Von Deetzen v Hauptzollamt Hamburg-Jonas (Von Deetzen II)* [1991] ECR I-5119 at para 27.

[104] [1995] ECR I-3875.

in particular to the national arrangements for implementing the rules in question and the national rules governing the relationship between landlord and tenant.

Finally, in Case C-63/93 *Duff & Others v Minister for Agriculture and Food, Ireland & the Attorney General*,[105] where it was alleged inter alia that the failure to grant additional milk quota to producers who had adopted development plans under Community law infringed their property rights, the Court held that the rules in question did not affect the *substance* of the right to property as the rules were aimed at the general Community interest and allowed the producers to continue to produce milk at the level of their production prior to the entry into force of the new rules.

Under art 5 of Regulation 3950/92, as amended by Regulation 1256/1999, quotas available to producers who have not marketed milk or other milk products during one of the twelve-month periods (ie 1 April to 31 March) are to be allocated to the national reserve and may be reallocated to producers determined in accordance with objective criteria agreed with the Commission. It is further provided that where a producer does not make use of at least 70 per cent of his quota, Member States may decide, in accordance with general principles of Community law,[106] whether all or part of the unused quota should revert to the national reserve, and under which conditions a quota may be reallocated to the producers concerned. However, this does not apply where the loss of production is due to force majeure or is otherwise justified.

While under the original scheme it was only envisaged that quota could be transferred with the holding, a system of temporary transfers of quota as such, or 'quota leasing' was introduced in 1987,[107] and in its present form is governed by art 6 of Regulation 3950/92. This requires Member States for the twelve-month period concerned to authorize temporary transfers of that part of the individual reference quantity which the producer who was entitled thereto does not intend to use. However, under art 6(2), a Member State may decide not to implement this scheme either because of the need to facilitate structural developments and adjustments or because of overriding administrative needs. The UK has nevertheless applied the scheme from its inception, and continues to do so.[108]

There are also various more general provisions involving the reallocation of quota, including in effect a continuation of the outgoers' scheme: under art 8(a), Member States may 'with a view to completing restructuring of milk production or to environmental improvement' grant compensation to producers who undertake to abandon definitively all or part of their milk production, and place the quota released in the national reserve. Art 8(b) envisages what might be described either as a privatized outgoers' scheme or as a controlled system for selling quota as such: Member States may, within the same limits, lay down the conditions under

---

[105] [1996] ECR I-569.
[106] See JA Usher, *General Principles of EC Law* (1998).
[107] Council Regulation 2998/87 (OJ 1987 L285/1).
[108] See SI 1997/733, Reg 13.

which producers may obtain (for payment) the reallocation by the competent authority at the beginning of a twelve-month period of quota released definitively at the end of the preceding twelve-month period by other producers in return for compensation. It is required that the payment by the producer acquiring quota should be equal to the compensation paid to the producer relinquishing quota, which in turn may be paid in one or more annual instalments. Member States may also determine the regions or collection areas within which the definitive transfer of quota without transfer of the corresponding land is authorized, with the aim of improving the structure of milk production,[109] and may also authorize the definitive transfer of quota without transfer of the corresponding land, or vice versa, with the aim of improving the structure of milk production at the level of the holding, or to allow for extensification[110] of production.[111]

The national reserve, at the United Kingdom level, comprises such wholesale and direct sales quota as is not for the time being allocated to any person, including quota withdrawn under the regulations.[112] Under art 5 of Regulation 3950/92, a Member State has a general power to replenish the national reserve following an across-the-board reduction in all the individual reference quantities in order to grant additional or specific quantities to producers in accordance with objective criteria agreed with the Commission. Furthermore, as mentioned above, art 5 also provides that quotas available to producers who have not marketed milk or other milk products during one of the twelve-month periods (ie 1 April to 31 March) are to be allocated to the national reserve and may be reallocated to producers determined in accordance with objective criteria agreed with the Commission; where a producer does not make use of at least 70 per cent of his quota, Member States may decide whether all or part of the unused quota should revert to the national reserve, and under which conditions a quota may be reallocated to the producers concerned. However, this does not apply where the loss of production is due to force majeure or is otherwise justified.

In the context of transfers of the holding, any part of the quota which is not transferred with the holding is added to the national reserve.[113] Furthermore, under art 8a, added by Regulation 1256/1999, where quota has been or is transferred with or without the corresponding land by means of rural leases or other means having comparable legal effects, Member States may decide on the basis of

[109] Art 8(d) of Council Regulation 3950/92 (OJ 1992 L405/1) as amended by Council Regulation 1256/1999 (OJ 1999 L160/73).

[110] This term is used in the context of the common organization of the market in beef and veal in relation to payment for limiting the stocking density on the holding; however, under art 13(4) of Council Regulation 1254/1999 on the common organization of the market in beef and veal, extensification payments may be made for the dairy cows kept on a holding located in a mountain area in a Member State where more than 50% of milk production takes place in mountain areas.

[111] Art 8(e) of Council Regulation 3950/92 (OJ 1992 L405/1) as amended by Council Regulation 1256/1999 (OJ 1999 L160/73).

[112] SI 1997/733, Reg 12.

[113] Art 7(1) of Reg 3950/92, as amended by Reg 1256/1999.

objective criteria whether and under what conditions all or part of the transferred quota shall revert to the national reserve.

In any event, where Member States grant compensation to producers who undertake to abandon definitively all or part of their milk production, the quota released is placed in the national reserve.[114]

The rate of levy where the quotas are exceeded is fixed by the EC legislation itself.[115] Under the original scheme, in direct sales it was fixed at 75 per cent of the target price, the target price being higher than the guaranteed intervention prices. In the context of delivery quota (where it is paid by the purchaser) it was fixed at 100 per cent of the target price, on the basis that the levy would not in practice necessarily cover all the excess quantities delivered by each producer. For the same reasons, Council Regulation 1305/85[116] introduced levy at the rate of 100 per cent even for direct sales where reference quantities were allocated to producer groups rather than to individual producers. However, Regulation 3950/92 raised the levy to a uniform rate of 115 per cent of the target price in all cases.[117] Under art 10 of Regulation 3950/92, the levy is deemed to be intervention to stabilize agricultural markets, and must be used to finance expenditure in the milk sector.

Under the UK implementing regulations, the Intervention Board is required[118] to maintain a direct sales register entry in respect of each direct seller, and a wholesale register entry in respect of producers delivering to purchasers; this latter includes a list of the purchasers whose purchaser quota comprises all or part of a particular producer's total wholesale quota. Conversely, each direct seller is required to register his quota with the Intervention Board, each producer with wholesale quota (the name given to delivery quota in the UK implementing regulations) is required to register with a purchaser, and each purchaser is required to register with the Intervention Board.[119]

A final observation that might be made in the context of the dairy sector is that a protocol to the 1972 Act of Accession[120] laid down conditions for the access of New Zealand butter and cheese to the United Kingdom market. The protocol itself expired on 1 January 1978, but special arrangements continued for the importation of specific quantities from New Zealand.[121] These have evolved into a tariff quota for New Zealand butter[122] forming part of the WTO Uruguay Round.

---

[114] Art 8(a) of Reg 3950/92, as amended by Reg 1256/1999.
[115] Reg 3950/92, art 1.   [116] OJ 1985 L137/12.   [117] Art 1.
[118] SI 1997/733, Reg 24.   [119] Reg 26.
[120] Act of Accession (1972), Protocol 18.
[121] Council Regulation 3667/83 (OJ 1983 L366/16), amended by Council Regulation 2007/84 (OJ 1984 L187/6).
[122] Which includes 'spreadable' butter, see Council Regulation 2250/1999 (OJ 1999 L275/4).

Beef and veal

While the common organization of the market in beef and veal established under Council Regulation 805/68[123] took as its pivotal point a 'guide price' fixed for calves, and a 'guide price' fixed for adult bovine animals, prices which equated with the target price in cereals terminology, the aim of the version of the common organization introduced by Council Regulation 1254/1999[124] is to reduce the level of market support and to establish a comprehensive system of direct payments for producers,[125] with effect from 1 January 2000. These direct payments take the form of special premium, deseasonalization premium, suckler cow premium, slaughter premium, extensification payment, and additional payments which may take the form of headage payments and/or area payments.

The special premium[126] is an annual payment to a producer holding male bovine animals on his holding per calendar year and per holding, subject to regional ceilings for not more than 90 animals for each of the relevant age brackets. It is paid once in the life of a bull (an uncastrated male bovine animal) from the age of 9 months, and twice in the life of a steer (a castrated male bovine animal) at the age of 9 months and after it has reached the age of 21 months. Member States may make limited derogations from these criteria, and may grant the premium at the time of slaughter, in which case the age criterion for bulls is replaced by a minimum carcass weight of 185 kg. The premium rises from €160 for bulls and €122 for steers in 2000, to €185/136 in 2001 and €210/150 for 2002 and subsequent years. The deseasonalization premium relates to steers, and is intended to spread their slaughter over the year. It applies[127] in Member States where the number of steers slaughtered in a given year exceeds 60 per cent of annual slaughterings of male bovine animals and where the number of steers slaughtered during the period 1 September to 30 November exceeds 35 per cent of total annual slaughterings of steers. It involves the payment of a high premium for animals slaughtered in the first fifteen weeks of the year, then progressively lower premiums for animals slaughtered in the sixteenth and seventeenth weeks, the eighteenth to twenty-first weeks and the twenty-second and twenty-third weeks, with no premium thereafter. Member States whose producers have previously received the premium may pay it at 60 per cent of the basic rates, subject to reducing the special premium payable for the second age bracket of steers.

Suckler cow premium[128] is again an annual payment to producers keeping suckler cows (a cow of a meat breed or meat breed cross belonging to a herd intended for rearing calves for meat production), subject to conditions intended in particular to avoid overlap with the common organization of the market in milk. The producer either must not supply milk or milk products from his farm (except

---

[123] OJ 1968 L148/24 (sp edn 1968 (I), p 187).   [124] OJ 1999 L160/21.
[125] Recital (3).   [126] Art 4.   [127] Art 5.
[128] Art 6.

for direct sales to consumers) for twelve months after lodging the application for the premium, or must supply such products with a total quota which does not exceed 120,000 kg—though Member States may waive or change this limit. In any event the producer must keep for at least six consecutive months after lodging the application a number of suckler cows equal to at least 80 per cent of the number for which premium was requested, and a number of heifers (female bovine animals over 8 months old which have not yet calved) which are no more than 20 per cent of that number. The premium rises from €163 in 2000 to €182 in 2001 and €200 in 2002 and subsequent years, and Member States may grant an additional premium up to €50 per animal. Suckler cow premium rights may be transferred with or without the holding, but if they are transferred without the holding, up to 15 per cent may be required to be returned to the national reserve[129] without compensation.

The total number of animals qualifying for special premium and suckler cow premium is limited by rules on stocking density,[130] which is in principle set at 2 livestock units (LU) per hectare of forage area per calendar year, though this does not apply to producers with a number of animals equivalent to no more than 15 livestock units. In calculating these units account is taken not only of the bulls, steers, suckling cows, and heifers subject to this common organization, but also of dairy cows, and sheep and goats. Bulls, steers, and heifers over 24 months old, suckler cows, and dairy cows count as one unit each, and bulls, steers, and heifers from 6 months to 24 months count as 0.6 LU, while sheep and goats count as 0.15 LU each.[131] Furthermore, producers receiving special premium and/or suckler cow premium may qualify for an extensification payment[132] of €100 per special premium and suckling cow premium granted, provided the stocking density is 1.4 LU per hectare or less—in other words a financial inducement to have fewer animals on the holding. In the alternative, in 2000 and 2001, Member States may make lower payments but make them in respect of densities between 1.6 LU and 2 LU per hectare (€33) and less than 1.6 LU (€66), and from 2002 onwards from 1.4LU to 1.8 LU (€40) and less than 1.4 LU (€80).

The slaughter premium[133] is granted on the slaughter or export to a third country of eligible animals. It is payable on bulls, steers, cows, and heifers from the age of 8 months at a rate rising from €27 in 2000 to €53 in 2001 and €80 in 2002 and subsequent years; it is also payable on calves between 1 and 7 months old with a carcass weight less than 160 kg at the lower rate of €17 in 2000, €33 in 2001, and €50 in 2002 and subsequent years.

Member States are also to make additional payments of the amounts set out in Annex IV of the regulation, which can take the form of headage payments or area payments. For male bovine animals, headage payments may be granted as a supplement to the slaughter premium,[134] subject to overall limits, and only if they are older than 8 months or have a minimum carcass weight of at least 180 kg.[135] For

---

[129] Required under art 9.   [130] Art 12.   [131] Annex III.
[132] Art 13.   [133] Art 11.   [134] Art 15.
[135] Art 16.

suckler cows and heifers, headage payments may only be granted as supplement to the suckler cow premium, and headage payments for dairy cows may only be granted as an amount per tonne of dairy quota.

Storage aid and intervention have been reduced to a residual status. From July 2002 a decision to grant aid for private storage may be taken when the average Community market price is less than 103 per cent of a basic price initially set at €2,224 per tonne,[136] and from that same date public intervention will be opened if the average market price in a Member State or region of a Member State falls below a price fixed at €1,560 per tonne, but the buying-in prices and the quantities accepted for intervention are to be determined under tender procedures.[137]

In principle, external protection is through customs duties under the Common Customs Tariff,[138] though export refunds may still be paid.

Clearly a system of support in which payments are related to the ages and numbers of animals on a holding requires effective monitoring arrangements; at the same time the BSE crisis emphasized both the need for traceability and the need for a system of labelling which might help restore consumer confidence. Art 21 of Regulation 1254/1999 made it clear that, to qualify for any of the direct payments, an animal had to be identified and registered under Council Regulation 820/97,[139] which has in turn been repealed and replaced by Regulation 1760/2000[140] of the European Parliament and of the Council establishing a system for the identification and registration of bovine animals and regarding the labelling of beef and beef products.

The system for the identification and registration of bovine animals comprises a combination of ear tags for each animal, computerized databases, animal passports, and individual registers kept on each holding.[141] Ear tags on both ears enabling both the animal and the holding on which it was born to be identified are required for all animals born after 1997 or intended for intra-Community trade after 1 January 1998.[142] The tags must be applied within twenty days, and no animal born after 1997 may be moved from a holding unless it has been tagged; animals imported from third countries must also be tagged within twenty days of passing the check required by Community law, unless they are slaughtered within that period. The computerized databases required to be set up by the competent national authorities under arts 14 and 18 of Directive 64/432 as updated[143] and amended were required to be fully operational by the end of 1999,[144] and from 1 January 1998 the competent authorities are required to issue a passport for each tagged animal within fourteen days of notification of its birth (or within fourteen days of its re-identification in the case of an animal imported from a third country). In principle an animal must be accompanied by its passport whenever it is

---

[136] Art 26.   [137] Art 27.   [138] Art 30.
[139] OJ 1997 L117/1.   [140] OJ 2000 L204/1.   [141] Reg 1760/2000, art 3.
[142] Art 4.
[143] By Council Directive 97/12 (OJ 1997 L109/1).
[144] Art 5.

moved,[145] though Member States with a database that the Commission deems to be fully operational may provide that a passport is to be issued only for animal intended for intra-Community trade; the passport is to be surrendered on the death (including slaughter) of an animal or on its export to a third country. Each keeper of animals is required to keep an up-to-date register,[146] available to the competent authorities for at least three years. Once the computerized database is fully operational, each keeper is also required to report to the competent authority all movements to or from the holding and all births and deaths of animals on the holding within three to seven days of the event occurring.

So far as labelling of beef products is concerned, the regulation sets out both a compulsory beef labelling scheme and the parameters to be followed in any voluntary labelling scheme going beyond those requirements, applicable to beef from animals slaughtered on or after 1 September 2000. The aim of the compulsory scheme is to ensure a link between the identification of the meat and the individual animal, or in some cases group of animals, from which it came.[147] The label must contain a reference number or code linking the meat to the animal or animals from which it came, and it must indicate the approval number of the slaughterhouse and the cutting hall. As from 1 January 2002, the label itself must also indicate the Member States or third countries of birth, of fattening, and of slaughter.

With regard to the voluntary labelling scheme, operators or organizations must send a specification for approval by the competent national authorities,[149] and such a specification must indicate the information to be included on the label, measures taken to ensure its accuracy, the control system to be applied, including the controls to be carried out by an independent designated body complying with the criteria set out in European Standard EN/45011, and, in the case of an organization, the mea-sures to be taken in relation to any member failing to comply with the specifications.

Where a third country is involved in the production of the beef, operators and organizations are required also to obtain the approval of the competent authorities in the third countries[149] concerned before being entitled to operate a voluntary labelling scheme.

Sheepmeat

The sheepmeat regime was established, ten years after the expiry of the time limit for the introduction of common organizations, by Council Regulation 1837/80,[150] following, in particular, a dispute between the United Kingdom and France.[151] It had several distinctive features, notably its use both of aid and intervention systems, with further aid (notably a variable slaughter premium in Great Britain) permitted

[145] Art 6.   [146] Art 7.   [147] Art 13.
[148] Art 16.   [149] Art 17.
[150] OJ 1980 L183/1.   [151] Case 232/78 *Commission v France* [1979] ECR 2729.

initially as an alternative to intervention. However, a particular characteristic when it was introduced was that the 'basic price', on which the organization essentially rests, was to be converted into different 'reference prices' for specified regions of the Community, determined originally from previous local prices, with the aim that these prices should converge over a period of four years. These rather belated transitional arrangements for sheepmeat were nonetheless held to be valid by the Court of Justice in Case 106/81 *Julius Kind KG v EC*.[152] The separate reference prices were in fact abolished in 1984, when a single price system was introduced.[153] Like other common organizations, it has subsequently undergone considerable changes, with the emphasis moving more to direct payments to producers and away from intervention, which has only a very minor role in the current version of the common organization set out in Council Regulation 2647/98.[154] The basic price for the 2001 and following marketing years was set at €504.7 per 100 kg carcass weight by Council Regulation 1669/2000,[155] which also sets the seasonally adjusted basic prices.

The general system of aid instituted under the common organization has become known in English as the annual ewe headage payment. It is paid in so far as the average market price in a quotation area (ie a Member State, except that Great Britain and Northern Ireland are separate quotation areas[156]) is below the basic price per 100 kg carcass weight. The difference is, in principle, multiplied by a coefficient representing the normal average production of lamb meat per ewe for the Community as a whole expressed per 100 kg of carcass weight.[157] The full premium is payable per ewe to producers of heavy lambs (ie those fattened for meat[158]), but the coefficient is reduced to 80 per cent[159] for the premium payable per ewe to the producers of light lambs (ie those produced by a sheep farmer marketing sheep's milk or products based on sheep's milk[160]). However, if a sheep farmer marketing sheep's milk or products based on sheep's milk can prove that at least 40 per cent of the lambs born on his holding have been fattened as heavy carcasses for slaughter, he may request payment of a proportionate amount of the full premium. A half-yearly advance payment may be made of 30 per cent of the expected premium, following the half-yearly calculation by the Commission of the foreseeable income loss for the entire marketing year, and the foreseeable amount of the premium.[161]

These payments are however subject to overall limits. In principle, the premium is payable for the number of animals for which it was payable to the producer in 1991,[162] subject to a corrective coefficient. However, until 1994, the full premium was only payable within the limit of 1,000 animals per producer in less-favoured

---

[152] [1982] ECR 2885 at 2920.
[153] Council Regulation 871/84 (OJ L90, 1.4.84, p 35).
[154] OJ 1998 L312/1.   [155] OJ 2000 L193/8.
[156] Council Regulation 2647/98 (OJ 1998 L312/1).
[157] Art 5.   [158] Art 4.   [159] Art 5(3).
[160] Art 4(3).   [161] Art 5(6).   [162] Art 6(1).

areas and 500 animals elsewhere.[163] Outside those limits, premium was only payable at a rate of 50 per cent. It is therefore provided that, with effect from the 1995 marketing year, individual limits are to be recalculated in such a way that quantities above the respective limits of 1,000 or 500 animals are to be reduced by 50 per cent—producing the same overall effect with regard to Community expenditure. However, the premium rights thus allocated to each producer are, like milk quota, transferable.[164] There is also an overall maximum guaranteed level fixed in the regulation at 63,400,000 head of ewes,[165] and if the estimate for the marketing year exceeds that level, the premium is reduced by applying a reduction to the basic price of 7 per cent for each 1 per cent by which the level is exceeded.[166]

Intervention measures, on the other hand, are reduced to private storage aid.[167] Where the market price in a quotation area is less than 90 per cent of the seasonally adjusted basic price and it is likely to remain so, a decision may be taken to grant private storage aid to that quotation area, and where it is less than 70 per cent of the seasonally adjusted basic price, the private storage aid may be brought in for the quotation area in question, in the framework of a tendering procedure;[168] aid may also be granted in the framework of an advance-fixing procedure where urgent recourse to private storage proves necessary in the light of a particularly difficult market situation in one or more quotation areas, but only in those areas.

It is expressly provided that when a producer sells or otherwise transfers his holding, he may transfer all his premium rights to the person who takes over his holding.[169] He may also transfer his rights in whole or in part to other producers without transferring his holding, but in that case, some of the premium rights (up to 15 per cent) must be surrendered without compensation to the national reserve in the Member State where the holding is situated, to be used for free distribution to new entrants or other priority producers.[170] This compulsory surrender does not however apply, subject to detailed implementing rules, to transfers between members of the same group of producers.[171]

Member States may also authorize leases of premium rights which the producer entitled to them does not intend to use, but they are under an overall duty to ensure that premium rights are not moved away from sensitive zones or regions where sheep production is especially important for the local economy.[172]

In Case C-38/94 *R v Minister for Agriculture, Fisheries and Food, ex p Country Landowners' Association*,[173] the landowners claimed that Member States should be required to introduce a compensation mechanism for the loss suffered by the owners of agricultural land in particular where the premium right was transferred by producers who did not own the land on which they farmed. The landowners argued that the allocation of freely transferable quotas to tenant producers would

---

[163] See art 5(7).　　　　[164] Art 6(4).　　　　[165] Art 13(1).
[166] Art 13(2) and (4).　　　[167] Art 11.　　　　[168] Art 12.
[169] Council Regulation 2467/98 (OJ 1998 L312/1) art 6(4).
[170] Listed in art 7(2).　　　[171] Art 6(4)(b).　　　[172] Art 6(4)(c) and (d).
[173] [1995] ECR I-3875.

have the effect of reducing the capital value of the land. This point was accepted by MAFF but they refuted the existence of any obligation upon them to compensate the landowners for this loss. The Court reaffirmed that no general principle of law upheld by the Community legal order, in particular, the principle of protection of the right to property, required that such compensation be paid. On the other hand, it stated that it was for each Member State to assess the need for such measures having regard in particular to the national arrangements for implementing the rules in question and the national rules governing the relationship between landlord and tenant.

Member States were required to establish a national reserve initially equal to between 1 and 3 per cent of the sum of the individual limits applicable to producers whose holdings were in its territory.[174] This reserve also receives the compulsory top-slice discussed in the previous paragraph where premium rights are transferred without transfer of the holding. The reserves may be used to grant entitlements to certain producers; many of the situations on the priority list in the regulation relate to the early 1990s,[175] but they include producers who submit a first application after 1993, and producers who acquire part of an area formerly used for sheep and/or goat production by other producers.[176] An additional reserve must also be created equal to 1 per cent of the sum of the individual limits of producers in the less-favoured areas in each Member State; this reserve must be allocated exclusively to producers in those same areas.[177]

Pigmeat, poultry, and eggs

Pigmeat, poultry, and eggs may be considered together to the extent that they have traditionally been treated as ancillary to the common organization of the market in cereals, and that the legislation governing them[178] was adopted in parallel with the legislation governing the common organization of the market in cereals. This parallelism was, however, broken in the 1979 Act of Accession,[179] where accession compensatory amounts were calculated from the prices of the products themselves, rather than from the prices of feed grain, which was the method used in the 1972 Act of Accession, and new versions of the basic regulation were not adopted when Council Regulation 1766/92 changed the emphasis of cereal market support to producer payments. The three common organizations originally rested essentially on external protection, with 'sluice-gate' prices and levies, but

---

[174] Council Regulation 2467/98 (OJ 1998 L312/1) art 7(1).
[175] Reg 2467/98 takes the form of a consolidation of the amendments to Reg 3013/89.
[176] Art 7(2)(d) and (e).
[177] Art 7(3).
[178] Council Regulation 2759/75 (OJ 1975 L282/1) (pigmeat), Council Regulation 2771/75 (OJ 1975 L282/49) (eggs), and Council Regulation 2777/75 (OJ 1975 L282/77) (poultrymeat).
[179] Act of Accession (1979), arts 99–101.

following the implementation of the Uruguay Round Agreement by Council Regulation 3290/94,[180] Common Customs Tariff duties apply in all three markets.

The most developed of these three common organizations relates to pigmeat. The pigmeat organization is founded on a 'basic price' which, as a matter of express legislation, must not lead to structural surpluses and is fixed at a level which contributes towards stabilizing market prices.[181] Intervention measures may be taken if the market price falls below 103 per cent of the basic price, but the Commission has a discretion whether to introduce such measures; furthermore, buying-in prices range from 78 per cent to 92 per cent of the basic price.[182]

For eggs and poultrymeat, there is no internal guaranteed price support. However, all three products may benefit from export refunds where appropriate.

Sugar

The legal interest of the common organization of the market in sugar lies in the fact that, apart from its use of the usual mechanisms of intervention, import levies, and export refunds, it has from the outset been subject to a system of production quotas, now copied to some extent in other common organizations, even though the quota system was intended only to last until 1975.[183]

Under the original version of the sugar market established by Council Regulation 1009/67,[184] a basic quota was allotted to each undertaking for each marketing year, and from this a maximum quota was calculated. Production outside the maximum quota was not to be disposed of on the internal market, and was subject to a levy if it was so disposed of. Even production within the maximum quota but outside the basic quota could be subject to a production levy to help cover the costs of its disposal. Under the current Council Regulation 1260/2001,[185] which continues the quota system until the marketing year 2005–2006, the basic and maximum quotas are renamed A and B quotas, and the surplus is referred to as C production, and even production within the A quota may be subject to a levy to help meet the costs of disposing of the surplus within the A and B quotas, whilst an additional levy may be imposed on the B production. This levy is, of course, only relevant when world prices are lower than Community prices, which has not always been the case with regard to sugar.

The legal basis of the system of quotas was considered by the Court in Case 250/84 Eridania[186] in relation to the Italian market in sugar, with regard to which the Court concluded that it was legitimate to base the quotas on historical

---

[180] OJ 1994 L349/105.
[181] Council Regulation 2759/75 (OJ 1975 L282/1), art 4.
[182] Art 5(1).
[183] Council Regulation 1009/67 (JO 1967 No 308, p 1 (sp edn 1967, p 304)), art 22.
[184] JO 1967 No 308 p 1 (sp edn 1967, p 304).
[185] OJ 2001 L178/1.   [186] [1986] ECR 117.

production rather than current consumption, so that the Italian production quota could be less than Italian consumption. The underlying rationale appears to be that it is a legitimate Community objective to encourage regional specialization, and that the quota system is not intended to benefit the least efficient producers. Most important of all, the Court stated that Italian producers could not complain about being required to co-finance the disposal of the Community surplus when they did not even meet Italian consumption, on the basis that to claim that producers should be able to limit their liability to surpluses for which those producers were themselves responsible was incompatible with the very concept of a common market. This clear affirmation that quotas serve the interests of Community, rather than national, policy, even when historically derived, may be regarded as being of particular importance given the extension of the quota system to the milk sector.

Under the 1972 Act of Accession the United Kingdom was permitted to continue imports under the Commonwealth Sugar Agreement until the end of February 1975,[187] when the first Lomé Convention was signed. This allowed guaranteed access to the Community for specified annual quantities of sugar from named developing countries, and has been followed in successive Lomé Conventions, despite the Community's own surplus production. In the Cotonou Agreement,[188] signed on 23 June 2000, it has been agreed to maintain the protocol on sugar, but to review it in the framework of negotiations for new trading arrangements.

Special features of other organizations

The basic features of a number of the other common organizations have already been described. The market in fruit and vegetables under Council Regulation 2200/96[189] is characterized by the important role entrusted to producers' organizations,[190] which may organize the withdrawal of products from the market,[191] and their marketing rules in certain circumstances may be extended to non-members,[192] provided they are compatible with Community law.[193] Withdrawal is however limited and degressive. The amount paid is set out as a fixed sum in euro per 100 kg in Annex V to the regulation, reducing over the period 1997 to 2002. Thus cauliflowers go from €9.34 per 100 kg in 1997–1998 to €7.01 per 100 kg from 2002 onwards, tomatoes from €6.44 to €4.83, and apples from €10.69 to €8.81. Furthermore, in principle the volume which may be withdrawn is reduced from 50 per cent of marketed production in 1997–1998 to 10 per cent of marketed production from 2002 onwards,[194] and 8.5 per cent in the case of apples and pears (though for melons and watermelons the 10 per cent ceiling has applied from 1997–1998).

---

[187] Act of Accession (1972), Protocol 17.   [188] OJ 2000 L317.
[189] OJ 1996 L297/1.   [190] Art 11.   [191] Arts 15 and 23.
[192] Art 18.
[193] Case 218/85 *Le Campion* [1986] ECR 3513.   [194] Art 23.

Whilst, traditionally, the common organization of the market in wine might seem to have been of interest in the United Kingdom from the point of view of the consumer rather than of the producer, the consolidated text in Council Regulation 1493/1999 on the common organization of the market in wine[195] expressly includes the United Kingdom in Zone A along with German areas other than Baden, Luxembourg, and such well-known wine-producing countries as Belgium, the Netherlands, Denmark, Sweden, and Ireland. The basic system of support involves storage aid[196] and distillation.[197] The long-term method of restricting surplus production is a prohibition on the planting of defined varieties of new vines currently in force until the end of 2010,[198] subject to narrowly defined new planting rights, replanting rights, and planting rights granted from a reserve. However, under art 21 this restriction does not apply in Member States where wine production does not exceed 25,000 hectolitres per wine year. The original version of this prohibition was upheld by the European Court in Case 44/79 *Hauer v Land Rheinland-Pfalz*[199] after observing that in all the Member States property ownership may be subjected to the requirements of the common good, and that all the wine-producing countries of the Community themselves imposed restrictions on the planting of vines, on the basis that the Community measure was not an undue restriction on the exercise of property rights, being justified by the aims the Community was pursuing in the general interest.

The common organization of the market in bananas was introduced only in 1993, in Council Regulation 404/93,[200] and has become notorious for the disputes to which it has given rise in the WTO context, which were discussed in the previous chapter.[201] It was there suggested that the timing of its introduction may be related to the completion of the single internal market by the end of 1992 under art 14 of the EC Treaty, in that the UK and France had had quota regimes giving preference to imports from their former colonies, and had previously been authorized not to grant Community treatment to bananas from other countries in free circulation in other Member States. At the domestic level, the common organization provided for limited financial support through producers' organizations, but only for a fixed level of production,[202] and it also provided for the payment of a premium to Community producers who cease to produce bananas.[203] However, the vast majority of bananas consumed in the EU are imported from third countries, and was with regard to these imports that the conflicts with WTO rules occurred. The regulation provided differential treatment for traditional imports from ACP countries,[204] for non-traditional imports from ACP countries, and for imports from non-ACP third countries. The traditional ACP imports were free of duty, and a further tariff quota, originally of 2 million tonnes, was established, within which imports from non-ACP third countries paid a reduced tariff,

---

[195] OJ 1999 L179/1.   [196] Arts 24–26.   [197] Arts 27–33.
[198] Art 2.   [199] [1979] ECR 3727.   [200] OJ 1993 L47/1.
[201] See pp 72–74 above.   [202] Art 12.   [203] Art 13.
[204] Listed in Annex I.

and non-traditional imports from ACP countries were free of duty. Outside this quota, imports were subject to the Common Customs Tariff duty, subject to a deduction of €100 per tonne for non-traditional imports from ACP countries.

The problems to which this and the associated licensing scheme[205] gave rise were discussed in the previous chapter. However, in 2001 changes were made to the import aspects of the common organization, and agreement was reached with the USA and other complainants as to the shape of a longer-term policy.

A transitional regime was introduced by Council Regulation 216/2001,[206] the recitals to which refer expressly to the recommendations of the dispute settlement body. So far as the import licensing question is concerned, a new art 19 provides that the tariff quotas may be managed in accordance with 'the method based on taking account of traditional trade flows . . . and/or other methods'. It would appear that the agreement with the USA was to use historic references,[207] but following further negotiations with Ecuador, 83 per cent of the quotas are to be managed this way and 17 per cent will be reserved for operators who do not have a suitable historic reference.[208] With regard to the quotas themselves, three bands of quota are envisaged, but under a new art 18, they are in principle open for imports of products originating in all third countries: quota A is for 2.2 million tonnes at a duty of €75 per tonne, quota B is for 353,000 tonnes at the same duty, and quota C is for 850,000 tonnes at a duty of €300. However, provision is made for a tariff preference of €300 per tonne for all imports from ACP countries, both inside and outside the quota, which would effectively allow duty-free access to ACP bananas under all three quotas.

However, under the agreement with the USA, 100,000 tonnes is to be moved from quota C to quota B, and the reduced quota C is then to be reserved exclusively for bananas of ACP origin[209]—which will require a waiver from art XIII of GATT, which the USA and Ecuador[210] have agreed to help to achieve. Longer term, it is proposed that a flat-tariff system will be introduced in 2006.[211]

Products not subject to common organizations

The general principles governing agricultural products which are not subject to common organizations have been considered in the context of the application of the general rules of the EC Treaty to agricultural products and in the context of the legal requirement for common policies. However, products which are not

---

[205] Art 17.   [206] OJ 2001 L31/2.
[207] Commission MEMO/01/135 (11 April 2001).
[208] Commission IP/01/628 (2 May 2001).
[209] Commission MEMO/01/135 (11 April 2001).
[210] Commission IP/01/628 (2 May 2001).
[211] Commission MEMO/01/135 (11 April 2001).

subject to a common organization may nevertheless still be regulated to some extent by legislation made under arts 32 to 38 of the EC Treaty. Hence, the regulation on the common organization of the market in cereals provides for a minimum price for potatoes intended for the manufacture of potato starch and a system of payments for producers of such potatoes,[212] even though potatoes themselves are not subject to a common organization.

---

[212] Council Regulation 1766/92 (OJ 1992 L181/21), art 8 as amended by Council Regulation 1253/1999 (OJ 1999 L160/18).

5

Agricultural support: financial mechanisms

The European Agricultural Guidance and Guarantee Fund

The EC Treaty expressly provides that in order to enable the common organizations to attain their objectives, one or more agricultural guidance and guarantee funds may be set up.[1] In fact the European Agricultural Guidance and Guarantee Fund was established by Council Regulation 25 of 4 April 1962,[2] the same date as that of Council Regulation 19[3] on the gradual establishment of the common organization of the markets in cereals, the first regulation dealing with common organizations of the market. Regulation 25 provided that the fund should form part of the Community budget and that, as single market organizations were established, the revenue from import levies should accrue to the Community budget and the fund should finance export refunds and intervention purchases.

The fact that the levies accrued to the budget and the fund financed refunds and intervention did not, however, make the agricultural policy self-financing, because there was and is no correlation at all between income and expenditure. If there was a high level of production of a particular agricultural product, it was quite likely that there would be a high level of intervention buying, meaning high expenditure for the fund, whereas at the same time there would be a low level of imports, therefore little in the way of import levies, and little income for the fund.

In 1964[4] the fund was split into a Guarantee Section, which included expenditure relating to refunds and intervention, and a Guidance Section, which included expenditure relating to measures undertaken in order to attain the objectives of the common agricultural policy,[5] in particular matters of structural policy. However, the current version in Council Regulation 1258/1999[6] makes a slightly

---

[1] EC Treaty, art 34(4).
[2] JO 1962, p 991 (sp edn 1959–1962, p 126).
[3] JO 1962, p 933.
[4] Council Regulation 17/64 (OJ 1964, p 586 (sp edn 1963–1964, p 103)), repealed and replaced by Council Regulation 729/70 (OJ 1970 L94/13 (sp edn 1970 (I), p 218)), in turn repealed and replaced by Council Regulation 1258/1999 (OJ 1999 L160/103).
[5] See EC Treaty, art 33.   [6] OJ 1999 L160/103.

different division: rural development measures outside Objective 1 programmes[7] except the rural development Community initiative are moved to the Guarantee Section, leaving the Guidance Section to finance other rural development measures. Council Regulation 1258/1999 on the financing of the common agricultural policy expressly states that both sections are to form part of the general budget of the Communities. The total revenue from agricultural levies, and other amounts and duties established in respect of trade with non-Member States within the framework of the CAP, is entered in the budget,[8] as are CCT customs duties, contributions, and duties under the common organization of the market in sugar. However, the day-to-day administration of the common agricultural policy is the responsibility of the national authorities, who both collect money on behalf of the Community[9] and make payments where so required under the various common organizations. Indeed, the Court of Justice has held that the liability of Member States to make payments required under a common organization exists even where the fund refuses, or is unable, to reimburse such payments.[10] The details of the relationship between the fund and the national authorities will be considered in the context of the administration of the common agricultural policy, but Community financing of that policy manifests the principle of financial solidarity. However, overall financial limits for the common agricultural policy and rural development policy (the 'agricultural guideline') were agreed in the Interinstitutional Agreement on budgetary discipline[11] concluded on 6 May 1999 by the European Parliament, the Council, and the Commission, and the reference base for this agricultural guideline was set out in Council Regulation 2040/2000[12] on budgetary discipline.

Common prices

The introduction of the euro as the unit in which EC agricultural prices are to be expressed by Council Regulation 2799/98[13] means that for the first time in the long history of the common agricultural policy common prices and payments are expressed in a unit which is the national currency of the Member States with no risk of fluctuation due to exchange risks; in other words common prices and payments are genuinely common. Regrettably, however, that is only the situation

---

[7] Under Reg 1260/1999 (OJ 1999 L161/1) on the Structural Funds, Objective 1 is defined as covering those areas where GDP per capita in terms of purchasing power is less than 75% of the Community average.

[8] Council Decision 94/728 on the system of the Communities' own resources (OJ 1994 L293/9), art 2.

[9] Council Decision 94/728 on the system of the Communities' own resources (OJ 1994 L293/9), art 8, implemented by Council Regulation 1150/2000 (OJ 2000 L130/1).

[10] Case 99/74 *Société des Grands Moulins des Antilles v Commission* [1975] ECR 1531.

[11] OJ 1999 C172/1.   [12] OJ 2000 L244/27.   [13] OJ 1998 L349/1.

for the twelve Member States which participate in the euro; exchange risks do remain for the other three Member States, Denmark,[14] Sweden, and the United Kingdom. This dichotomy makes it particularly appropriate to take an overview of the ways in which the EC has, in the context of the common agricultural policy, dealt with the phenomenon of floating currencies and the determination of criteria of value in that context, and the burden of monetary risk, looking in particular at the changes resulting from the introduction of the euro.

The particular importance of monetary movements in the context of the common agricultural policy arises from the fact that the more developed organizations of agricultural markets have taken the form of a price structure, albeit one which is now evolving into more of a payments structure. Thus, as mentioned in the previous chapter, at the heart of the original version of the common organization of which the market in cereals was the archetype were a target price and an intervention price, which were protected by a threshold price for imports, representing the minimum price at which the relevant goods might enter the Community. If (as was usually the case) the world price was lower than the threshold price, the difference had to be covered by an import levy. In the converse situation, if a Community producer wished to export into lower-priced world markets, there was power under the Community legislation to pay an export refund to cover the difference.

The EC's obligations to convert levies to tariffs and to reduce support under the Uruguay Round Agreement were effected under Council Regulation 3290/94,[15] though in the cereals market, and other major agricultural markets, the customs duties tend to be of a flat-rate nature. As a consequence of the change to customs duties, there was no longer a threshold price, and the target price therefore no longer served any practical purpose, and was abolished by Council Regulation 1528/95.[16]

This has been accompanied, as noted in the previous chapter, by a move away from a system of product support (intervention) to a system involving an element of producer support (eg area payments and set-aside). The Community has nevertheless decided to maintain the system of export levies (now called export taxes) designed to prevent Community producers taking advantage of world prices when they are higher than Community prices.

The concept of a common price policy led to the development of common organizations based on prices applicable throughout the Community and expressed in units of account rather than national currencies. Originally these units of account were defined in terms of the gold value of the United States dollar, and prices were converted into national currencies at the official parity. However, in 1971, the system of fixed exchange rates collapsed, and certain Community currencies floated upwards from their official parities. The overall unity of Community prices could

---

[14] Which however participates in the European Monetary System Mark II within a band of fluctuation of 2.25%.

[15] OJ 1994 L349/105.   [16] OJ 1995 L148/3.

have been maintained by reducing the prices expressed in those national curren-cies, which is the logical consequence of using units of account, but this was not done. Presumably it was hardly considered feasible politically at the time, though it has been and is the result of the revised rules set out in Council Regulation 3813/92,[17] and of the current rules set out in Council Regulation 2799/98[18] which introduce the euro as the unit used for fixing agricultural prices. Instead, Council Regulation 974/71[19] introduced a system of 'monetary compensatory amounts' (hereinafter MCAs) designed to cover the difference in real prices caused by the difference between agricultural exchange rates and current exchange rates. For currencies which appreciated in value, the MCA constituted a charge on imports and a subsidy on exports, but following the accession of the United Kingdom in 1973, MCAs were also introduced in a form appropriate to currencies which had depreciated, ie as a subsidy on imports and as a charge on exports.

In 1979 the old unit of account was replaced by the European Currency Unit (ECU) based on the value of a basket of Community currencies and used to deter-mine the central rates for currencies participating in the exchange rate mechanism of the European Monetary System. However, by then the divergences between prices expressed in national currencies were so great that the ECU had to be converted into national currencies at special agricultural rates of exchange rather than at the central rate, thus maintaining the need for MCAs. A conscious effort was thereafter made to bring conversion rates into line with reality and to dismantle the system of MCAs. The price settlements agreed from 1989 onwards involved very little monetary compensation, but it might have been thought that MCAs could not be totally eliminated while some national currencies still floated freely and could therefore alter in value during the course of the marketing year. Nevertheless, at the end of 1992 the concept of the area without internal frontiers prevailed, and the system of MCAs was in principle eliminated by Council Regulation 3813/92.[20] The 1992 regulation provided for the conversion of ECUs into national currency and vice versa at an agricultural conversion rate based on representative market rates, and recognized that a sum in national currency representing a common price fixed in ECUs might have to be altered even during the course of a marketing year if the representative market rate diverged from the agricultural conversion rate by more than a fixed amount. This policy has continued following the introduction of the euro as the unit to be used in the CAP by Council Regulation 2799/98.[21] Community agricultural prices are now fixed in euro for the whole Community, and granted and collected in euro in the twelve Member States which participate in the single currency. However, these prices are converted into national currency at a money-market exchange rate for the other Member States. Producers in the non-participating states therefore bear the exchange risk, subject to the power to grant compensatory aid to farmers in cases of appreciable revaluation.

[17] OJ 1992 L387/1.   [18] OJ 1998 L349/1.   [19] JO 1971 L106/1.
[20] OJ 1992 L387/1.   [21] OJ 1998 L349/1.

There have, however, been exceptions to the principle of single prices expressed in units of account. In Case 8/78 *Milac v HZA Freiburg*,[22] despite the reference in art 34(2) to a common price policy, the Court was prepared to accept that different prices could be set in units of account for different Member States when, as a result of floating exchange rates, this would give rise to greater uniformity in terms of national currencies—although this could be said to add a further corrective element to the correction already carried out by monetary compensatory amounts. On the other hand, Council Regulation 1889/87 introduced differentiation of prices expressed in ECUs as a method of trying to eliminate 'negative MCAs'.[23] For different, but still pragmatic, reasons, the Court also accepted in Case 106/81 *Kind v EEC*[24] that the widely differing reference prices for sheepmeat in different regions of the Community could be accepted in the initial stages of the common organization of the market in sheepmeat, provided the aim was to achieve an eventual coordination of prices.

The problems of floating currencies

The monetary problems encountered in the common agricultural system therefore resulted from the system of floating currencies without fixed exchange rates. Given the continuing difficulties, at least with regard to the Member States which do not participate in the euro, caused by floating currencies within the EC and in particular in the context of the common agricultural policy, it may be observed that the original version of the EEC Treaty stated in art 3 that the activities of the Community should include 'the application of procedures by which the economic policies of the Member States can be coordinated and disequilibria in their balances of payments remedied'. This was reflected in the original art 104, requiring each Member State to pursue the economic policy needed to ensure the equilibrium of its overall balance of payments and to maintain confidence on its currency, and under the original art 105(1), Member States were to coordinate their economic policies so as to facilitate the attainment of those objectives.[25] Those obligations can hardly be said to have been universally observed, and indeed in the context of the common agricultural policy the European Court held in 1978 that the floating of exchange rates and the underlying failure to coordinate divergent monetary policies constituted a breach of the obligation set out in art 105(1).[26]

It may or may not be a coincidence therefore that the structure of the original European Monetary System was laid down in a resolution of the European Council

---

[22] [1978] ECR 1721.
[23] OJ 1987 L182/1.   [24] [1982] ECR 2885.
[25] The relevant part of the original art 105(1) became art 109m after the Treaty of Maastricht, and continues in force for the 'outs' as art 124 following the Treaty of Amsterdam.
[26] See eg Cases 80–81/77 *Ramel v Receveur des Douanes* [1978] ECR 927.

dated 5 December 1978,[27] backed up by an agreement between the central banks of the Member States of 13 March 1979 laying down the operating procedures for the EMS. Given its continuing importance as one of the convergence criteria for Member States that wish to accede to EMU in the future, the European Monetary Institute prepared a draft framework for a European Monetary System Mark II,[28] and this formed the basis of an agreement in principle on its structure at the Dublin European Council in December 1996. This framework was adopted in a European Council Resolution of 16 June 1997,[29] following exactly the same pattern as the 1978 resolution of the European Council on the original European Monetary System.[30]

What distinguishes the resolutions establishing the European Monetary Systems from most binding Community acts is that they do not in themselves create a comprehensive set of obligations for every Member State; in effect, it was for each Member State to decide whether to join the exchange rate mechanism[31] under the original version, and under the current version participation in the exchange rate mechanism is voluntary for the Member States outside the euro area, although 'Member States with a derogation can be expected to join the mechanism'.[32]

While the details of the original version of the European Monetary System are now a matter of history, a brief outline of its exchange rate mechanism may be given if only because of its relevance to monetary compensation and agricultural conversion rates. The ECU was at the heart of the exchange rate mechanism,[33] even if the bands of fluctuation related to bilateral exchange rates between participating currencies. This unit was first created, under the name of the European Unit of Account (EUA) in April 1975[34] as a method of calculating the amount of aid payable under the first Lomé Convention.

Despite fundamental differences in conception, the 1975 EUA was not totally divorced from the old gold parity unit of account. It was defined in Council Decision 75/250[35] as being the sum of 0.828 German marks, plus 0.0885 pounds sterling, plus 1.15 French francs, plus 109 Italian lire, plus 0.286 Dutch guilders, plus 3.66 Belgian francs, plus 0.14 Luxembourg francs, plus 0.217 Danish kroner, plus 0.00759 Irish pounds. However, in the recitals to the decision it was made clear that the sum of this cocktail had an initial value equivalent to the value set by the International Monetary Fund on 28 June 1974 for the Special Drawing Right, otherwise known as the SDR. As then defined, this was also a basket unit, but one which gave a heavy weighting to the United States dollar which, of course,

---

[27] EC Bulletin 1978 No 12, point 1.1.11.
[28] Report of the EMI to the informal ECOFIN Council, Verona, 12–13 April 1996.
[29] 'Rapid' Information Service, 18 June 1997.
[30] European Council Resolution of 5 December 1978 (EC Bulletin 1978 No 12, point 1.1.11).
[31] Art 3 of the 1978 resolution.
[32] European Council Resolution of 16 June 1997, para 1.6.
[33] Art 2(2).
[34] Council Decision 75/250 (OJ 1975 L104/35).
[35] OJ 1975 L104/35.

was not included in the European EUA basket. Until the summer of 1974, the value of an SDR had however been based on the gold value of the United States dollar, in other words, 0.888671 grammes of fine gold, which was also, of course, the definition of the value of the old EC unit of account. There is therefore a clear linkage between the dollar, the ECU, and the euro.

The fundamental characteristic of the EC's basket unit was that it comprised fixed sums of national currencies, not fixed percentages of national currencies. These fixed sums did not change automatically when central rates were altered in an EMS realignment or when market values fluctuated, so that the percentage composition of the unit in terms of national currencies did in fact change. The percentage share of a currency which rose in value would, since the EUA and now ECU comprised a fixed element of that currency, increase, and the percentage share of a currency whose value diminished would inevitably decrease, since there was still the same nominal sum in that currency represented in the unit. For example, during the period 1975 to 1983, when the definition of the EUA/ECU remained unchanged, the percentage of the unit represented by the same fixed sum of German currency rose from about 27 per cent to about 37 per cent.[36] By way of comparison, in the last definition in 1989, its share was set at 30.1 per cent.[37] When the ECU was created in the context of the European Monetary System, the European Council's resolution of 5 December 1978[38] expressly provided that the value and composition of the ECU would be identical with the value of the EUA at the outset of the system, so that Council Regulation 3180/78,[39] changing the value of the unit of account used by the European Monetary Cooperation Fund,[40] defined the ECU as the sum of exactly the same currency elements as the EUA. Under the 1978 resolution, the weightings of the currencies used in the definition of the ECU could be revised within six months after the entry into force of the European Monetary System and thereafter every five years, although a revision could be requested at any other time if the weight of any currency had changed by 25 per cent or more.[41] A revision was in fact effected in September 1984 by Council Regulation 2626/84,[42] which took the opportunity to include Greek drachmas in the definition, and also reduced the nominal amount of German marks, presumably because of their increase in value in the meantime, whilst increasing the nominal value of the sum of Italian lire and Irish pounds for example. A further revision took place in 1989, when the opportunity was taken to incorporate the Spanish peseta and the Portuguese escudo.

Whereas one of the basic characteristics of the ECU was that its composition could be changed, even if in principle only every five years, art 118 introduced by

[36] Commission of the EC, *The ECU* (1984) 12.
[37] Council Regulation 1971/89 (OJ 1989 L189/1), art 1.
[38] EC Bulletin 1978 No 12, point 1.1.11.
[39] OJ 1978 L379/1.
[40] Created by Council Regulation 907/73 (OJ 1973 L89/2).
[41] Art 2(3).
[42] OJ 1984 L247/1.

the Maastricht Treaty stated categorically that the currency composition of the ECU basket should not be changed, no doubt with the intention of building confidence in the international money markets. The result of this is that the September 1989 definition remained in force and could not be altered, since it could not in principle be revised until September 1994 under the previous rules, and this date was after the entry into force of art 118. This means that the definition of the ECU could not and did not reflect an element of the currencies of the Member States which have joined since that date: Austria, Finland, and Sweden.

Art 118 further provided that from the start of the third stage, the value of the ECU should be irrevocably fixed in accordance with art 123(4), which in turn required that from that date, the Council should, acting with the unanimity of the Member States which were able and willing to participate, adopt the conversion rates at which their currencies were irrevocably fixed and at which irrevocably fixed rate the ECU was substituted for these currencies. It further provided that the ECU should become a currency in its own right, although this occurred under the label of the 'euro'. It nevertheless still provided, in terms redolent of the 1978 resolution, that this measure should by itself not modify the external value of the ECU. The irrevocable fixing of the value of the ECU related only to those currencies which it replaced, but the fundamental consequence is that from the start of the third stage of Economic and Monetary Union, the ECU/euro ceased to be a basket in which the currencies of all Member States were represented.

Returning to the role of the ECU in the original exchange rate mechanism, first, it was used as the denominator of the exchange rate mechanism, in other words the central rates of the national currencies were fixed against it and not against other national currencies; bilateral exchange rates were then calculated from those central rates. Secondly, the ECU formed the basis or reference against which the so-called divergence indicator operates. In a sense these roles were, of course, linked. Basically, in the original version, fluctuation margins of plus or minus 2.25 per cent were established round the bilateral exchange rates with regard to the other participating currencies derived from the central rates of a currency in relation to the ECU, although countries with previously floating currencies, ie those that were not in the 'snake', could opt for wider margins of up to plus or minus 6 per cent.[43] Initially, only Italy took advantage of this wider margin, moving to the narrow band of 2.25 per cent in January 1990,[44] only to have to leave the system in 1992. Spain when it joined in 1989,[45] Portugal, and the UK for its two years of membership also took advantage of the wider band. However, following turbulence on the money markets, in August 1993 a general margin of fluctuation of 15 per cent was adopted on a 'temporary' basis subject to a bilateral arrangement between Germany and the Netherlands to maintain a 2.25 per

---

[43] Art 3(1).
[44] Agence Europe 8/9 January 1990 No 5167, p 5.
[45] Agence Europe 19/20 June 1989 No 5039, p 7.

cent margin between their currencies.[46] It may be observed that Italy was then able to rejoin the mechanism in November 1996.

Intervention was compulsory when the intervention points defined by these margins of fluctuation were reached, but as a kind of early warning system a threshold of divergence was fixed at 75 per cent of the maximum spread of divergence against the ECU[47] calculated for each currency on an individual basis.[48] The idea behind this appears to have been that in a bilateral relationship there might be room for argument as to whether a widening gap was caused by one currency going up or by another going down. The existence of the central rate against the ECU meant that it could be determined objectively which currency was moving in which direction, thus indicating which authorities needed to take action. The spread of divergence was calculated in such a way as to eliminate the effect of the weighting of the currency in the ECU basket,[49] which in practice meant the heavier the weighting, the narrower the spread of divergence, so that the original spread for the DM was only 1.51 per cent.[50] It would appear that in practice this system of thresholds was not much used, although the September 1987 agreement on strengthening the European Monetary System provided for an increased use of 'intramarginal' intervention,[51] and the widening of the band of fluctuation to 15 per cent might appear to have had the effect of virtually eliminating the need for intervention.

Under the European Monetary System Mark II, the exchange rate mechanism is based on central rates against the euro,[52] which means that Member States outside the euro area participating in the exchange rate mechanism have to stay in a defined relationship with the euro which is for them a foreign currency but nevertheless is the currency in which EC agricultural prices and payments are expressed, rather than in a relationship with a basket ECU in which their currency is represented. Furthermore, there are no bilateral exchange rates with other national currencies with regard to which bands of fluctuation are fixed under the 1997 resolution: rather, the margins of fluctuation are based on the central rates against the euro itself. In other words, what matters is the relationship between the currency of a Member State outside the euro area participating in the exchange rate mechanism and the euro, not the relationship between the currency of a Member State outside the euro area participating in the exchange rate mechanism and the currency of another Member State outside the euro area participating in the exchange rate mechanism. The standard fluctuation band is plus or minus 15 per cent around the central rates,[53] a figure continued from the original system after 1993, but 'on a case-by-case basis, formally agreed fluctuation bands narrower than the standard

[46] Agence Europe 2/3 August 1993 No 6034, pp 3–4.
[47] Art 3(5).
[48] See P Coffey, *The European Monetary System: Past, Present and Future* (2nd edn, 1987), 22–25.
[49] Art 3(5).   [50] Coffey (n 48 above).
[51] EC Bulletin 1987 No 9, point 1.3.5.
[52] Para 2.1.   [53] Para 2.1.

one and backed up in principle by automatic intervention and financing may be set at the request of the non-euro area Member State concerned.'[54] In fact, in September 1998 agreement was reached between the finance ministers of the Euro-11, the ECB, and the ministers and Central Bank governors of Denmark and Greece that Denmark would participate in ERM II within a narrow band of fluctuation of 2.25 per cent, and that Greece would participate within the standard band of plus or minus 15 per cent.[55] However, it is also stated that 'the standard and narrower bands shall not prejudice the interpretation of the third indent of Article 109j(1)[56] of the EC Treaty',[57] ie they do not prejudice the question of what is the 'normal' margin of fluctuation.

While membership of the current exchange rate mechanism may be voluntary for the 'outs', it is worth remembering so far as they are concerned that art 124 of the EC Treaty remains in force,[58] requiring them to treat their exchange rate policy as a matter of common interest. It may be suggested that non-participant Member States which purport not to have an exchange rate policy are in breach of that obligation.

The determination of criteria of value

As indicated above, it was hardly politically feasible to fix Community agricultural prices in the currency of a particular Member State. Therefore a criterion of value which was neutral as between the Member States was chosen. Under Regulation 129, of 23 October 1962,[59] the unit of account used for the agricultural policy was defined at a value of 0.88867088 grammes of fine gold, which happened to be the official value of the United States dollar. Art 2 of that regulation provided that where sums given in one currency are required to be expressed in another currency the exchange rate to be applied should be that which corresponded to the par value communicated to and recognized by the International Monetary Fund.

While this formula was not immediately changed to reflect the collapse of this fixed exchange rate system in 1971, a new factor was introduced following the accession of the UK, Ireland, and Denmark in 1973, recognizing that, for the purposes of converting prices and amounts under the common agricultural policy, 'conversion rates should be applied which are not based on parities but are more in line with economic realities'. Council Regulation 222/73,[60] on the exchange rates to be applied in agriculture for the currencies of the new Member States, created representative rates for the conversion of the currencies of the United Kingdom and Ireland. As a matter of history, the conversion rate therein established

---

[54] Para 2.4.
[55] Bulletin Quotidien Europe No 7310, 28 and 29 September 1998.
[56] Now art 121(1).   [57] Para 2.5.
[58] In the case of the UK, this is confirmed by art 6 of the UK Protocol.
[59] JO 1962, p 2553.   [60] OJ 1973 L27/4.

was that £1 was equal to 2.3499 United States dollars. Following this, Council Regulation 509/73[61] introduced a new paragraph 1(a) into art 1 of Regulation 974/71, the basic regulation governing monetary compensation, recognizing the existence of conversion rates other than the official parity and allowing, in appropriate cases, for these conversion rates to replace the official parity for the purposes of the calculations under that regulation. The next amending Regulation 1112/73[62] introduced a new version of art 2 of the 1971 regulation using a global formulation, 'the conversion rate used under the common agricultural policy', which was apt to cover conversion both at the official parity and at representative rates where applicable. This regulation also introduced a much more important reform in the system of calculating MCAs.

Following the introduction of the joint float known as the 'snake', under which the majority of Member States' currencies floated together in relation to other currencies, maintaining as between themselves a maximum variation in their spot-market rates at any given moment of 2.25 per cent, Regulation 1112/73 took account of the introduction of this system to use the snake currencies instead of the gold definition of the United States dollar as a reference for the calculation of monetary compensatory amounts. Art 2(1) of the 1971 regulation, as amended by this regulation, used a double method of calculating MCAs. For Member States whose currencies were within the snake, the MCAs were obtained by applying to the relevant prices the percentage difference between the conversion rate used under the common agricultural policy and the conversion rate resulting from the central rates of those currencies. For the other Member States it was, in reality, the relationship of their currencies to the snake currencies that was important. The MCAs for these Member States were obtained by applying to the relevant prices the average of the percentage differences between the relationship of their agricultural conversion rates to the parities or central rates of the snake currencies and the relationship of the spot-market rates of their currencies to the snake currencies. In other words, the currencies remaining within a band of 2.25 per cent were used as the standard for determining the real value of other Member States' currencies, and also for determining the value such currencies were deemed to have for the purposes of the common agricultural policy, and this system was continued even after the introduction of the European Monetary System. Monetary compensatory amounts were obtained by multiplying the relevant Community prices of individual products by the difference between these two values expressed as a percentage.

In September of that same year, Council Regulation 2543/73[63] amended the old Regulation 129[64] so as to simplify the procedure for making derogations from that regulation. Under this procedure Council Regulation 2544/73[65] was made, introducing a representative rate for the conversion under the common agricultural policy of the currency of one of the original Member States, the Dutch guilder. According to the recitals to that regulation, this was done so as to avoid

[61] OJ 1973 L50/1.   [62] OJ 1973 L114/4.
[63] OJ 1973 L263/1.   [64] JO 1962, p 2553.   [65] OJ 1973 L263/2.

introducing monetary compensatory amounts in the internal trade of the Benelux Customs Union. Subsequently, in October, Regulation 2985/73[66] introduced a representative rate for the Italian lira, noting in its recitals that the system of applying MCAs to prices converted at official parities 'has led to different price levels in the Member States affected' and that the MCAs applicable in trade with Italy could be reduced by fixing a representative conversion rate of the Italian lira at a level more closely related to the actual economic situation.

Eventually Council Regulation 475/75[67] fixed, for the first time, representative rates for the conversion of the currencies of all the Member States, creating what are popularly referred to as 'green' currencies. Hence, agricultural conversion rates became as much a matter for political decision as agricultural prices under common organizations. By 1978–1979, for example, German prices in national currency were some 45 per cent higher than UK prices in national currency,[68] in terms of market exchange rates.

The introduction of the European Monetary System,[69] and the use of the ECU[70] in agriculture by virtue of Council Regulation 652/79,[71] made no real difference, since the ECU continued to be converted at agricultural conversion rates like the old unit of account, and, as discussed above, one of the characteristics of the original European Monetary System was that, like the old 'snake', its members (except for Italy) maintained their currencies within a spread of 2.25 per cent, the criterion used for determining whether there had been monetary movements.

The system of conversion eventually consolidated in Council Regulation 1676/85[72] was that the agricultural conversion rate was used for conversion between the ECU and national currencies—and it clearly appeared from the contemporaneous Council Regulation 1678/85,[73] fixing the agricultural conversion rates, that the same Member State might have different rates for different products—but for conversion between ECU and non-Member State currencies or world prices the central rate was used for Member States within the 2.25 per cent band, and for other Member States use was made of the average relationship between their spot-market rates against the currencies of those Member States within the 2.25 per cent band and their central rates. With regard to the system of MCAs under Council Regulation 1677/85,[74] the basic system of calculation was as described above. Whilst the calculation of monetary compensatory amounts for currencies within the 2.25 per cent band was relatively straightforward, for the other currencies it was more complex. Taking the United Kingdom milk sector at the relevant period[75] as an

[66] OJ 1973 L303/1.

[67] OJ 1975 L52/28.

[68] See JA Usher, 'Agricultural Markets: Their Price Systems and Financial Mechanisms' (1979) EL Rev 147, 152.

[69] Resolution of the European Council of 5 December 1978 (EC Bulletin 1978 No 12, point 1.1.11). See p 116.

[70] See above p 116.   [71] OJ 1979 L84/1.   [72] OJ 1985 L164/1.

[73] OJ 1985 L164/11.   [74] OJ 1985 L164/6.

[75] Example taken in March 1987.

example, if the agricultural conversion rate was 1 ECU=£0.618655, and the central rate of, for example, the Deutschmark was 1 ECU=2.05853 DM, then the agricultural value of the pound expressed in terms of the central rate of the Deutschmark was that £0.618655=2.05853 DM, so that £1=3.327428 DM. If the spot-market rate for the pound was, however, £1=2.9275 DM, the percentage difference was 12.019133 per cent. This calculation had to be repeated in terms of the other currencies falling within the narrow band of the European Monetary System, and the MCA for the pound was the average of those percentage differences.

Certain aspects were however described in simpler terminology. In particular, the regulation specifically defined 'positive' MCAs, which constituted a charge on imports and a subsidy on exports and arose where the central or market rate was higher than the agricultural conversion rate, and 'negative' MCAs, which constituted a subsidy on imports and a charge on exports, and arose where the central or market rate was lower than the agricultural conversion rate. Further, the MCA was defined as filling the 'monetary gap', which was the real monetary gap between agricultural conversion rates and central or market rates, minus a small 'neutral margin', to allow for small fluctuations without changing the MCAs.

This system was, however, subject to a further corrective factor introduced initially for a three-year period by Council Regulation 855/84[76] on the calculation and 'dismantlement' of MCAs, and reproduced in Regulation 1677/85.[77] This regulation reflected a political will to narrow the differences in representative rates, and was intended to eliminate 'positive' MCAs, which had a tendency to encourage over-production by allowing producers to be paid more than their competitors in other Member States.[78] This corrective factor had the effect of taking the strongest Community currencies as the basis for calculation, and had the result of reducing, therefore, 'positive' MCAs, even if it initially increased 'negative' MCAs.

The 1987 target date proved optimistic, and in 1987 a graduated programme was adopted to phase out positive MCAs by the beginning of the 1989–1990 marketing year, under Council Regulation 1889/87.[79] This provided for the corrective coefficient to be increased and in case of a realignment of currencies to be altered automatically in line with the currency the revaluation of which against the ECU was the highest. Conversely, it introduced provisions for the elimination of 'transferred negative' MCAs, that is, those created by the operation of this coefficient, over a three-year period following the revaluation, and for the elimination of other negative MCAs created since the last realignment of parities. However, recognizing that the devaluation of the 'green rate' of a national currency to eliminate negative MCAs would increase prices in national terms, hence possibly leading to further over-production, provision was made for the 'common' prices in ECUs to be reduced for the Member States concerned, to neutralize any increase

[76] OJ 1984 L90/1.   [77] OJ 1985 L164/6.
[78] See R Strauss, 'The Economic Effects of Monetary Compensatory Amounts' (1983) JCMS 261.
[79] OJ 1987 L182/1.

in terms of national prices which would otherwise result from the devaluation of the 'green rate' necessary to eliminate the transferred negative MCAs.

It was only on the eve of the date set for the completion of the internal market at the end of 1992[80] that Council Regulation 3813/92[81] was enacted following the logic of what, it may respectfully be submitted, should have happened in 1971. The 1992 regulation provided for the conversion of ECUs into national currency and vice versa at an agricultural conversion rate based on representative market rates,[82] although making express reference back to Regulation 1677/85 in continuing to require the use of a corrective factor.[83] Furthermore it recognized that a sum in national currency representing a Community price fixed in ECUs might have to be altered even during the course of a marketing year if the representative market rate diverged from the agricultural conversion rate by more than 2 per cent of the latter, subject to short-term transitional arrangements,[84] although following the widening of the margin of fluctuation under the European Monetary System in 1993, this range of divergence was raised to 3 per cent where the monetary gap was positive.[85] The problem of a possible reduction in farmers' incomes in terms of national currency if that currency increased in relative value was dealt with by permitting Member States with floating currencies to grant farmers compensatory aid in such circumstances,[86] with a possible Community contribution to that aid.

For the twelve Member States participating in Economic and Monetary Union, such problems largely disappeared with the introduction of the euro. Under Council Regulation 2799/98 on agrimonetary arrangements for the euro,[87] prices and amounts fixed in legal instruments relating to the common agricultural policy are expressed in euro, and granted and collected in euro in the participating Member States. For the other Member States, however, the amounts fixed in euro are converted into their national currency, in principle at the market exchange rate, so they alone face an exchange risk, subject to general transitional arrangements where the conversion rate or exchange rate for the euro on 1 January 1999 represented an 'appreciable revaluation' against the agricultural conversion rate in force on 31 December 1998.[88]

Who takes the monetary risk?

Whilst the need at the outset of the CAP to use a unit of account which was not the currency of any one Member State may seem to be politically self-evident, it

---

[80] EC Treaty, art 14, originally art 8a when introduced by the Single European Act.
[81] OJ 1992 L387/1.
[82] Art 3(1).   [83] See above p 123.   [84] Art 4.
[85] Council Regulation 3528/93 (OJ 1993 L320.32). See above p 127.
[86] Art 8.   [87] OJ 1998 L349/1.
[88] Council Regulation 2800/98 on transitional measures under the CAP with regard to the euro (OJ 1998 L349/8).

would appear that the regulations which led to the establishment of market organizations based on a single Community price were conducted in terms of
Deutschmarks,[89] and the Deutschmark continued in practice to play an important
role in the calculation of agricultural prices until its replacement by the euro.
Under Regulation 129, of 23 October 1962,[90] the unit of account used for the
agricultural policy was defined at a value of 0.88867088 grammes of fine gold,
which happened to be the official value of the United States dollar. Art 2 of that
regulation provided that where sums given in one currency were required to be
expressed in another currency the exchange rate to be applied should be that
which corresponded to the par value communicated to and recognized by the
International Monetary Fund.

The basic financial mechanism, then, was that agricultural prices were fixed in
uniform units of account converted into national currencies at the official parity. The
logic of such a system is that if parities change, the risk falls on producers in the
country whose parity has changed; if the national currency rises in value they will
receive less in terms of national currency. However, this logic was not followed when
currencies began to float in 1971. By way of contrast, the system of monetary
compensation allowed prices in terms of national currency to remain the same
throughout a marketing year, irrespective of the exchange rate. It may however be
suggested that its fundamental and intended aim was to protect the system of intervention in such circumstances rather than to protect producers against exchange risks.

Under the scheme of Regulation 974/71,[91] as re-enacted in Council
Regulation 1677/85,[92] the system of MCAs applied only to products covered by
intervention arrangements or to products whose price depended on the price of
intervention products, and MCAs could only be applied where application of the
monetary measures in question would lead to disturbances in trade in the relevant
agricultural products. The aim of the system was stated in Case 46/84 *Nordgetreide*[93]
to be to protect the single price system, not national markets. Similarly, in Case
236/84 *Malt*,[94] the Court made clear that monetary compensatory amounts were
not intended to produce a protective effect with regard to imports from third countries, but that there was no obligation to offer equal treatment to all third countries.
On the other hand, where MCAs were payable on import into a Member State,
they were only attracted if the goods actually entered the market of the Member
State of import.[95] The Court consistently held that the Commission enjoyed a wide
discretion in assessing the risk of disturbance. So, in Case 55/75 *Balkan v
Hauptzollamt Berlin-Packhof*,[96] it was stated that the regulation could not be interpreted as obliging the Commission to decide case by case or in respect of each
product individually whether there was a risk of disturbance. Further, the Court

[89] E Neville-Rolfe, *The Politics of Agriculture in the European Community* (1984) 231.
[90] JO 1962, p 2553.   [91] JO 1971 L106/1.   [92] OJ 1985 L164/6.
[93] [1985] ECR 3127.   [94] [1986] ECR 1923.
[95] Case 254/85 *Irish Grain Board* [1986] ECR 3309.
[96] [1976] ECR 19.

held that in reviewing the legality of the exercise of such discretion it must confine itself to examining whether it contained a manifest error or constituted a misuse of power or whether the authority did not clearly exceed the bounds of its discretion. The only cases in which a manifest error was shown concerned price dependency rather than the risk of disturbance. In Case 131/77 *Milac*,[97] a Commission regulation was held to be invalid in so far as it applied MCAs to trade in powdered whey, it being shown that there was no correlation of prices between powdered whey and skimmed milk powder, the relevant intervention product.

In the context of protecting the intervention system, the particular problem of derived products was at issue in Case 4/79 *Providence Agricole de la Champagne*,[98] and Case 145/79 *Roquette v Administration des Douanes*.[99] Under the regulations, the MCA on the dependent product should have been equal to the incidence on its price of the MCA on the intervention product. The Court started from the premiss that the aim of the system of MCAs was to 'neutralise' the difference between the current exchange rate for a currency and its 'representative' or 'green' rate expressed in units of account, and went on to emphasize that MCAs must be strictly neutral in character, unlike import levies which could be protective in nature. From this it concluded that MCAs which obviously went beyond what was necessary to compensate the difference between prices expressed in real and representative exchange rates would no longer be helping to maintain the single price system, but would become akin to charges having equivalent effect to customs duties. Similarly, whilst recognizing that there were difficult technical and economic problems in calculating MCAs on derived or dependent products, and that flat-rate MCAs might not give exactly the right degree of compensation for each undertaking or producer, the Court held that, in this context, the Commission would exceed the limits of its discretion if it used a method of calculation which consistently went beyond what was necessary to take account of the incidence on the price of the dependent product of the MCA on the intervention product.

In those cases, where it was admitted by the Commission that the sum of the MCAs on the derived products exceeded the MCA on the basic product, the Court stated as an overall limit on the Commission's discretion that, whatever the difficulties in calculating the precise MCA for each derived product, this should not occur; it made clear, however, that the mathematical limit on the sum of the MCAs on derived products only applied where these products could be obtained from the same manufacturing process. Hence, it distinguished the process by which maize was made into meal, flour, germs, and bran and sharps from that by which it was made into starch, gluten, and germs. On the other hand, the Court suggested that the mathematical limitation on the MCAs on dependent products should not apply where the MCA on the processed product was calculated not from that on the basic product (indeed, the Court put forward the hypothesis of a basic product not subject to MCAs) but from that on a competing product.

---

[97] [1978] ECR 1041.   [98] [1980] ECR 2823.   [99] [1980] ECR 2917.

This was the situation in the *Roquette* case with regard to potato starch. Although there was no intervention price for potatoes, and, hence, no MCA on potatoes as such, it was agreed that the price of potato starch depended on that of maize starch, and the Court deduced from this that the incidence of the MCA in maize on the price of potato starch must be regarded as being the same as its incidence on the price of maize starch, and, hence, that the MCA on potato starch could not exceed that on maize starch. These judgments did not, however, mean that the Commission had to achieve absolute mathematical equilibrium in calculating MCAs on derived products. In *Providence Agricole* the error was of the order of 30 per cent, and in *Roquette* the error was about 12 per cent, albeit involving also a wrong basis of calculation, but in Case 39/84 *Maizena*,[100] and Case 46/84 *Nordgetreide*,[101] it was held that divergences respectively of 5.9 per cent and 4.3 per cent were not sufficient to invalidate the calculation.

The Court's basic approach was clearly summarized in Case 97/76 *Merkur v Commission*.[102] It was there said that the aim of the system of compensatory amounts was, in particular, to obviate the difficulties which monetary instability might create for the proper functioning of the common organizations of the market, rather than to protect the individual interests of traders. The Court, further, said that although the possibility of protecting the legitimate interests of the trader could not be excluded, nevertheless, the Community could only be rendered liable for the damage suffered by such traders as a result of the adoption of legitimate measures governing the system of MCAs if in the absence of any overriding public interest the Commission were to abolish or modify the compensatory amounts applicable in a specific sector with immediate effect, and without warning, and in the absence of any appropriate transitional measures, and if such abolition or modification was not foreseeable by a prudent trader. This may be contrasted with Case 74/74 *CNTA v Commission*,[103] which arose in the days when MCAs were calculated on the basis of the values of Member States' currencies calculated in terms of the dollar. The harm in that case was alleged to have been caused by the withdrawal by Commission Regulation of MCAs applicable to colza and rape seeds, thus causing loss to the applicants in performing certain contracts for the sale of these seeds to purchasers in non-Member States.

The Court there held that the application of MCAs in practice avoided the exchange risk, so that even a prudent trader might be induced to omit to cover himself against such risk. However, whilst it may be that a reasonable trader could regard MCAs based on the values of national currencies in terms of the dollar as covering the exchange risk, it may be doubted whether any reasonable trader could regard an MCA designed to cover the difference between a politically, rather than economically, calculated representative rate[104] and the real value of a national currency in terms of a basket of other Community currencies as being in any way

[100] [1985] ECR 2115.   [101] [1985] ECR 3127.   [102] [1977] ECR 1063.
[103] [1975] ECR 533.   [104] See above p 122.

necessarily related to exchange risks. In so far as the analogy may be appropriate, it was held in Case 299/84 *Neumann*[105] that when the agricultural conversion rates themselves were changed there was no necessary implication that the Council intended to avoid a purchaser tendering before the change in 'green' rates paying more in terms of national currency than a purchaser tendering after that change.

It may however be suggested that the risk was put firmly back on producers (and traders), subject to limited cushioning for their protection rather than that of the intervention system, when MCAs were abolished at the end of 1992. Art 3(1) of Council Regulation 3813/92[106] provided that the agricultural conversion rate should be fixed by the Commission on the basis of the representative market rate, defined[107] in the case of a fixed currency (ie a currency within the narrow band of the original European Monetary System[108]), the central rate for the ECU fixed within the framework of the European Monetary System, multiplied by a correcting factor,[109] and in the case of a floating currency (ie those not within that band), the average exchange rate for the ECU with respect to that currency, recorded over a reference period and multiplied by the correcting factor. It was further provided in art 4(1) that the agricultural conversion rate for a floating currency should be adjusted where the monetary gap (the percentage of the agricultural conversion rate representing the difference between that rate and the representative market rate) exceeded two points for the last referenced period of a month, and in art 4(2) that in the event of a monetary realignment affecting the central rates determined for the Member States with fixed currencies, the agricultural conversion rates should be adjusted immediately so as to eliminate the monetary gaps of the fixed currencies. The prices in national currencies could therefore be changed during the marketing year for currencies within the narrow band only if there was a monetary realignment, but for the other currencies they could be changed whenever the representative market rates moved beyond the trigger level, subject to the power of Member States with floating currencies under art 8(1) for three years to grant farmers compensatory aid when the average agricultural conversion rate over the previous twelve months was lower than the average agricultural conversion rate over the twelve months preceding that period. This in turn was subject to a Community contribution up to a maximum of 50 per cent under art 8(3) or a maximum of 75 per cent in areas qualifying for Objective 1 status under the structural fund legislation.

This distinction between fixed and floating currencies was however short-lived. Following the decision in 1993 'temporarily' to widen the margin of fluctuation under the European Monetary System to 15 per cent,[110] Council Regulation 3258/93[111] noted in its recital that 'all the currencies of the Member States must temporarily be considered to be floating currencies' and widened the monetary

---

[105] [1985] ECR 3663.   [106] OJ 1992 L387/1.   [107] In art 1(d).
[108] See above p 118.   [109] See above p 118.   [110] See above p 118.
[111] OJ 1993 L320/32.

gap triggering an adjustment of the agricultural conversion rate to three points where the gap was positive.[112]

Following the introduction of the euro by Council Regulation 2799/98,[113] prices and amounts fixed in legal instruments relating to the common agricultural policy are expressed in euro, and they are granted or collected in euro in the participating Member States. There is therefore no question of any monetary risk (except with regard to the wider world) for the participating Member States. However, in the other Member States, the prices in euro are converted into their national currency by means of an exchange rate (the currency market exchange rate between the euro and the national currency), and in principle granted or collected in national currency. For producers in the 'outs' therefore there remains an exchange risk, though under art 4 the Member State concerned may grant compensatory aid to farmers in cases of appreciable revaluation, defined as a situation where the annual average exchange rate is below a threshold constituted by the lowest average annual conversion rate applied during the preceding three years and the exchange rate of 1 January 1999. This aid is however different in nature from its predecessors, reflecting, it may be suggested, the influence of the Uruguay Round Agreement on Agriculture.

In order presumably to avoid its inclusion in the domestic support the Community is required to reduce under that agreement,[114] being calculated on a flat-rate basis decoupled from actual production, thus falling within the exemptions from the reduction commitments listed in Annex 2 to the agreement. Under art 4(1) of Regulation 2799/98, it is made clear that the compensatory aid payments that Member States may grant to farmers in the case of appreciable revaluation 'shall not take the form of aid linked to production, other than production during a stipulated, prior period. They shall not favour any particular type of production or be dependent on production subsequent to the period stipulated.' Such payments are to be made in three twelve-month tranches, and art 4(2) provides for the maximum amount of the first tranche of compensatory aid to be established, for the Member State concerned as a whole, by multiplying the appreciable part of the revaluation by the *flat-rate income loss* (emphasis added) calculated according to a formula set out in the annex to the regulation. The disregard for small fluctuations under the previous system is however continued in spirit under art 4(4) which requires that no aid shall be granted for the portion of that amount that does not exceed an appreciable revaluation of 2.6 per cent, and the amounts paid out under the second and third tranches are to be reduced, *vis-à-vis* the level of the previous tranche, by at least a third of the amount paid out in the first tranche.[115]

There is separate provision for compensation in relation to flat-rate aid calculated per hectare or per livestock unit, compensatory premiums per sheep or goat, and amounts of a structural or environmental nature[116] where the exchange rate

[112] See above p 124. [113] OJ 1998 L349/1. [114] Art 6 of the Agreement.
[115] Art 4(5). [116] Art 5.

applicable on the date of the operative event is below that applicable previously. Again the payments are in three tranches, calculated in accordance with the annex and subject to progressive reduction, but it is specified that such compensatory aid must be granted in the form of an addition to the aid, premiums, and amounts concerned—which of course are themselves of a flat-rate nature. For these specific payments and amounts, the Community's contribution is 50 per cent of the aid which may be granted, even if the Member State withdraws from participation in financing the aid, but otherwise the general rule is that the Community's contribution is 50 per cent of the amounts actually paid by the Member State concerned.[117]

It might finally be observed that Regulation 2799/98 also provides that if a non-participating Member State decides to pay the expenditure resulting from legal instruments relating to the common agricultural policy in euro rather than in its national currency 'the Member State shall take such kind of measures that the use of the euro does not provide a systematic advantage compared with the use of national currency'.

Conclusions

The history of the common agricultural policy shows all too clearly the perils of trying to operate a single price system without a single currency. However, for producers in the twelve Member States which participate in the euro, there is now a genuine single price system in each common organization of an agricultural market, given that prices and payments are fixed in what is their national currency. Difficulties remain for producers in the non-participant Member States which maintain a freely floating currency, but although limited compensation is admissible, the twin pressures of the EC's single internal market programme and the Uruguay Round Agreement on Agriculture mean that the system of monetary compensation used between 1971 and the end of 1992 is unlikely to be seen again.

---

[117] Art 6.

6

Fisheries

Introduction

By its very nature, fisheries legislation gives rise to problems not encountered in land-based agriculture, requiring not only the organization of a market in goods but also the conservation of natural resources and the resolution of questions of territorial competence and of external relations. Hence the Community's common fisheries policy can only be regarded as having been completed on the adoption of EC Council Regulation 170/83[1] establishing a Community system for the conservation and management of fishery resources.

The current legislative framework is set by Council Regulation 3760/92[2] establishing a Community system for fisheries and aquaculture, which describes the general objectives of the common fisheries policy as being 'to protect and conserve available and accessible living marine aquatic resources, and to provide for rational and responsible exploitation on a sustainable basis, in appropriate economic and social conditions for the sector, taking account of its implications for the marine eco-system, and in particular taking account of the needs of both producers and consumers'.[3] So far as its scope is concerned, it is stated to cover 'exploitation activities involving living aquatic resources', and aquaculture, as well as the processing and marketing of fishery and aquaculture products 'where practised on the territory of Member States or in Community fishing waters or by Community fishing vessels',[4] Community fishing waters being defined as waters under the sovereignty or jurisdiction of the Member States,[5] and Community fishing vessels being defined as fishing vessels (ie vessels equipped for commercial exploitation of resources[6]) flying the flag of a Member State and registered in the Community.[7]

The regulation enables measures to be adopted laying down the conditions of access to waters and resources and of the pursuit of exploitation activities.[8] Under art 4(2), these measures may restrict or prohibit fishing activities in certain zones, limit exploitation rates, set limits on the quantities of fish that may be caught, limit the time spent at sea, fix the number and type of fishing vessels authorized to fish, lay down technical measures regarding fishing gear, set minimum sizes or weights of fish that may be caught, and establish incentives to promote more selective fishing.

[1] OJ 1983 L24/1.   [2] OJ 1992 L389/1.   [3] Art 2(1).
[4] Art 1.   [5] Art 3(a).   [6] Art 3(c).
[7] Art 3(d).   [8] Art 4(1).

Market support

A common organization of the market in fishery products was originally introduced by EC Council Regulation 2142/70[9] as part of the common agricultural
policy, and the current version is contained in EC Council Regulation
104/2000.[10] Fish is a product which is not covered by the WTO Agreement on
Agriculture,[11] and among other things, this common organization consists of a
price system, involving a guide price and a 'withdrawal' price not exceeding 90
per cent of the guide price,[12] at or around which products may be withdrawn
from the market. Externally, the basic Common Customs Tariff duties are rein-
forced by a reference price system, under which various tariff reductions or suspen-
sions and other arrangements will not be available for quantities imported below
the reference price. The particular feature of the system, however, is the role played
by producer organizations, which are empowered to operate the withdrawal
system. Non-members may be required to abide by the rules of such organizations[13] and to pay fees covering their administrative costs, and the organizations
may levy contributions to finance their intervention measures.[14] On the other
hand, aid may be granted to new producer organizations, and member states are
required, within strict limits, to grant compensation for intervention measures.[15]
However, this compensation is on a diminishing scale as the proportion of fish
withdrawn increases.

Territorial competence

Before the accession to the Community of the United Kingdom, Council
Regulation 2141/70[16] was adopted, laying down a common structural policy for
the fishing industry. It set out the basic principle that rules applied by each Member
State in respect of fishing in 'the maritime waters coming under its sovereignty or
within its jurisdiction' should not lead to differences in treatment of other Member
States, and that there should be equal conditions of access to fishing grounds
situated in these waters, subject to a five-year exemption for certain zones within
a 3-mile limit.[17] However, one of the few derogations from established Community
policy to be given in the 1972 Act of Accession permitted Member States until 31
December 1982 to restrict fishing within a 6-mile limit to vessels which traditionally fished in these waters, with an extension to 12 miles in certain defined

---

[9] JO 1970 L236/5 (sp edn 1970 (III), p 707).
[10] OJ 2000 L17/22.
[11] Agreement on Agriculture Annex I(1)(i).
[12] Council Regulation 104/2000, art 20.
[13] Art 7.   [14] Art 17.   [15] Art 21.
[16] JO 1970 L236/1 (sp edn 1970 (III), p 703).
[17] Council Regulation 2141/70, arts 2, 4.

zones.[18] These provisions were drafted as a derogation from Regulation 2141/70, which was replaced, following the expiry of the five-year period for which it provided, by Council Regulation 101/76,[19] which repeated the basic principles. However, the importance of the Act of Accession derogation was considerably diminished by the resolution of the Council that the Member States should act in concert to extend their fishing zones to 200 nautical miles with effect from 1 January 1977 along their North Sea and North Atlantic coastlines,[20] with the result that thereafter most Community waters were not subject to the Act of Accession derogations. In Case 812/79 *Burgoa*,[21] Advocate General Capotorti suggested, with regard to third country rights in the 6- to 12-mile zone, that it was 'wholly untenable' to argue that such rights should apply by analogy in the 12- to 200-mile zone.

Although the deadline of the end of 1982 may therefore seem of little relevance for the greater part of the fishing zones of the Member States, art 103 of the 1972 Act of Accession enabled the Council to examine the provisions which could follow the derogations in force until the end of 1982. In fact Council Regulation 170/83[22] provided for the generalization of the exclusive zone up to a limit of 12 nautical miles rather than 6, subject to the other derogation conditions of the 1972 Act of Accession.[23] That regulation was not adopted until 25 January 1983, however, and for the intervening period, the Commission purported to authorize the Member States to continue their exclusive zones under the Act of Accession. The validity of this authorization came before the Court of Justice in Case 63/83 *R v Kirk*,[24] which arose from the prosecution of a Danish MEP for fishing in United Kingdom coastal waters in January 1983, before the enactment of Regulation 170/83. The Court held that following the expiry of the derogation under the Act of Accession, the basic principle of equal access re-enacted in Regulation 101/76 was fully applicable, so that there was no legal vacuum which the Commission could authorize the Member States to fill, even as trustees of the Community interest. However, the extended exclusive zone has been continued until the end of 2002 by Council Regulation 3760/92.[25]

A further territorial problem arises from the fact that certain of the territories of the Member States are excluded from the Community,[26] or at least excluded from the scope of the common agricultural policy,[27] or included subject to specific measures adopted by the Council.[28] The problem then arises whether the fishery

---

[18] Act of Accession (1972), arts 100, 101.
[19] OJ 1976 L20/9.
[20] Council Resolution of 3 November 1976 (XV International Legal Materials 1425).
[21] [1980] ECR 2787.
[22] OJ 1983 L24/1.
[23] Council Regulation 170/83, art 6(1).
[24] [1984] ECR 2689.
[25] OJ 1992 L389/1.
[26] EC Treaty, art 299(6), and 1972 Act of Accession Protocol no 2 (Faeroes).
[27] EC Treaty, art 299(6), and 1972 Act of Accession Protocol no 3 (Channel Islands and Isle of Man).
[28] EC Treaty, art 299(2) (the Azores, Madeira, and the Canary Islands).

zones calculated from baselines in the excluded territories are themselves excluded from the scope of the common fisheries policy. Such a view would appear, with one exception, to be supported by Community Treaty practice: the exclusion of the Faeroes under art 26(3) of the 1972 Act of Accession, introducing art 299(6)(a) into the EC Treaty, appears to have been accepted as excluding also the fishery limits measured from the Faeroes, since in 1977 the Community negotiated an agreement with the Danish government acting on behalf of the Faeroese home government, in order to obtain access for Community vessels to Faeroese waters and vice versa.[29] Similarly, the Treaty amendment taking Greenland out of the Community must have been accepted as also taking out Greenland waters, since a contemporaneous agreement was negotiated again to allow Community access to Greenland waters.[30] The exception is that Faeroese waters are expressly included in art 101 of the 1972 Act of Accession as benefiting from the 12-mile exemption from equal access, which would not have been necessary if Faeroese waters were not within the Community. However, since, conversely, the 1977 Agreement would not have been necessary if Faeroese waters were within the Community, the better view may be either to regard the provision in art 101 as redundant, or as a precaution in anticipation of Faeroese accession.

With regard to the Isle of Man and the Channel Islands, art 299(6) of the EC Treaty provides that that Treaty shall apply 'only to the extent necessary to ensure the implementation of arrangements for those islands' set out in the 1972 Act of Accession. Protocol No 3 to that Act, on the Channel Islands and the Isle of Man, provides in art 1(2) that 'in respect of agricultural products and products processed therefrom which are the subject of a special trade regime' the islands shall apply the levies and other import measures applied by the United Kingdom under Community law in trade with third countries, and also shall apply 'such provisions of Community rules, in particular those of the Act of Accession, as are necessary to allow free movement and observance of normal conditions of competition in trade in these products'. It being now indisputable that sea fish and sea fisheries fall within the scope of the common agricultural policy,[31] the basic legal situation of the Isle of Man and the Channel Islands may be summarized as being that they are in principle excluded from the common agricultural policy, subject to this exclusion being disapplied in the specific instances mentioned in the protocol.

That the old 12-mile limits round the Isle of Man were excluded in principle from Community law was accepted— indeed, urged—by the UK government in Case 32/79 *Commission v United Kingdom*[32] which involved the legitimacy of UK fisheries legislation part of which purported to apply to Isle of Man waters. Such a view appears also to have been accepted by the Commission in that case, since the Commission argued that Community rules applied by virtue of Protocol No 3,[33]

[29] OJ 1980 L226/12.   [30] OJ 1985 L29/9.
[31] Case 141/78 *France v UK* [1979] ECR 2923.
[32] [1980] ECR 2403.   [33] Ibid, at 2420.

which is only relevant if the waters in question are not prima facie subject to Community law. It appears, similarly, to have been accepted by AG Reischl.[34] The Court itself recognized that the 12-mile belt round the Isle of Man was 'subject to special rules',[35] but after having had Protocol No 3 drawn to its attention the Court expressly asserted that it was not necessary 'to consider the constitutional position of the Isle of Man and the relationship of that territory to the Community', so that its judgment can hardly be of authority on that point. Rather, the Court decided the case on mechanical requirements of consultation and the principle of non-discrimination; no doubt, bearing in mind the Commission's submission that even if Isle of Man waters were not subject to the CFP, the United Kingdom was still in breach of its Treaty obligations.

Internal Community competence

Although Council Regulation 2141/70[36] had foreseen the enactment of measures 'to encourage rational use of the biological resources of the sea', the 1972 Act of Accession specifically provided that 'from the sixth year after Accession at the latest, the Council, acting on a proposal from the Commission, should determine conditions for fishing with a view to ensuring protection of the fishing grounds and conservation of the biological resources of the sea',[37] thus laying down a time limit which expired on 31 December 1978.[38] The view has been put forward that this provision conferred a new competence on the Community,[39] but in the view of the Court of Justice fisheries as such fall within the common agricultural policy as defined in the EC Treaty.[40] So far as Community legislation is concerned, there existed skeletal legislation even before the end of 1978, but comprehensive legislation was not adopted until 1983, as has been noted. On the question of competence, however, the situation may be summarized as being that in principle Member States could enact their own measures until the end of 1978, subject to their being compatible with such Community legislation as existed, but that thereafter competence has resided in the Community.

The position during the first period, until the end of 1978, was considered by the Court of Justice in a group of references from Dutch courts concerned with the application of Dutch catch quotas.[41] The Court's approach was to see if those quotas jeopardized the objectives and functioning of the system established by the regulations laying down a common structural policy for the fishing industry and

---

[34] Ibid, at 2472–2473.   [35] Ibid, at 2439.
[36] JO 1970 L236/1 (sp edn 1970 (III), p 703).
[37] Act of Accession (1972), art 102.
[38] Cases 185–204/78 *J Van Dam en Zonen* [1979] ECR 2345.
[39] E Hiester, 'The Legal Position of the European Community with Regard to the Conservation of the Living Resources of the Sea' [1976] LIEI 55.
[40] Case 141/78 *France v United Kingdom* [1979] ECR 2923.
[41] Cases 3, 4, and 6/76 *Officier van Justitie v Kramer* [1976] ECR 1279.

the common organization of the market in fishery products, and pointed out that the regulations themselves and art 102 of the 1972 Act of Accession provided for comparable measures and that indeed Council Regulation 811/76[42] adopted after the questions were referred to the Court expressly authorized Member States to limit the catches of their fishing fleets. It concluded that measures for the limitation of catches of fish and the possibility of taking such measures formed an integral part of the general system established by the regulations.

Similar Dutch catch quotas were again at issue in Cases 185–204/78 J Van Dam en Zonen,[43] and the Court repeated that during the year 1978 (in that instance) the Member States had the right and duty to adopt, within their respective spheres of jurisdiction, any measure compatible with Community law to protect the biological resources of the sea and in particular to fix fishing quotas. Further, in Case 61/77 Commission v Ireland,[44] the Court had said that the Member States were entitled to take appropriate conservation measures so long as the transitional period laid down in the 1972 Act of Accession had not expired and the Community had not yet fully exercised its power in the matter. However, this position of principle was affected by the Hague Resolution of November 1976,[45] it having been held that the Member States must in enacting new fisheries measures comply with the requirements of the resolution pending implementation of a Community fisheries policy, on the grounds that that resolution made specific the duties of cooperation imposed on Member States under art 10 of the EC Treaty. Annex VI to that resolution required a member state taking unilateral fisheries measures to consult the EC Commission and seek its approval. In Case 141/78 France v United Kingdom,[46] the United Kingdom was held to be in breach of its Treaty obligations by bringing into force the Fishing Nets (North-East Atlantic) Order 1977[47] without so doing. Hence, even from November 1976, any new national fisheries measure would appear to have required Council approval. If, however, such approval were sought and obtained, then a Member State could set total allowable catches, and divide them among other Member States, at least where it followed the Commission's approval, as was held in Case 287/81 Anklagemyndigheden v Kerr[48] with regard to Danish catch quotas.

The position after the end of 1978 had to be considered by the Court of Justice in Case 804/79 Commission v United Kingdom[49] where, as has already been observed in the context of the legal requirement for common policies,[50] it was held (1) that Member States were no longer entitled to exercise any power of their own in the matter of conservation measures in the waters under their jurisdiction at least with regard to resources to which the fishermen of the other Member States have an equal right of access (which left the question open with regard to exclusive zones); and (2) that although the EC Council had not taken the relevant conservation

---

[42] OJ 1976 L94/1.   [43] [1979] ECR 2345.   [44] [1978] ECR 417.
[45] EC Council Resolution of 3 November 1976 (XV International Legal Materials 1425).
[46] [1979] ECR 2923.   [47] SI 1977/440 (revoked).   [48] [1982] ECR 4053.
[49] [1981] ECR 1045.   [50] See Chapter 1.

measures, the transfer to the Community of powers in this matter was total and definitive, so that such a failure to act could not in any case restore to the Member States the power and freedom to act unilaterally in this matter. Hence conservation measures must in principle, until Community rules were enacted, remain as they were at the end of 1978, subject to amendment to take account of biological and technological developments.

Member States accordingly had no power to lay down new conservation policies. With regard to mere amendments, or the introduction of necessary interim conservation measures, the Member States may only act 'as trustees of the common interest' so that they became under a duty 'not only . . . to undertake detailed consultations with the Commission and to seek its approval in good faith, but also . . . not to lay down national conservation measures in spite of objections, reservations or conditions which might be formulated by the Commission'. This approach may perhaps be explained by the fact that, as will be seen, the Court of Justice has derived an exclusive external competence from the Community's internal competence, and the internal and external aspects of fisheries policy are so interlinked that the exclusivity of the one must be reflected in the other. This view was reaffirmed by the Court in *Opinion 1/94*[51] on the question of competence to conclude the Uruguay Round Agreements, where the case of fisheries was distinguished from other areas where the Community would only acquire exclusive competence once common internal rules had been adopted.[52] One consequence therefore is that the concepts of subsidiarity under art 5 of the EC Treaty and of closer cooperation under art 11 of the EC Treaty are not relevant in the context of fisheries, since they both apply only to matters which do not fall under the exclusive competence of the Community.

Be that as it may, this principle was at issue in the first reference for a preliminary ruling to be ordered by a Scottish court, Case 24/83 *Gewiese and Mehlich v Mackenzie*,[53] which concerned the prosecution of German fishermen for fishing for herring off the west coast of Scotland in 1981 under a 1981 Order which re-enacted a 1978 Order forbidding herring fishing in the relevant area. It was held that no fresh consultation of the Commission was required in the case of the re-enactment, without substantive amendment, of a national measure for the conservation of fishery resources which had previously been adopted in conformity with the procedural and substantive conditions laid down by Community law.

It would appear that, until the adoption of EC Council Regulation 170/83,[54] the system prescribed in Case 804/79 *Commission v United Kingdom*[55] was applied in practice, the EC Commission from time to time publishing lists of national conservation measures which had been the subject of decisions by it.[56] Certain relatively limited Community measures were enacted, such as Council Regulation

---

[51] [1994] ECR I-5267.
[52] See JA Usher, *EC Institutions and Legislation* (1998) chapter 5.
[53] [1984] ECR 817.   [54] OJ 1983 L24/1.   [55] [1981] ECR 1045.
[56] See eg EC Commission Communication OJ 1981 C218/2.

2527/80[57] on technical measures for the conservation of fishery resources dealing with such matters as net mesh sizes, which in turn enabled the issue of specific measures such as Commission Regulation 2962/81[58] regulating the use of trawls, Danish seines, or similar nets off the west of Scotland for the six-month period to 31 March 1982. More generally, the Commission put forward proposals for a general policy, from time to time amending them, and, failing the adoption of these measures as such, the Council at regular intervals issued decisions[59] on fisheries activities in waters under the sovereignty or jurisdiction of Member States ('sovereignty' here being of a rather titular nature) requiring Member States, among other things, to observe the total allowable catches (TACs) laid down in the Commission's proposals. The Commission itself even issued a declaration to the effect that it considered these proposals to be legally binding on the Member States.[60]

How far this declaration accurately stated the law seemed unlikely to be determined, following the adoption of a Community policy in EC Council Regulation 170/83,[61] the basic function of which was to enable total allowable catches to be set and to be distributed among the Member States 'in a manner which assumes in each member state relative stability of fishing activities for each of the stocks considered'. However, the point was directly raised before the Court in Case 346/85 *UK v Commission*[62] arising out of the refusal of the European Agricultural Guidance and Guarantee Fund[63] to finance UK fishery activities which were alleged to contravene the Commission's proposals. In its judgment, the Court stated categorically that unilateral proposals by the Commission were not rules of Community law, emphasizing, in particular, that legislation having financial consequences should be certain and of foreseeable application.

Control and monitoring of fisheries activities

As mentioned earlier in this chapter, Regulation 170/83 has been repealed and replaced by Council Regulation 3760/92[64] establishing a Community system for fisheries and aquaculture, which, like its predecessor, is essentially a framework regulation enabling the Council by qualified majority to enact catch quotas, in the light of the advice of a Scientific, Technical, and Economic Committee for Fisheries set up under the auspices of the Commission,[65] these quotas being calculated on a Community basis and then distributed among the Member States.[66]

---

[57] OJ 1980 L258/1.   [58] OJ 1981 L297/13.
[59] eg EC Council Decision 82/807 (OJ 1982 L339/57).
[60] EC Commission Declaration of 27 July 1981 (OJ 1981 C224/1).
[61] OJ 1983 L24/1.
[62] Case 346/85 *United Kingdom v EC Commission* [1987] ECR 5197.
[63] See Chapter 5 above.   [64] OJ 1992 L389/1.   [65] Art 16.
[66] Art 8(4).

One practical problem which emerged was that over-fishing by vessels of certain Member States could lead to the closure of a fishery where other Member States had not yet used up their quota. However, Member States may exchange quotas by mutual arrangement, subject to notifying the Commission.[67] The quotas are normally set on an annual basis, and the quotas for 2001 were set by Council Regulation 2484/2000.[68]

To the extent that quotas are allocated for use by vessels flying the flag of a Member State, it is now clear that nationals of other Member States may by virtue of the basic Treaty freedom of establishment own and operate such vessels.[69] This provides a stark illustration of the dichotomy between the allocation of quota on a national basis, and the fundamental rule prohibiting discrimination on grounds of nationality in the context of the Treaty freedoms.[70]

It has already been observed that Council Regulation 3760/92 enables measures to be adopted laying down the conditions of access to waters and resources and of the pursuit of exploitation activities.[71] Under art 4(2), these measures may restrict or prohibit fishing activities in certain zones, limit exploitation rates, set limits on the quantities of fish that may be caught, limit the time spent at sea, fix the number and type of fishing vessels authorized to fish, lay down technical measures regarding fishing gear, set minimum sizes or weights of fish that may be caught, and establish incentives to promote more selective fishing.

A number of examples of the Community legislation which pursues these objectives may be given. Under art 3 of Council Regulation 2847/93[72] on a control system applicable to the common fisheries policy, as amended by Council Regulation 686/97,[73] Member States are required to establish a satellite-based vessel monitoring system (VMS) to monitor the position of Community fishing vessels. This requirement came into general application in 2000 for all vessels exceeding 20 metres between perpendiculars or 24 metres overall, unless they operate exclusively within the 12-mile limit or never spend more than twenty-four hours at sea. Art 5 of the 1993 regulation, as amended by Council Regulation 2846/98,[74] provides for measures to be adopted as to the identification of officially designated inspectors and inspection vessels, aircraft, and such other means of inspection as may be used by Member States. Art 6 requires the masters of Community fishing vessels to keep a logbook of their operations, and art 6(2) as amended by Council Regulation 2846/98[75] requires any amount greater than 50 kg of live-weight equivalent of any species retained on board to be recorded in the logbook, except in the Mediterranean, where any amount greater than 50 kg of live-weight equivalent of any species indicated on a list adopted under that provision and retained on board must be recorded in the logbook.

---

[67] Art 9.   [68] OJ 2000 L334/1.
[69] Case C-48/93 *R v SoS Transport ex p Factortame* [1996] ECR I-1029.
[70] EC Treaty, art 12.   [71] Art 4(1).   [72] OJ 1993 L261/1.
[73] OJ 1997 L102/1.   [74] OJ 1998 L358/5.   [75] Ibid.

Council Regulation 2846/98[76] has also introduced a new Title VIa into Regulation 2847/93[77] on the monitoring of the fishing activities of third country vessels operating in the Community fishing zone; inter alia, such vessels are required to comply with the requirement to keep records in a logbook and, if they fall within the size limits, to be equipped with a VMS position monitoring system approved by the Commission. They are also required to comply with the Community rules on fishing licences and special fishing permits.

The basic rules on Community fishing licences are laid down in Council Regulation 3690/93,[78] which prohibits catching, retaining on board, transferring, or landing fish where a fishing licence has not been granted or has been withdrawn or suspended. It requires that the flag Member State certifies in the licence certain information required in the annex to the regulation. The issue of special fishing permits to Community vessels, and of fishing licences and special fishing permits to third country vessels, is governed by Council Regulation 1627/94.[79] A special fishing permit for a Community vessel enables it to carry out fishing activities during a specified period, in a given area, for a given fishery, in accordance with measures adopted by the Council,[80] and can only be issued if the vessel already has a fishing licence.[81] On the other hand, so far as the issue of fishing licences and special fishing permits to third country vessels is concerned, art 9 of the regulation requires applications to be transmitted to the Commission by the competent authorities of the third country in question, and the Commission issues the licences and permits in accordance with the measures adopted by the Council and the provisions contained in the agreement with the country in question or adopted in the framework of that agreement.

Legislation on technical measures for the conservation of fishery resources is laid down by Council Regulation 894/97,[82] much of which has been replaced by Council Regulation 850/98,[83] for the waters defined in that regulation. It lays down rules on mesh sizes,[84] restricts the use of driftnets,[85] lays down rules determining the minimum size of marine organisms which may be caught,[86] lists fish which may not be caught in certain defined areas and imposes restrictions on the use of certain types of vessels and gear in fishing for certain species during certain periods and in certain geographical areas,[87] notably salmon and sea-trout, herring, sprats, mackerel, anchovy, shrimps, pout, hake, and plaice, though its rules on tuna have been replaced by Council Regulation 973/2001 on the conservation of certain stocks of highly migratory species.[88] Regulations 894/97 and 850/98, like their predecessors, do not however apply in the Mediterranean, which is subject

---

[76] OJ 1998 L358/5. [77] OJ 1993 L261/1. [78] OJ 1993 L341/93.
[79] OJ 1994 L171/7. [80] Art 2(1)(a). [81] Art 5(1).
[82] OJ 1997 L132/1. [83] OJ 1998 L125/1.
[84] Arts 4–10 of the 1998 regulation.
[85] Art 11 of the 1997 regulation.
[86] Arts 17–19 of the 1998 regulation.
[87] Arts 20–29 of the 1998 regulation.
[88] OJ 2001 L137/1.

to a separate regime of technical measures for the conservation of fishery resources introduced by Council Regulation 1626/94.[89] This regime applies not just to fisheries but also to 'related activities', and it applies not just in Community Mediterranean waters, but also to Community vessels pursuing such activities elsewhere in the Mediterranean.[90] It also deals with some rather different problems: for example, it prohibits the use for fishing purposes of 'toxic, soporific or corrosive substances, of electric shock generators and of explosives',[91] the use of St Andrew's crosses and similar towed gear for harvesting coral, and the use of pneumatic hammers or other percussive instruments for the collection of lithophagous molluscs,[92] as well as limits on the types and sizes of nets which may be used in particular areas.

Finally, with the aim of providing information for the regular assessment of the situation as regards fishery resources and its economic implications by the Scientific, Technical, and Economic Committee for Fisheries, Council Regulation 1543/2000,[93] establishing a Community framework for the collection and management of the data needed to conduct the common fisheries policy, requires Member States to establish 'multiannual aggregated and science-based datasets' which incorporate biological and economic information.[94] More particularly, the data to be collected relates to the activities of the various fishing fleets, the total volume of catches, the abundance and distribution of stocks, the prices associated with the various landings, and data needed to evaluate the economic state of the industry.[95] Member States are further required to ensure that the aggregated data relating to Community programmes is fed into computerized databases, and it is envisaged that by the end of 2003, the Commission will review whether the range of data should be extended to such areas as aquaculture, or the relationship of fisheries and aquaculture with the environment.[96]

The question however arises as to whose fishing activities are governed by this legislation, in particular whether it applies in the context of non-commercial fishing. While under Council Regulation 3760/92[97] the common fisheries policy might appear to be aimed at commercial fishing activity, the definition of Community fishing vessels as vessels equipped for commercial exploitation of resources[98] is stated to be 'for the purposes of this Regulation', and the question arises as to whether this definition is also applicable in the context of other fisheries legislation. Here two distinct models may be observed: some of the legislation declares that it is made in implementation of Council Regulation 3760/92,[99] and does not contain its own set of definitions, and may therefore be regarded as applying within the parameters of the parent regulation. Examples of this model are the annual

---

[89] OJ 1994 L171/1.
[90] Art 1(1), now however followed in art 31 of Council Regulation 850/98 (OJ 1998 L125/1).
[91] Art 2(1).   [92] Art 2(2).   [93] OJ 2000 L176/1.
[94] Art 3(1).   [95] Art 4.   [96] Art 10(3).
[97] OJ 1992 L389/1.   [98] Art 3(c).   [99] OJ 1992 L389/1.

quota regulations, the quotas for 2001 being set by Council Regulation 2484/2000,[100] Council Regulation 2847/93[101] on a control system applicable to the common fisheries policy, which, as amended by Council Regulation 686/97,[102] requires Member States to establish a satellite-based vessel monitoring system (VMS) to monitor the position of Community fishing vessels, and art 6 of which requires the masters of Community fishing vessels to keep a logbook of their operations; Council Regulation 3690/93,[103] laying down the basic rules on Community fishing licences, which prohibits catching, retaining on board, transferring, or landing fish where a fishing licence has not been granted or has been withdrawn or suspended; Council Regulation 1627/94,[104] governing the issue of special fishing permits to Community vessels, and of fishing licences and special fishing permits to third country vessels; and Council Regulation 1543/2000,[105] establishing a Community framework for the collection and management of the data needed to conduct the common fisheries policy.

The second model, on the other hand, comprises legislation which, while it might appear to fall within the general framework of Council Regulation 3760/92,[106] does not state that it is made in implementation of that regulation, and which contains rules which arguably might be regarded as having wider application. This may be illustrated by the series of regulations on technical measures for the conservation of fishery resources, the legislation which governs the equipment which may be used for fishing purposes, such as Council Regulation 894/97,[107] now largely replaced by Council Regulation 850/98[108] on the conservation of fishery resources through technical measures for the protection of juveniles of marine organisms. As mentioned above the Mediterranean area is subject to a separate regime of technical measures for the conservation of fishery resources introduced by Council Regulation 1626/94.[109] Aspects of fishing in both areas are covered by Council Regulation 973/2001[110] laying down certain technical measures for the conservation of certain stocks of highly migratory species, which defines 'Community fishing vessels' simply as 'vessels flying the flag of Member States and registered in the Community'.

It may be suggested that these regulations contain rules many of which may be regarded as being of general application and not limited to commercial fisheries. This appears particularly to be the case with regard to Council Regulation 1626/94[111] on the conservation of fishery resources in the Mediterranean. Art 1(1) of that regulation states that it applies 'to all fisheries *and related activities* [emphasis added] pursued within the territory or the maritime waters of the Mediterranean of the east of line 5° 36′ west falling under the sovereignty or jurisdiction of Member States with the exception of pools and lagoons'. It also applies to such activities pursued in the Mediterranean outside those waters by Community vessels.

---

[100] OJ 2000 L334/1.
[101] OJ 1993 L261/1.
[102] OJ 1997 L102/1.
[103] OJ 1993 L341/93.
[104] OJ 1994 L171/7.
[105] OJ 2000 L176/1.
[106] OJ 1992 L389/1.
[107] OJ 1997 L132/1.
[108] OJ 1998 L125/1.
[109] OJ 1994 L171/1.
[110] OJ 2001 L137/1.
[111] OJ 1994 L171/1.

By way of illustration of related activities, art 2(2) prohibits the use of St Andrew's crosses and similar towed gear for harvesting coral. More specifically, art 1(2), permitting Member States to adopt certain measures, arguably indicates the extent to which non-professional fishing falls within its scope: art 1(2) provides that:

Member States with a Mediterranean coastline may continue to legislate in the areas[112] covered by paragraph 1, including that of non-commercial fisheries, by adopting measures supplementary to, or going beyond the minimum requirements of, the system established by this Regulation, provided such measures are compatible with Community law and in conformity with the common fisheries policy.

The implication appears to be that non-commercial fisheries do fall within the Community rules under art 1(1), otherwise there would be no need to give Member States permission to legislate. Indeed, it might be argued that the aim of this legislation is to prevent the use of certain fishing methods regarded as having harmful effects, irrespective of the status of those using them, even though some of them by their very nature may only be relevant to those fishing commercially. There is however, no case law on the subject. It does however raise the related question of the duties of Member States in relation to fisheries conservation.

In this context, art 2(2) of Council Regulation 3760/92[113] establishing a Community system for fisheries and aquaculture provides that the purpose of the regulation is to establish a framework for the conservation and protection of resources, and that 'Member States shall ensure that non-commercial activities do not jeopardize the conservation and management of resources covered by the common fisheries policy'. It goes on to declare that to that end, and in order to ensure sustainable exploitation activities, the regulation establishes a framework for the regulation of access, management, and monitoring of exploitation activities, as well as the requisite means and procedures.

While there appears to be no decision of the European Court concerning the interpretation of this provision, it may be suggested that its aim is to ensure that, although the regulation itself is aimed only at commercial fishing activities, the conservation and management of resources aspects of the common fisheries policy should not be circumvented by non-commercial fishing activities. In other words, although non-commercial fishermen may not be required to have satellite tracking systems, or to carry a logbook of their fishing activity, or to obtain a special fishing permit, they should not be allowed to use methods of fishing which breach the Community's ecological or conservation objectives, and it is the duty of the Member States to ensure that non-commercial activities do not breach these objectives. In fact, it was argued above that much of this conservation legislation could be interpreted as being of general application, but if that argument is incorrect, it is submitted that the effect of art 2(2) is to require Member States to ensure that the objectives of this legislation are observed by non-commercial fishermen.

[112] 'Domaines' in the French text.
[113] OJ 1992 L389/1.

In any event, in the context of the Mediterranean, art 2(2) of Council Regulation 3760/92[114] should be read with Council Regulation 1626/94[115] on the conservation of fishery resources in the Mediterranean. The recitals to this regulation refer to the fact that art 2(2) of Council Regulation 3760/92 establishing a Community system for fisheries and aquaculture obliges Member States to ensure that non-commercial fisheries activities do not jeopardize the conservation and management of resources covered by the common fisheries policy, and then add that 'this obligation is of particular importance in the Mediterranean owing to the considerable extent of such activities in that sea' and the fact that 'it is important to limit any negative affects thereof on the state of stocks'.

As well as reinforcing the obligation under art 2(2) of Council Regulation 3760/92, art 1(2) of Council Regulation 1626/94 also provides, as mentioned in the first section, that 'Member States with a Mediterranean coastline may continue to legislate in the areas covered by paragraph 1, including that of non-commercial fisheries, by adopting measures supplementary to, or going beyond the minimum requirements of, the system established by this Regulation, provided such measures are compatible with Community law and in conformity with the common fisheries policy'. When adopting such measures, Member States are required to pay attention to the conservation of fragile or endangered species or environments, in particular those listed in Annex I of Regulation 1626/94. It was suggested earlier that art 1(2) could be interpreted as implying that the provisions of Council Regulation 1626/94 extended to non-commercial fishing activities, and if that is correct then Member States still have the power to enact stricter (but not less strict) measures. If on the other hand that view is wrong, the effect of art 2(2) of Council Regulation 3760/92 would nevertheless be to require Member States to ensure that non-commercial fishermen are not allowed to breach the conservation objectives of Council Regulation 1626/94 on the conservation of fishery resources in the Mediterranean.

External Community competence

It will be clear from this discussion of monitoring and control measures that the common fisheries policy is not purely domestic: aspects of it govern third country vessels in Community waters and Community vessels in third country waters, as well as Community vessels in Community waters, and this interrelationship has long been recognized by the European Court. That exclusive implied external competence may derive from the exercise of internal Community competence is a concept first enunciated by the Court in 1971[116] in the context of the European

---

[114] OJ 1992 L389/1.   [115] OJ 1994 L171/1.
[116] Case 22/70 *Commission v Council* [1971] ECR 263.

Road Transport Agreement (AETR).[117] That exclusive implied external competence may also arise once the time for implementing the internal policy has expired is a concept which has largely developed in the context of fisheries policy.

The point arose in Cases 3, 4, and 6/76 *Officier van Justitie v Kramer*.[118] These were references from Dutch courts in the context of criminal proceedings brought against fishermen accused of having breached Dutch legislation aimed at ensuring the conservation of stocks of sole and plaice in the North-East Atlantic in pursuance of the obligations of the Netherlands under the North-East Atlantic Fisheries Convention of 1959 (NEAFC).[119] Summarizing the questions which are here relevant, the Court was asked in effect whether the Community alone had authority to enter into commitments such as that convention. It was found that in the absence of specific provisions of the EC Treaty authorizing the Community to enter into international commitments in the sphere of conservation of the biological resources of the sea, it was necessary to look at the general system of Community law in the sphere of external relations of the Community. The Court then considered the relevant Treaty provisions and also the regulations then in force laying down a common structural policy for the fishing industry and the common organization of the market in fishery products. From this it deduced that the Community had at its disposal, on the internal level, the power to take any measures for the conservation of the biological resources of the sea, including the fixing of catch quotas. It also said that the only way to ensure the conservation of the biological resources of the sea, both effectively and equitably, was through a system of rules binding on all the states concerned, including non–Member States. In these circumstances, it followed from the very duties and powers which Community law had established and assigned to the institutions of the Community on the internal level that the Community had authority to enter into international commitments for the conservation of the resources of the sea.

However, the Court then turned to the question whether the Community had in fact, rather than as a possibility, assumed the functions and obligations arising from the convention and from decisions taken under it, and found that at the time the convention was entered into in 1959 the Community had not adopted any regulations relating to the sea fishing industry, that those regulations which had eventually been adopted were limited to providing the Community institutions with the power to take measures similar to those which the Member States concerned had committed themselves to taking and did take, and that so far the institutions had not made use of that power. The Court concluded that since the Community had not yet fully exercised its functions in the matter at the time the question arose, the Member States had the power to assume commitments within

---

[117] European Agreement Concerning the Work of Crews of Vehicles Engaged in International Road Transport (AETR) (Geneva, 1 July 1970–31 March 1971; TS 103 (1978); Cmnd 7401).

[118] [1976] ECR 1279.

[119] North-East Atlantic Fisheries Convention (NEAFC) (London, 24 January 1959; TS 68 (1963); Cmnd 2190).

the framework of the convention and consequently had the right to ensure the application of those commitments within the area of their jurisdiction. However, the Court added a rider that this authority of the Member States was only of a transitional nature and that the Member States concerned were by the time of the judgment bound by Community obligations in their negotiations within the framework of the convention and other comparable agreements. The Court pointed out that the authority of the Member States should end from the sixth year after accession at the latest, because under the 1972 Act of Accession the Council was required by then to have adopted measures for the conservation of the resources of the sea.[120]

That thereafter the Community has had exclusive external authority with regard to fisheries was confirmed in the European Court's Opinion on the Uruguay Round Agreement,[121] and, more importantly, this has also been accepted by other negotiating parties. So the Community as such became a party to the Northwest Atlantic Fisheries Convention 1978[122] and to the North-East Atlantic Fisheries Convention 1981,[123] the latter replacing the old NEAFC.

So far as bilateral relations are concerned, the Council adopted a series of regulations laying down interim measures for the conservation and management of fisheries resources applicable to vessels flying the flags of various non-Member States, which in turn were followed by formal agreements with such states, including neighbours with a particular interest in fisheries such as Norway[124] and Greenland,[125] as well as more distant countries such as Canada.[126] It may be observed that these agreements were based on the total allowable catch system even though they antedated any overtly binding internal Community measure giving effect to TACs. Bilateral agreements have also been made to enable Community fishermen to fish off developing countries such as Senegal,[127] Equatorial Guinea,[128] and Angola,[129] paying compensation to those countries for the privilege.

---

[120] Act of Accession 1972, art 102.

[121] Opinion 1/94 [1994] ECR I-5267.

[122] Convention on Future Multilateral Cooperation in the Northwest Atlantic Fisheries (Ottawa, 24 October–31 December 1978; Misc 9 (1979); Cmnd 7569; OJ 1978 L378/16).

[123] Convention on Future Multilateral Cooperation in North-East Atlantic Fisheries (London, 18 November 1980–28 February 1981; Misc 2 (1982); Cmnd 8474; OJ 1981 L227/22).

[124] Agreement on Fisheries between the EC and Norway (OJ 1980 L226/48).

[125] For recent developments see Agreement on the Provisional Application of the Fourth Protocol to the Fisheries Agreement with Denmark and the Local Government of Greenland (OJ 2000 L329/47).

[126] Agreement on Fisheries between the EC and Canada (OJ 1981 L379/54).

[127] Agreement between Senegal and the EC on Fishing off the Coast of Senegal (OJ 1980 L226/17; OJ 1985 L361/87).

[128] Agreement on the Provisional Application of the Protocol Setting out Fishing Opportunities and Financial Contributions under the Agreement with Equatorial Guinea for 2000–2003 (OJ 2000 L329/3).

[129] Agreement on the Provisional Application of the Protocol Setting out Fishing Opportunities and Financial Contributions under the Agreement with Angola for 2000–2002 (OJ 2000 L329/18).

Relationship to previous international arrangements

Under art 307 of the EC Treaty, rights and obligations arising from agreements concluded before the entry into force of that Treaty between one or more Member States on the one hand, and one or more third countries on the other, are not to be affected by the provisions of that Treaty, and under the Act of Accession (1972) this protection applies to agreements or conventions concluded by the United Kingdom, Ireland, and Denmark before accession.[130] Hence in Case 812/79 *AG v Burgoa*[131] the Court held that this provision applied to the 1964 London Fisheries Convention[132] with regard to the relationship between Ireland and Spain. However, the case involved a Spanish vessel caught fishing 20 miles off the Irish coast, and the Court, acting on the basis that it was accepted that the convention applied only to the zone up to 12 miles from the Irish coast, held that the 12- to 200-mile zone was governed by the relevant Council regulation applying interim measures for the conservation and management of fishery resources applicable to vessels flying the flag of Spain, which was 'superimposed' on the regime previously applied in that zone, as to which the Court did not commit itself.

Although it has subsequently been overtaken by Spanish accession, the Community did enter into a formal agreement with Spain,[133] which contained an express declaration to the effect that 'the purpose of this Agreement is to establish the principles and rules which will govern, in all respects, the fishing activities of vessels of either Party within the fishing zones falling under the jurisdiction of the other Party' subject to one defined exception. On the other hand, the agreements with Norway[134] and Sweden[135] (the latter again overtaken by accession) were expressed to be without prejudice to other existing agreements concerning fishing by vessels of one party within the area of fisheries jurisdiction of the other. Whatever the latter may mean, it was held that the effect of the Spanish agreement was to replace earlier international agreements so that Spanish fishermen could no longer rely on the London Convention in EC waters.[136] However, more contentious, and possibly of wider relevance, is the attitude taken to the status of agreements not protected by the EC Treaty within the 12-mile zone (but outside the 6-mile exclusive zone) as against Community regulations imposing interim measures with regard to vessels flying the flag of a relevant non-Member State. This was the problem faced in Case 181/80 *Procureur Général v Arbelaiz-Emazabel*,[137] which involved a Spanish vessel caught fishing in 1977 between 6 and 12 miles

---

[130] Act of Accession 1972 art 5. [131] [1980] ECR 2787.
[132] Fisheries Convention (London, 9 March–10 April 1964; TS 35 (1966); Cmnd 3011).
[133] Agreement on Fisheries between the EC and Spain (OJ 1980 L322/4).
[134] Agreement on Fisheries between the EC and Norway (OJ 1980 L226/48), art 4.
[135] Agreement on Fisheries between the EC and Sweden (OJ 1980 L226/2), art 5.
[136] Cases 50–58/82 *Administrateur des Affaires Maritimes, Bayonne v Dorca Marina* [1982] ECR 3949.
[137] [1981] ECR 2961.

from the French coast off Bayonne without being in possession of the licence required by the relevant Council regulation laying down interim measures for vessels flying the Spanish flag. It was argued on behalf of the Spanish skipper that under a 1967 agreement between France and Spain, concluded within the framework of the 1964 London Fisheries Convention, Spanish nationals were entitled to fish in the area in question. Although these agreements clearly did not fall within the protection of art 307 of the EC Treaty, the Court of Justice accepted, on the basis of its judgment in the *Kramer* case,[138] that since the Community had not at that stage exercised its powers in the matter and its competence had not then become exclusive, France could validly enter into the agreements in question. It was also clear that the new agreement between the Community and Spain was not signed until 1980; however, the Court took account of the fact that the interim measures were expressed to be adopted 'pending the conclusion of the fishing agreements currently being negotiated' and of the fact that the Spanish authorities collaborated in the implementation of the Community interim measures, passing lists of licence applications to the Commission, and distributing the licences granted, so that they fell 'within the framework of the relations established between the Community and Spain in order to resolve the problems inherent in conservation measures and the extension of fishery limits'. The Court thus concluded that these relations 'replaced' the prior international obligations existing between certain Member States (such as France) and Spain.

Whether a different view would have been taken if the Community's negotiating partners had been less cooperative remains a matter of speculation, although it must be said that in the context of general commercial policy the Court of Justice has held that measures of commercial policy of a national character are permissible after the end of the transitional period only by virtue of specific authorization by the Community.[139] Transposed to fisheries, this would appear to mean that previous arrangements made at the national level must at least after 1978 give way to Community measures unless protected by art 307 of the EC Treaty or specifically authorized. It has indeed been suggested that the situation could have arisen where the Member State would have been in breach of its Treaty obligations if it had not applied the Community interim measures, but would have been in breach of its Treaty obligations to the non-Member State under general international law if it had applied these measures.[140]

The sensitivity of the fisheries issue may be evidenced by the fact that the 1985 Act of Accession listed by name the Spanish boats entitled to their initially very limited right of access to the waters of the older Member States[141]—a restriction to some extent circumvented by those taking advantage of freedom of establishment under the Treaty to own and operate vessels flying the flag of another Member State.[142]

---

[138] Cases 3, 4, and 6/76 *Officier van Justitie v Kramer* [1976] ECR 1279.
[139] Case 41/76 *Donkerwolcke v Procureur de la République* [1976] ECR 1921.
[140] E White, 'Fishery Rights of Non-Member States in Community Waters' [1982] EL Rev 415.
[141] Act of Accession 1985, art 158, Annex IX.
[142] Case C-48/93 *R v SoS Transport ex p Factortame* [1996] ECR I-1029.

7

Common organizations of the market: legal consequences

Introduction: the powers of national authorities

The situations where common organizations themselves confer powers on national authorities or require action on the part of national authorities will be considered in the context of the administration of the common agricultural policy.[1] Greater legal problems have, however, been raised in determining the extent to which national authorities retain the power to act in their own right in relation to products governed by common organizations. Here, two different approaches may be detected in the case law of the Court of Justice. On one view, the existence of a common organization precludes unilateral national legislation within its scope. On the other view, unilateral national legislation may be permitted provided it is not incompatible with the rules of the common organization. The development of these views may be illustrated in relation to certain specific aspects of common organizations.

Problems created by rules of common organizations

It is not unknown for the provisions of a common organization to create a new problem which they fail to resolve. This came clearly to light in Case 159/73 *Hannoversche Zucker v Hauptzollamt Hannover*[2] in relation to the common organization of the market in sugar, which provided for a system of annual production quotas, and laid down the consequences of over-production, but failed to make provision for determining the marketing year to which an excess should be attributed when discovered on a stocktaking which might occur at intervals of several years. The problem being created by the Community rules themselves, the Court held that the rules of the common organization must be regarded as forming a complete system in the sense that it did not leave to the Member States the power to fill such a lacuna by resorting to their national laws. The Court therefore sought a Community

---

[1] See Chapter 9 below.   [2] [1974] ECR 121.

solution in the light of the aims and objectives of the common organization. It concluded that an excess must be treated as arising during the marketing year in which it was ascertained, which happened to be the solution that the Commission had in the meantime adopted by way of regulation.

This refusal to allow national solutions to such problems was repeated in the context of the system operated in the beef market which required security to be lodged to guarantee the performance of contracts for the private storage of certain products subject to Community aids. In Case 117/83 *Karl Könecke GmbH v Bundesanstalt für Landwirtschaftliche Marktordnung*[3] a trader in Germany had obtained the release of such a security by fraud, and the goods had been removed from storage. The German authorities sought to recover the security from the trader. They faced the difficulty that the Community legislation failed to provide for such recovery, and they therefore wished to invoke the relevant German legislation. Again, the Court held that the storage system for beef must be regarded as a complete system, so that it did not allow Member States to resort to their national laws to fill the lacuna unless they were so authorized under the Community legislation, although the national authorities had both the right and the duty to apply the rules of their national criminal law with regard to the fraud itself.

However, it was held in Case 124/83 *Corman*[4] that where a security was wrongly released, allowing a tenderer to acquire goods at a reduced price, he could be required as a matter of Community law to pay the difference between the reduced price and the normal intervention price.

Price systems of common organizations

The question of the legal effects of the price systems of common organizations with regard to the powers of national authorities first arose in Case 31/74 *Galli*.[5] Galli was charged with breaches of Italian prices legislation in relation to the sale of cereals subject to the common organization of the market in cereals and in relation to the sale of flour derived from oilseeds subject to the common organization of the market in oils and fats. The European Court was in effect asked to what extent the Community price system established within the context of the common organization of the market may exclude a national price control system. Its view was expressed in rather wide-ranging terms: 'It must be concluded that in sectors covered by a common organisation of the market . . . Member States can no longer interfere through national provisions taken unilaterally in the machinery of price formation as established under the common organisation.' Even more strongly it was stated that 'the only way compatible with Community law of enabling Member States to attain, in a sector covered by a common organization of the market, the objectives sought by the national legislation and intended to combat a rise in prices,

---

[3] [1984] ECR 3291.   [4] [1985] ECR 3777.   [5] [1975] ECR 47.

is for those states to take, at the Community level, the necessary action for the purpose of prompting the competent Community authority to institute or authorise measures which are consistent with the requirements of the single market' set up by the regulations in question. However, the Court also stated that the price system established by the regulations in question was applicable solely at the production and wholesale stage. The result was that those provisions left Member States free to take the appropriate measures relating to price formation at the retail and consumption stages, provided they did not jeopardize the aims or functioning of the common organization of the market in question.

Shortly afterwards, the Court was again faced with the effects of price systems, this time under the common organization of the market in sugar, in Case 65/75 *Tasca*[6] and in Cases 88–90/75 *Società SADAM v Comitato Interministeriale dei Prezzi*.[7] In its judgments the Court expressly repeated certain of the passages from its *Galli* judgment quoted above. It then went on to say however that a distinction between maximum consumer prices and maximum prices applicable at previous marketing stages was difficult, and concluded that the unilateral fixing by a Member State of maximum prices for the sale of sugar, whatever the marketing stage in question, was incompatible with the regulation[8] introducing the common organization of the market in sugar, once it jeopardized the objectives and the functioning of this organization and in particular its system of prices. The Court then went on to consider how such incompatibility could arise. Having looked at the structure of the sugar market and the sugar price system in the common organization, it held that a Member State would jeopardize the objectives and functioning of the sugar markets if it regulated prices in such a way as, directly or indirectly, to make it difficult for the sugar manufacturers to obtain an ex-factory price at least equal to the intervention price. The Court added that such an indirect obstruction would exist when a Member State, without regulating the prices at the production stage, fixed maximum selling prices for the wholesale and retail stages at such a low level that the grower found it practically impossible to sell at the intervention price. It was finally concluded that it was for the national court to decide, having regard to these considerations, whether the maximum prices which it was called upon to consider produced such effects as to make them incompatible with the Community provisions on sugar.

Nevertheless, the Court returned to the distinction it had made in *Galli* in two cases decided in 1979. In Case 10/79 *Toffoli v Regione Veneto*,[9] which involved local legislation by the Region of Venice fixing a regional price for milk at the production level, it was repeated that Member States may no longer interfere through national provisions taken unilaterally in the machinery of price formation established under a common organization. But in the judgment delivered the same day

---

[6] [1976] ECR 291.   [7] [1976] ECR 323.
[8] Council Regulation 1009/67 (JO 1967 No 308, p 1 (sp edn 1967, p 304)).
[9] [1979] ECR 3301.

on references from the Belgian Cour de Cassation in Cases 16–20/79 *Openbaar Ministerie v Danis*,[10] the Court of Justice again added the rider that Member States still have the power to take unilateral measures relating to price formation at the retail and consumption stages, provided that they do not jeopardize the aims or functioning of the common organization of the market in question.

In the result, despite the difficulties of distinguishing the economic effects of price controls at different levels in the chain of distribution, it would appear that in areas subject to common organizations based on production prices, Member States have no power to enact legislation relating to prices at the production level: such legislation is presumed incompatible with the Community rules, whereas the compatibility of national legislation governing prices at other marketing stages with the Community rules must be considered in the light of the circumstances of each case. It may however be suggested that the importance of this case law has somewhat diminished as the Community has moved from product support to producer support.[11]

Other aspects of common organizations

The approach described in the preceding paragraph is one which has been followed with regard to other aspects of common organizations. Here, it was not said that national legislation was excluded, but rather, as the Court of Justice put it in Case 111/76 *Officier van Justitie v Van den Hazel*,[12] that once a common organization of the market had been established it was the duty of Member States to refrain from taking any measures which might derogate from or harm that organization. This approach was illustrated in Case 50/76 *Amsterdam Bulb BV v Produktschap voor Siergewassen*,[13] which was concerned with Dutch legislation providing (1) for a minimum export price for bulbs smaller than those for which Commission Regulation 369/75[14] laid down a minimum price, and (2) for a minimum price for bulbs of a type not covered by that regulation. The Court held again that the compatibility of these provisions with the Community regulations must be examined having regard not only to the express provisions of the regulations but also to their aims and objects. With regard to the first problem, that of the small bulbs, the Court found that under the Community scheme, bulbs smaller than those specified in Council Regulation 315/68[15] could not in fact be exported, and that the minimum price for those falling within that regulation but not mentioned in Regulation 369/75 should be the lowest price fixed in that regulation. With regard to the second problem, that of the types of bulbs not covered by the Community regulations on prices, although falling within the scope of the common organization

---

[10] [1979] ECR 3327.   [11] See Chapter 4 above.   [12] [1977] ECR 901.
[13] [1977] ECR 137.   [14] OJ 1975 L41/1.
[15] JO 1968 L71/1 (sp edn 1968 (I), p 46).

as a whole, the Court found that there was no express prohibition on the fixing of national minimum prices for exports, and inferred from the minimum price system applied by the Commission that such prices could continue to be fixed until replaced at the Community level.

The situation can also arise where the practical problems involved in applying the rules of a common organization may lead the Court to infer that certain national legislation is compatible with that organization. In three sets of French wine cases heard in 1975[16] the question was asked, in effect, whether the Community rules in the wine sector enabled Member States to apply a presumption in law of over-alcoholization based on the proportion of alcohol to 'reduced extract' which in turn was obtained by the 'hundred degree' method. The Commission regulation determining Community methods for the analysis of wines provided for measuring the dry extract by the 'densimetric' method.[17] However, the Court found that under the regulations on the common organization of the market in wine the Member States were required to take effective measures of control. It also found that the use of the densimetric method laid down by the Community regulations is not an aim in itself and that in the absence of Community measures of control it would be contrary to the aims of the Community rules to require that this method be used at the cost of invalidating the only method of control then acknowledged to be appropriate for the detection of over-alcoholization. So it was stated that, until more appropriate methods had been worked out, Community rules in the wine sector did not prohibit Member States from using the hundred degree method to measure the dry extract of wine in order to apply a presumption in law of over-alcoholization based on the proportion of alcohol to dry extract.

Compatibility has been tested not only against the express provision of a regulation establishing a common organization, but also against its underlying principles, as in Case 83/78 *Pigs Marketing Board v Redmond*,[18] in relation to Council Regulation 2759/75[19] on the common organization of the market in pigmeat. This case was a reference from a Northern Irish resident magistrate in the context of a prosecution brought by the Northern Irish Pigs Marketing Board. Under the relevant Northern Irish legislation, only producers who were registered with the board could sell bacon pigs, and only to or through the agency of the board. In laying down the test for determining whether such a scheme was compatible with

---

[16] Cases 89/74 and 18, 19/75 *Procureur Général, Bordeaux v Arnaud* [1975] ECR 1023, Cases 10–14/75 *Procureur de la République, Aix-en-Provence v Lahaille* [1975] ECR 1053, Case 64/75 *Procureur Général, Lyon v Mommessin* [1975] ECR 1599.

[17] The 'hundred degree' method consists in weighing what is left after evaporating the volatile substances in the wine at 100 °C. The 'densimetric' method consists in calculating the dry extract indirectly from the specific gravity of the wine from which the alcohol has been removed and which has been brought up to the initial volume by adding water: see Cases 89/74 and 18, 19/75 *Procureur Général, Bordeaux v Arnaud* [1975] ECR 1023 at 1026.

[18] [1978] ECR 2347.

[19] OJ 1975 L282/1.

the common organization, the Court looked to what might be described as the underlying concept, stating that the common organization of the market in pigmeat was based on the concept of an open market to which every producer had free access, and the functioning of which was regulated solely by the instruments provided for by that organization. It concluded that 'any provisions or national practices which might alter the pattern of imports or exports or influence the formation of market prices by preventing producers from buying and selling freely within the state in which they are established, or in any other Member State, in conditions laid down by Community rules, and from taking advantage directly of intervention measures or any other measures for regulating the market laid down by the common organisation are incompatible with the principles of such organisation of the market'. In any event measures of the type there at issue were specifically found to contravene the EC Treaty provisions prohibiting measures having equivalent effect to quantitative restrictions on imports and exports.[20]

The idea of looking at the underlying concepts of a common organization rather than its express provisions was taken a step further in another judgment involving the common organization of the market in pigmeat in Case 177/78 *Pigs and Bacon Commission v McCarren & Co Ltd*,[21] which involved a marketing system in the Irish Republic under which the Pigs and Bacon Commission was empowered to impose a levy on the production of all pig carcasses intended for the manufacture of bacon, whilst paying a bonus to those exporting bacon through its agency. Council Regulation 2759/75, and the provisions on the free movement of goods held to be an integral part of it, do not appear expressly to prohibit the payment of bonuses. Nonetheless, the Court found that 'according to the idea on which the regulation dealing with the common organisation of the market in pigmeat is based, the products referred to therein are in fact required to move freely within the Community at the price level resulting from the operation of the machinery for the common organisation of the market, and neither Member States nor agencies on which they have conferred powers are entitled to create advantages for the marketing of national products as against those of other Member States by means of financial machinery such as the grant of bonuses'. However, earlier in the judgment, it was said that the marketing system established by the regulation precluded 'any intervention by Member States in the market otherwise than as expressly laid down by the regulation itself'. Taken literally, this would appear to exclude unilateral national competence in any market governed by a common organization. This would represent a considerable change in attitude, and would be difficult to reconcile with the contemporaneous cases allowing national prices legislation at the retail level so long as it did not interfere with the functioning of a common organization.

[20] Now arts 28 and 29.
[21] [1979] ECR 2161.

Development of exclusivity

The principle of exclusivity enunciated in the *McCarren* case[22] appears nevertheless to indicate the approach followed by the Court of Justice in its subsequent case law. Case 222/82 *Apple and Pear Development Council v KJ Lewis Ltd*[23] involved, among other things, the quality standards laid down by the United Kingdom Apple and Pear Development Council. The Court there stated that the common organization of the market in fruit and vegetables laid down an exhaustive system of quality standards for the relevant products, so that Member States and bodies such as the development council were prevented from imposing unilateral provisions concerning the quality of the fruit marketed by growers, although the development council might make simple recommendations. This view that the Community rules in the fruit sector on quality standards are exhaustive was repeated in Case 218/85 *Le Campion*[24] where it was held that a Member State could not make the rules of a national producers' organization compulsory with regard to weight, presentation, etc.

Furthermore, in Case 16/83 *Prantl*[25] involving the common organization of the market in wine, the Court stated categorically that where a common organization of the market constitutes a complete system, Member States no longer have any competence in the matter unless a provision of Community law provides otherwise. The dispute in that case involved German rules concerning bottle shapes, and it was found that a provision in the regulation establishing the common organization did authorize Member States to regulate bottle shapes, although it was then found that the German rules at issue constituted measures equivalent to quantitative reduction on imports which are prohibited under art 28 of the EC Treaty. Finally, in Cases 47 and 48/83 *Pluimveeslachterij Midden-Nederland BV*,[26] involving quality standards for poultrymeat, the Court applied the exclusivity theory as developed in the context of fisheries policy to a land-based common organization. The regulation establishing the common organization provided for the Council to lay down the relevant quality standards, but it had totally failed to do so. After referring to its decision in Case 804/79 *Commission v United Kingdom*[27] in relation to fisheries policy, the Court held that the Member States, faced with such a failure to act, had no competence of their own but could nonetheless act on behalf of the Community in taking interim measures on a provisional basis, although it added that their interim measures should themselves be compatible with the principles of the common organization.

Given this clear move towards the exclusivity of Community competence in areas covered by common organizations of agricultural markets, it is at first sight surprising that in Case 237/82 *Jongeneel Kaas BV v Netherlands*,[28] decided in the same period, concerning the common organization of the market in milk, it was

---

[22] Case 177/78 *Pigs and Bacon Commission v McCarren & Co Ltd* [1979] ECR 2161.
[23] [1983] ECR 4083.   [24] [1986] ECR 3513.   [25] [1984] ECR 1299.
[26] [1984] ECR 1721.   [27] [1981] ECR 1045.   [28] [1984] ECR 523.

held that, in the absence of any specific rules in the regulation establishing the common organization, Member States had power to lay down quality standards for cheese, provided they were compatible with the other provisions of the common organization. However, it may be argued either that the regulation was construed as authorizing Member States to take such measures, again therefore making it a matter of exclusive Community competence, or that there was not a complete common organization of the type described in the *Prantl* case with regard to quality standards for cheese. It may therefore be suggested that the modern principle is that the existence of a common organization precludes unilateral national legislation on the matters which it covers, unless it can be shown to be incomplete in the sense of not covering or not purporting to cover the matter at issue.

National legislation may be enacted only where required or permitted by the rules of the common organization. This was illustrated in the *de Boer* case,[29] where it was held that Council Regulation 1353/83[30] on herring quotas did empower Member States to lay down how the quota should be used, so that the Netherlands could determine how boats participating in the quota should be equipped; but that Council Regulation 3796/81[31] on the common organization of the market in fish products left Member States with no competence to determine how fish caught under the quota should be processed and marketed, so that the Netherlands could not require the fish caught to be sold in a particular form.

As summarized in Case 48/85 *Commission v Germany*[32] Member States are only competent in matters not governed by a common organization, or where they are authorized to act by the Community, although, as was pointed out in Case 118/86 *Nertsvoederfabriek*,[33] the existence of a common organization does not exempt producers from national legislation pursuing objectives different from those of the common organization. It may therefore be suggested that common organizations of agricultural markets and the common fisheries policy[34] represent the two distinct concepts from which the European Court recognized that the exclusivity of Community competence may be derived, in its *Opinion 2/91*[35] on competence to enter an ILO convention. It there suggested that these concepts were:

- the concept that the existence of Community legislation on a matter excludes national legislation on the same matter, which has been shown above in the context of the land-based common organizations of agricultural markets, and
- the concept that the duty of the Community to act in a particular matter from a particular date may exclude the possibility of Member States acting in that area from that date, which may particularly be illustrated in the context of the common fisheries policy under art 102 of the 1972 Act of Accession.

---

[29] Case 207/84 *Rederij L de Boer en Zonen BV v Produktschap voor Vis en Visprodukten* [1985] ECR 3203.
[30] OJ 1983 L139/54.   [31] OJ 1981 L379/1.   [32] [1986] ECR 2589.
[33] [1987] ECR 3883.   [34] Discussed in Chapter 6 above.
[35] [1993] ECR I-1061 at 1077.

The consequence in both cases is that the concepts of subsidiarity under art 5 of the EC Treaty and of closer cooperation under art 11 of the EC Treaty are not relevant in the context of common organizations of the market or of fisheries, since they both apply only to matters which do not fall under the exclusive competence of the Community. It is true that many modern common organizations do give Member States wide powers to determine eg whether particular forms of producer support should be provided; for example under art 16 of Council Regulation 1255/1999[36] on the common organization of the market in milk, an annual dairy premium is envisaged as starting in 2005, payable per tonne of individual reference quantity (ie quota) eligible for premium and available on the holding. These sums are low,[37] but it is envisaged that Member States may supplement them by premium supplements under art 18 and/or by area payments under art 19, provided they do not exceed the global amounts set out in Annex I to the regulation. It is stated in recital 12 to the regulation that a Community-wide scheme with uniform payments would be 'too rigid'. However, by way of illustration of the effect of exclusive Community competence in this area, Member States may make these supplementary payments only in so far as the regulation authorizes them so to do; they are not exercising their own original competence in this area.

There is however one respect in which the enactment of comprehensive Community legislation no longer appears totally to exclude national legislation. Following amendments made by the Treaty of Amsterdam, to the extent that measures adopted under the common agricultural policy may be regarded as measures of 'harmonization'—which is perhaps more likely to be the case with regard to the health measures considered in Chapter 1—art 95 of the EC Treaty envisages situations where Member States may be allowed to maintain national provisions or even introduce new national provisions despite the adoption of Community measures. Under art 95(4), if, after the adoption by the Council or by the Commission of a harmonization measure, a Member State deems it necessary to *maintain* national provisions on grounds of major needs referred to in art 30,[38] or relating to the protection of the environment or the working environment, it is required to notify the Commission of these provisions as well as the grounds for maintaining them. Furthermore, under art 95(5), if, after the adoption by the Council or by the Commission of a harmonization measure, a Member State deems it necessary to *introduce* national provisions based on new scientific evidence relating to the protection of the environment or the working environment on grounds of a problem specific to that Member State arising after the adoption of the harmonization measure, it is again required to notify the Commission of the envisaged provisions as well as the grounds for introducing them. In both cases, the

[36] OJ 1999 L160/48.
[37] See Chapter 4 above.
[38] For a discussion of this phrase see N Green, T Hartley, and J Usher, *Legal Foundations of the Single European Market* (1991) 85–86.

Commission is required within six months of the notifications to approve or reject the national provisions involved after having verified whether or not they are a means of arbitrary discrimination or a disguised restriction on trade between Member States and whether or not they constitute an obstacle to the functioning of the internal market, although in the absence of a decision by the Commission within this period the national provisions are deemed to have been approved, unless the Commission notifies the Member State concerned that the period should be extended for a further period of up to six months, when justified by the complexity of the matter and in the absence of danger for human health. It is also provided in art 95(7) and (8) that when a Member State is authorized to maintain or introduce national provisions derogating from a harmonization measure, the Commission must immediately examine whether to propose an adaptation to that measure, and that when a Member State raises a specific problem on public health in a field which has been the subject of prior harmonization measures, it must bring it to the attention of the Commission which must immediately examine whether to propose appropriate measures to the Council.

On the widest interpretation, the art 95 derogations only justify the maintenance of national provisions which would be justifiable as restrictions on the free movement of goods; they appear highly unlikely to justify measures relating to the structure of an agricultural market. Furthermore, new national measures can only be justified under the very narrow criteria laid down in art 95(5): new scientific evidence relating to the protection of the environment or the working environment on grounds of a problem specific to that Member State arising after the adoption of the harmonization measure. In any event, in both cases, the national measures in principle require the authorization of the Commission, which appears to confirm that it is a matter of Community rather than national competence.

Role of national organizations of the market

Whilst common organizations may expressly provide for a particular function to be performed by national organizations, in particular producer organizations,[39] the Court of Justice clearly stated in Case 83/78 *Pigs Marketing Board v Redmond*[40] that the institution of a common organization replaces any pre-existing national organization of the market, in the sense that the national organization ceases to have any special legal position, even if, as in that case, the overall time limit for the replacement of national organizations by common organizations under the Act of Accession (1972) had not yet expired. On the other hand, Community law itself may, as it did with the United Kingdom Milk Marketing Boards until their abolition, permit the continuance of national organizations within the limits of a common organization.

---

[39] See Chapter 8 below.   [40] [1978] ECR 2347.

8

Structural and guidance measures

General structural policy

The references in art 33 of the EC Treaty on the one hand to increasing agricultural productivity and on the other to the need to take account of the structural and natural disparities between the various agricultural regions themselves
have indicated from the outset that the common agricultural policy must do more
than simply offer a system of price or producer support. This view is further
evidenced by the reference in art 34(3) to an agricultural guidance fund as well
as to an agricultural guarantee fund. Indeed, the problems caused by large numbers
of small farms were well recognized even when Community agricultural legislation was first discussed, and the Commission did propose the establishment of a
separate European Fund for Structural Improvement. However, the Council
decided to add structural measures to the Guidance Section of the general European Agricultural Guidance and Guarantee Fund (EAGGF), when that was split
into two sections in Council Regulation 17/64.[1]

However, the Guidance Section received relatively little of the Community
funds spent on agriculture, the fundamental legal obligation under the common
organizations being to finance the guarantee measures provided under those
organizations. Indeed, under Council Regulation 1258/1999 on the financing of
the common agricultural policy,[2] in principle the Guidance Section finances only
rural development measures falling within Objective 1 programmes and the rural
development Community initiative. This however reflects the fact that the Single
European Act introduced what is now art 159 of the EC Treaty, under which the
Guidance Section of the EAGGF forms part of the Structural Funds of the
Community. Under Regulation 1260/1999[3] on the Structural Funds, Objective 1
is defined as covering those areas where GDP per capita in terms of purchasing
power is less that 75 per cent of the Community average,[4] and it is provided that
69.7 per cent of the €195 billion allocated to the Structural Funds for 2000–2006
should go on Objective 1 projects.[5]

Although Council Regulation 17/64[6] created the Guidance Section of the
European Agricultural Guidance and Guarantee Fund (EAGGF) and laid down a

---

[1] JO 1964, p 117 (sp edn 1963–1964, p 135).
[2] OJ 1999 L160/103. [3] OJ 1999 L161/1. [4] Art 3.
[5] Art 7. [6] JO 1964, p 117 (sp edn 1963–1964, p 135).

procedure under which particular projects could be submitted for aid, it was not immediately followed by any measures of structural policy. Then, in 1968, the Commission put forward its Memorandum on the Reform of Agriculture in the EC, commonly called the 'Mansholt Plan' after the name of the Commissioner responsible for agriculture. Its basic aim was to lead to the creation of larger farms, so that high guaranteed prices could be reduced, on the basis that a larger, more efficient unit could provide an adequate income at lower prices. This proposal also indicated that it would involve some 5 million people leaving farming, and that some 5 million hectares should be taken out of production. This proved politically unacceptable as such, but did lead to the enactment in 1972 of a trio of directives which remained in force as the backbone of Community structural policy until 1985.

Council Directive 72/159[7] on the modernization of farms was basically intended to help farmers with low incomes, a criterion adopted also in the new legislation. It was largely implemented in the United Kingdom through the Farm and Horticulture Development Schemes. Council Directive 72/160[8] on measures to encourage the cessation of farming and the reallocation of utilized agricultural area enabled payments to be made to farmers aged between 55 and 65 who left farming, it being required that their land should either be leased or sold to farmers falling within Directive 72/159 or that it should be withdrawn from agricultural use. This was implemented in the United Kingdom under the Farm Amalgamation Scheme. The third of this series was Council Directive 72/161[9] on the provision of socio-economic guidance for and the acquisition of occupational skills by persons engaged in agriculture, the improvement of agricultural skills remaining an objective of the new legislation.

The validity of these directives was successively extended until they were replaced in 1985 by Council Regulation 797/85[10] on improving the efficiency of agricultural structures. This regulation replaced not only the three 1972 directives but also the aid provisions of Council Directive 75/268[11] on mountain and hill farming and farming in less-favoured areas, although, even as originally drafted, these had been treated as 'common measures' under Directive 72/159. While, according to its recitals, Council Regulation 797/85 was made under the agricultural provisions of the EC Treaty, it may be said that in some respects it appeared to be as much related to rural social policy as to agricultural policy in the strict sense. The following year the Single European Act introduced what is now art 159 of the EC Treaty, under which the Guidance Section of the EAGGF forms part of the Structural Funds of the Community, and it is perhaps appropriate that the current legislation in this area, Council Regulation 1257/1999,[12] describes itself as being 'on support for rural development from the EAGGF'. Reflecting also the pervasive nature of environmental protection under art 6 of the EC Treaty, its aim

---

[7] JO 1972 L96/1 (sp edn 1972 (II), p 324).
[8] JO 1972 L96/9 (sp edn 1972 (II), p 332).
[9] JO 1972 L96/15 (sp edn 1972 (II), p 339).
[10] OJ 1985 L93/1.   [11] OJ 1975 L128/1.   [12] OJ 1999 L160/80.

is stated to be to establish the 'framework of Community support for sustainable rural development'.

Investment aid for agricultural holdings may be granted to reduce production costs, to improve and redeploy production, to increase quality, to preserve and improve the natural environment, hygiene conditions, and animal welfare standards, or to promote the diversification of farm activities.[13] To be eligible, the economic viability of the holding must be demonstrated, minimum standards with regard to the environment, hygiene conditions, and animal welfare standards must be complied with, and the farmer must possess adequate occupational skill and competence. Support must not be given however for investment which has as its objective an increase in production for which no normal market outlet can be found.[14] The amount of support is limited to 40 per cent, or 50 per cent in less-favoured areas,[15] though these figures rise to 45 per cent and 55 per cent for investments by young farmers. Young farmers are defined as those under 40 setting up on an agricultural holding for the first time,[16] and, subject to similar conditions as to viability and standards, they may benefit from setting-up aid, either in the form of a single premium or an interest subsidy on loans taken out with a view to covering the costs arising from setting-up. Support may also be given for training, and, at the other end of the scale, for early retirement, which is available for farmers (and farm workers) over 55 but under the normal age of retirement.[17]

Provision is also made for compensatory allowances for farmers in less-favoured areas and in areas with environmental restrictions. Less-favoured areas include both mountain areas[18] (ie areas where either (1) because of altitude, difficult weather conditions substantially shorten the growing season, or (2) at lower altitudes, the slopes are too steep for the use of machinery or require the use of very expensive equipment) and areas which are in danger of abandonment of land-use.[19] They also include areas in which farming should be continued to conserve or improve the environment, maintain the countryside, and preserve the tourist potential of the area, or in order to protect the coastline.[20] Support may also be given for agri-environmental commitments, ie commitments to use agricultural production methods designed to protect the environment and to maintain the countryside.[21] Provision is also made for support for investments to improve the processing and marketing of agricultural products,[22] for forestry, in so far as it contributes to the maintenance and development of the economic, ecological, and social functions of forests in rural areas,[23] and for certain other measures promoting the adaptation and development of rural areas.[24] Overall, Regulation 1257/1999 envisages the drawing up of integrated plans for rural development support measures to be applied in a particular area. These should be drawn up at the most appropriate geographical level, and cover a period of seven years from 1 January 2000.

[13] Art 4.   [14] Art 6.   [15] Art 7.
[16] Art 8.   [17] Arts 10–12.   [18] Art 18.
[19] Art 19.   [20] Art 20.   [21] Art 22.
[22] Art 25.   [23] Art 29.   [24] Art 33.

So far as other national aid measures are concerned, it is expressly provided that the state aid rules in the EC Treaty apply to aid granted by Member States to support rural development. More particularly, investment aids beyond the percentages permitted by the regulation are prohibited, and aids to compensate for natural handicaps in less-favoured areas are prohibited if they do not meet the conditions laid down in the regulation.[25]

Hill farming

One of the more obvious legislative consequences of United Kingdom accession to the Communities was the adoption of Council Directive 75/268[26] on mountain and hill farming and farming in less-favoured areas. The benefits now accorded to such areas under the general structural policy have been explained in the preceding section. Of particular interest in the UK is the definition of 'mountain areas' as areas where either (1) because of altitude, difficult weather conditions substantially shorten the growing season, or (2) at lower altitudes, the slopes are too steep for the use of machinery or require the use of very expensive equipment. Such areas are in fact listed in further directives, which have been continued in force by art 55(4) of Council Regulation 1257/1999. The United Kingdom list is set out in Council Directive 84/169[27] as amended by Council Directive 91/125.[28] This defines the relevant areas by reference in England and Scotland to named parishes falling wholly or partly within such areas (with the additional refinement of certain land falling outside parishes, and isolated farms in some instances), in Wales to 'communities', and in Northern Ireland to 'district electoral divisions'. These units are listed under county names, the names in the English and Welsh list being those which resulted from local government reorganization in the 1970s, the names of the Scottish list however, being those which preceded the introduction of 'regions' under such reorganization, and the further reorganization of the 1990s. In effect, the 'less-favoured areas' would appear to include most of Scotland, apart from the east coast, most of Wales, most of Northern Ireland, the parts of England bordering Scotland and Wales, and much of the north-east, north-west, and south-west of England, in so far as a generalization may be made.

Fisheries

Special structural measures for fisheries are contained in Council Regulation 1263/1999[29] on a Financial Instrument for Fisheries Guidance. This also forms part of the Structural Funds under Council Regulation 1260/1999,[30] and in principle

---

[25] Art 51.   [26] OJ 1975 L128/1.   [27] OJ 1984 L82/67.
[28] OJ 1991 L16/25.   [29] OJ 1999 L161/54.   [30] OJ 1999 L161/1.

it applies to Objective 1 areas.[31] It enables a number of measures to be supported, including fleet renewal and modernization, socio-economic measures, and measures to find and promote new market outlets; it has been further implemented by Council Regulation 2792/1999[32] on structural assistance in the fisheries sector.

The background to this legislation, as with its predecessors,[33] is the adoption by the Commission of multiannual guidance programmes for individual Member States,[34] which are to be implemented through the measures set out in arts 6–12 of the regulation.

Art 6 deals with fleet renewal and modernization, and requires each Member State to submit to the Commission permanent arrangements for monitoring fleet renewal and modernization. Within the framework of these arrangements Member States must either demonstrate that entries and exits from the fleet will be managed in such a way that the capacity does not exceed the annual objectives fixed in the multiannual guidance programme, overall and for the segments concerned, or, where appropriate, that fishing capacity is gradually reduced to attain these objectives. These arrangements must, in particular, take into account that capacity, other than that of vessels of less than 12 metres overall length (excluding trawlers), which has been withdrawn with public aid cannot be replaced. Increases in capacity may only be requested for measures to improve safety, navigation at sea, hygiene, product quality, and working conditions provided that these measures do not result in an increase in the exploitation rate of the resources concerned.

Member States are required under art 7 to take appropriate measures to adjust fishing effort to achieve the objectives of the multiannual guidance programmes. This is to be achieved, where necessary, by stopping vessels' fishing activities permanently or restricting them or a combination of both measures. Measures to stop vessels' fishing activities may be applied only to vessels ten years old or more, and it is provided that the permanent cessation of vessels' fishing activities may be achieved either by the scrapping of the vessel or by its permanent transfer to a third country, including in the framework of a joint enterprise within the meaning of art 8, which is essentially a commercial enterprise registered in a third country involving a Community partner usually with 25–75 per cent of the share capital, and nationals of that third country, operating in the fisheries sector in waters subject to the jurisdiction of that third country. Such a transfer requires the agreement of the competent authorities of the country concerned, provided all the following criteria are met:

- there exist appropriate guarantees that international law is not likely to be infringed, in particular with respect to the conservation and management of marine resources or other objectives of the common fisheries policy and with respect to working conditions of fishermen;

---

[31] Council Regulation 1263/1999, art 2.   [32] OJ 1999 L337/10.
[33] See eg Council Regulation 2908/83 (OJ 1983 L290/1) and Council Regulation 4028/86 (OJ 1986 L376/7).
[34] Council Regulation 2792/1999, art 4.

- the third country to which the vessel is to be transferred is not a country which is a candidate for accession;
- the transfer results in a reduction of fishing effort on the resources previously exploited by the vessel transferred; however, this criterion shall not apply when the vessel transferred has lost fishing possibilities under a fisheries agreement with the Community or under another agreement;
- permanent reassignment of the vessel for purposes other than fishing.

Member States must ensure that the fishing licences of all vessels withdrawn are cancelled and that the withdrawals of the vessels are communicated to the fishing vessel register of the Community. They must also ensure that vessels transferred to third countries and declared as deleted from the register are permanently excluded from fishing in Community waters. Art 7(5) sets out limits on the public aid for final cessation paid to beneficiaries differing according to the age of the vessel and the method of withdrawal.

Furthermore, art 7(7) provides that measures to restrict fishing activities may include restrictions on the fishing days or days at sea authorized for a specific period. Such measures may not give rise to any public aid. On the other hand, art 16 envisages that the Member States may grant compensation to fishermen and owners of vessels for the temporary cessation of activities in the following circumstances:

- in the event of unforeseeable circumstances, particularly those caused by biological factors; the granting of compensation may however last for no more than two months per year or six months over the entire period from 2000 to 2006;
- where a fisheries agreement is not renewed, or where it is suspended, for the Community fleets dependent on the agreement; the granting of compensation may not last longer than six months; it may be extended by a further six months provided a conversion plan approved by the Commission is implemented for the fleet concerned;
- where a plan is introduced for the recovery of a resource threatened with exhaustion, decided by the Commission or by one or some Member States; the granting of compensation may last for no more than two years and may be extended by a further year.

Under art 16(2), the Member States may also grant financial compensation to fishermen and owners of vessels where a Council decision imposes technical restrictions on the use of certain gear or fishing methods; this aid is intended to cover the technical adjustment and may not be paid for more than six months. However, none of the aid under art 16 may be invoked as contributing to the attainment of the objectives of the multiannual guidance programme, and the financial contribution from the FIFG to the measures referred to in art 16 per Member State for the entire period from 2000 to 2006 may not exceed the higher of €1 million or 4 per cent of the Community financial assistance allocated to the sector in the Member State concerned.

Returning to the objectives of the multiannual guidance programme, there is very restricted provision for public aid for fleet renewal and modernization of fishing vessels. Under art 9, and only provided that the overall annual objectives of the multiannual guidance programme are respected, Member States must ensure that during the programming period from 2000 to 2006 the entry of new capacity with public aid is compensated by the withdrawal of a capacity without public aid which is at least equal to the new capacity introduced in the segments concerned. However, public aid may also be granted for the equipping or modernizing of vessels where this does not concern capacity measured in terms of either tonnage or power.

On the other hand, where a group of owners of vessels or families of fishermen involved in small-scale coastal fisheries (fishing carried on by vessels of an overall length of less than 12 metres) cooperatively implement an integrated collective project to develop or modernize this fishing activity, a lump-sum premium part-financed by the FIFG may be granted to the participants.[35] Integrated collective projects in this context include: safety equipment on board and improvement of sanitary and working conditions; technological innovations (more selective fishing techniques); organization of the production, processing, and marketing chain (promotion and added value of the products); and professional requalification or training.

What are termed 'socio-economic' measures are also envisaged, some of them paralleling what is available under Council Regulation 1257/1999[36] on rural development discussed above. Under art 12 of Council Regulation 2792/1999,[37] financial assistance from the FIFG may be granted for part-financing of national early retirement schemes for fishermen, provided that, at the time of early retirement, the age of the beneficiaries of the measure must be not more than ten years from the legal retirement age within the meaning of the legislation in force in the Member State, or the beneficiaries must be aged at least 55, and the beneficiaries can show that they have worked for at least ten years as fishermen. However, in each Member State, for the entire programming period the number of beneficiaries may not exceed the number of jobs eliminated on board fishing vessels as a result of those vessels permanently stopping fishing activities within the meaning of art 7.

Financial assistance from the FIFG may also be granted for part-financing of individual compensatory payments to fishermen who can show that they have worked for at least twelve months as fishermen, on the basis of an eligible cost limited to €10,000 per individual beneficiary, provided the vessel on which the beneficiaries were employed has been the object of measures permanently stopping its activities, within the meaning of art 7. Such assistance is also available to grant non-renewable individual compensatory payments to fishermen who can show that they have worked for at least five years as fishermen, to help them retrain or diversify their activities outside maritime fisheries under an individual or

---

[35] Art 11.   [36] OJ 1999 L160/80.   [37] OJ 1999 L337/10.

collective social plan, on the basis of an eligible cost limited to €50,000 per individual beneficiary.

FIFG financial assistance is also available to grant individual premiums to fishermen younger than 35 years who can demonstrate that they have worked at least five years as fishermen or can demonstrate equivalent vocational training and who acquire for the first time part or total ownership in a fishing vessel, provided that the fishing vessel has an overall length between 7 and 24 metres, it is aged between ten and twenty years at the time of acquisition of ownership, operational and registered in the fishing vessel register of the Community; also, the transfer of ownership must not occur within the same family up to the second degree. In any event, the amount of the premium may not exceed 10 per cent of the cost of acquisition of ownership nor exceed the amount of €50,000.

Outside the multiannual guidance programme, art 13 of Council Regulation 2792/1999[38] empowers Member States to take measures to encourage capital investment in the fields of: fixed or movable facilities aimed at the protection and development of aquatic resources, except restocking; aquaculture; fishing port facilities; processing and marketing of fishery and aquaculture products; and inland fishing. However, in this context, financial assistance from the FIFG may be granted only for projects which contribute to lasting economic benefits from the structural improvement in question, offer an adequate guarantee of technical and economic viability, and avoid counterproductive effects, particularly the risk of creating surplus production capacity.

Finally, arts 14 and 15 respectively encourage measures to find and promote new markets, and to encourage the operation of producer organizations, which will be considered in the following sections, and art 17 encourages certain innovative measures and technical assistance, including experimental fishing projects, 'provided their aim is the conservation of fishery resources and they implement more selective techniques'. The pervasive influence of the requirement to take account of environmental considerations under art 6 of the EC Treaty is therefore felt here as elsewhere in the context of structural measures of agricultural policy.

Processing and marketing

Council Regulation 1257/1999[39] on support for rural development from the EAGGF has subsumed within itself the previously separate legislation on common measures to improve the conditions under which agricultural products are processed and marketed.[40] Art 25 provides for support for investment which facilitates the improvement and rationalization of processing and marketing of agricultural

---

[38] OJ 1999 L337/10.   [39] OJ 1999 L160/80.
[40] Council Regulations 355/77 (OJ 1977 L51/1), 866/90 (OJ 1990 L91/1), and 951/97 (OJ 1997 L142/1).

products, thereby contributing to increasing the competitiveness and added value of such products. Such support must contribute to one or more of the following objectives: to guide production in line with foreseeable market trends or encourage the development of new outlets for agricultural products; to improve or rationalize marketing channels or processing procedures; to improve the presentation and preparation of products or encourage the better use or elimination of by-products or waste; to apply new technologies; to favour innovative investments; to improve and monitor quality; to improve and monitor health conditions; and to protect the environment—whose pervasive influence is therefore again clearly shown.

Under art 26, support is to be granted to those persons ultimately responsible for financing the investment in enterprises for which economic viability can be demonstrated, and which comply with minimum standards regarding the environment, hygiene, and animal welfare. Furthermore, sufficient evidence must be shown that normal market outlets for the products concerned can be found. This system of support for investment does not however apply to fishery products,[41] which rather fall within the scope of Council Regulation 2792/1999[42] on structural assistance in the fisheries sector; neither does it apply to investment at the retail level, or (fairly obviously) to investment in the processing or marketing of products from third countries.[43] In any event, the total amount of support, expressed as a percentage of the volume of eligible investment, is limited to a maximum of 50 per cent in Objective 1 regions and 40 per cent in the other regions.[44]

More specific promotional measures are envisaged in Council Regulation 2826/2000 on information and promotion actions for agricultural products on the internal market[45] and Council Regulation 2702/1999 on measures to provide information on, and promote, agricultural products in third countries.[46] In many ways these are similarly drafted, and have the common concern of ensuring that they do not promote brand names or the products of any one Member State.[47] The internal market regulation allows Community finance, in whole or in part, of: public relations work, promotion, and advertising, which in particular draws attention to intrinsic features and advantages of Community products, notably the quality and safety of food, specific production methods, nutritional and health value, labelling, high animal welfare standards, and respect for the environment; participation in events, fairs, and exhibitions of national or European importance, in particular with stands aimed at upgrading the image of Community products; actions of information notably on the Community systems covering protected designation of origin (PDO), protected geographical indication (PGI), guaranteed traditional specialities (GTSs), organic production, labelling, as well as on the graphic symbols laid down in legislation, in particular for extremely remote regions; actions of information on the Community system covering quality wines produced

---

[41] Art 27(1).   [42] OJ 1999 L337/10.   [43] Art 28(1).
[44] Art 28(2).   [45] OJ 2000 L328/2.   [46] OJ 1999 L327/7.
[47] Art 1 of both regulations.

in specified regions (quality wines psr), wines with geographical indication and spirit drinks with geographical indication, or reserved traditional indication; and studies to assess the results of the promotion and information activities.[48] The sectors and products which may be covered by these actions are to be determined having regard to: the desirability of drawing attention to the quality, typical features, specific production method, nutritional and health value, safety, welfare or environment-friendliness of the products in question, by means of thematic or target-specific campaigns; the implementation of a consumer information labelling system and of product traceability and control systems; the need to tackle specific or short-term difficulties in individual sectors; the desirability of providing information on the Community PDO/PGI, GTS, and organic production schemes; the desirability of providing information on the Community system covering quality wines psr, wines with geographical indication and spirit drinks with geographical indication, or reserved traditional indication.[49] It is further envisaged that the professional and/or interprofessional organizations representing the sectors concerned are to draw up an information and promotion programme of a maximum duration of thirty-six months. Such a programme may cover one or more interested Member States, and may be from a European-level organization or an organization spanning one or more Member States;[50] the latter programmes are to have priority.

Council Regulation 2702/1999 on measures to provide information on, and promote, agricultural products in third countries[51] follows much the same pattern, except that it is expressly required that products intended for direct consumption or processing for which export opportunities or potential new market outlets in third countries exist, especially where export refunds will not be required, and typical or quality products displaying high added value in particular shall be eligible for the measures referred to.[52] It is also provided that in choosing the third countries in which the measures will be carried out, account shall be taken of the markets of countries where there is actual or potential demand.[53]

So far as fishery products are concerned, art 14 of Council Regulation 2792/1999[54] on structural assistance in the fisheries sector empowers Member States to take measures to encourage collective operations to find and promote new market outlets for fishery and aquaculture products, in particular: operations associated with quality certification, product labelling, rationalization of product names, and product standardization; promotion campaigns, including those highlighting quality; projects to test consumer and market reactions; organization of and participation in trade fairs and exhibitions; organization of study and sales visits; market studies and surveys, including studies relating to the prospects for marketing Community products in third countries; campaigns improving marketing conditions; sales advice and aids, services provided to wholesalers, retailers, and producer organizations.

---

[48] Art 2.   [49] Art 3.   [50] Art 6.
[51] OJ 1999 L327/7.   [52] Art 3.   [53] Art 4.
[54] OJ 1999 L337/10.

However, art 14(2) makes it clear that priority is to be given to investments to encourage the sale of surplus or underexploited species, or implemented by producer organizations officially recognized under Council Regulation 104/2000,[55] or jointly implemented by several producer organizations or other organizations of the sector recognized by national authorities, or pursuing a quality policy for fishery and aquaculture products, or to promote products obtained using environmentally friendly methods.

As under Council Regulation 2826/2000 on information and promotion actions for agricultural products on the internal market[56] and Council Regulation 2702/1999 on measures to provide information on, and promote, agricultural products in third countries,[57] the measures supported under art 14 of Council Regulation 2792/1999[58] on structural assistance in the fisheries sector must not be based around commercial brands nor make reference to particular countries or a geographic zone, except in specific cases where official recognition of origin with reference to a specified geographical zone for a product or process is granted pursuant to Council Regulation 2081/92 on the protection of geographical indications and designations of origin for agricultural products and foodstuffs.[59]

It might finally be observed that although it is not a marketing measure as such, Council Regulation 2092/91 on organic production[60] may be seen as serving a structural purpose. Its recitals explain that the market price for such products is higher, and the way in which they are produced involves less intensive use of land. Therefore, in the context of the reorientation of the common agricultural policy, 'this type of production may contribute towards the attainment of a better balance between supply of, and demand for, agricultural products, the protection of the environment and the conservation of the countryside'.

Producer organizations

Mention has already been made of the role to be played by producer organizations in the support mechanisms of certain common organizations of the market, such as those concerned with the marketing of fishery products under Council Regulation 104/2000[61] or with the marketing of fruit and vegetables, where, under Council Regulation 2200/96,[62] certain marketing rules can even be extended to non-members. Their role will also be considered in the context of the administration of the common agricultural policy.[63]

The encouragement of producer organizations may also be regarded as aiding the improvement of agricultural structures, although the recitals to Council Regulation 1257/1999 on support for rural development from the EAGGF[64]

[55] OJ 2000 L17/22.   [56] OJ 2000 L328/2.   [57] OJ 1999 L327/7.
[58] OJ 1999 L337/10.   [59] OJ 1992 L208/1.   [60] OJ 1992 L198/1.
[61] OJ 2000 L17/22.   [62] OJ 1996 L297/1.   [63] See Chapter 9 below.
[64] OJ 1999 L160/80.

declare that in view of existing aid to producer groups and their associations in several common organizations of the market, specific support to producer groups in the framework of rural development 'no longer appears to be necessary', and that the aid scheme under Council Regulation 952/97[65] on producer groups and associations thereof (which can be traced back to 1978[66]) should be discontinued.[67]

However, a clear example of sector-specific support for producer organizations may be found in the fisheries market. Art 15 of Council Regulation 2792/1999[68] on structural assistance in the fisheries sector authorizes Member States to encourage the creation and facilitate the operation of producer organizations recognized under Council Regulation 104/2000 on the common organization of the market in fishery and aquaculture products.[69] More specifically, aid can be granted to producer organizations created after 1 January 2000 for three years following the date of recognition. This aid for the first, second, and third years must be within both the following limits: 3 per cent, 2 per cent, and 1 per cent respectively of the value of the products marketed by the producer organization, and 60 per cent, 40 per cent, and 20 per cent respectively of the administrative costs of the producer organization. Such aid is to be paid to the final beneficiaries during the year following that for which it was granted, and not later than 31 December 2008.

The Member States may also encourage short-term operations of collective interest with a broader scope than operations normally undertaken by private businesses, carried out with the active contribution of members of the trade themselves or carried out by organizations acting on behalf of the producers or by other organizations having been recognized by the management authority, and serving to attain the objectives of the common fisheries policy. Under art 15(3), eligible operations relate in particular to: management and control of conditions for access to certain fishing zones and quota management; management of fishing effort; promotion of gear or methods recognized by the management authority as being more selective; promotion of technical measures for the conservation of resources; promotion of measures improving the working conditions and the sanitary conditions concerning the products, on board and landed; collective aquaculture facilities, restructuring or improvement of aquaculture sites, collective treatment of aquaculture effluent; eradication of the pathological risks of fish farming or parasites in catchment areas or coastal ecosystems; collection of basic data and/or preparation of environmental management models for fisheries and aquaculture with a view to drawing up integrated management plans for coastal areas; organization of electronic trade and other information technologies to disseminate technical and commercial information; creation of 'business incubators' in the sector and/or centres for the collection of fishery and aquaculture products; access to training, particularly in quality, and organization of transmission of know-how on board

[65] OJ 1997 L142/30.
[66] Council Regulation 1360/78 (OJ 1978 L166/1).
[67] Recital 44.   [68] OJ 1999 L337/10.   [69] OJ 2000 L17/22.

vessels and on land; design and application of systems to improve and control quality, traceability, health conditions, statistical instruments, and environmental impact; creation of added value in products (inter alia, through experimentation, innovation, the addition of value to by-products and co-products); and, finally, improvement of knowledge and transparency in production and in the market. Despite the breadth of this list, it is made clear that expenditure incurred in the normal production process is not eligible.

Structural Funds

It has long been realized that there is an obvious utility, at least in the poorer areas of the Community, in bringing together the various sources of Community finance to promote common activity. However, the first group of measures to refer expressly to integrated programmes, which included Council Regulation 1939/81[70] on an integrated development programme for the Western Isles (Outer Hebrides), eventually involved only the financial participation of the Guidance Section of the European Agricultural Guidance and Guarantee Fund (EAGGF). It was intended to aid agriculture, fisheries, tourist amenities, crafts, and industrial and 'other complementary activities essential to the improvement of the socio-economic situation', and enabled the Guidance Section of the EAGGF to finance up to 40 per cent of the costs of projects for the improvement of agricultural structures, the planting of windbreaks, the improvement of marketing and processing of agricultural products, the improvement of agricultural infrastructure, the provision of shore facilities for inshore fisheries, and the development of aquaculture.

The pilot actions for integrated Mediterranean programmes, on the other hand, initiated by Council Decisions 84/70 to 84/82,[71] whilst clearly only pilot actions, did enable the Commission to use EAGGF, Social Fund, Regional Development Fund, or fisheries restructuring appropriations, or a special budgetary line within the limits of available budgetary resources. These pilot schemes were subject to specific decisions of the Commission on individual projects, the decisions themselves fixing the Community's contributions to their financing. The schemes eventually led to the adoption of Council Regulation 2088/85[72] concerning integrated Mediterranean programmes, and may be regarded as the precursors of the current system of Structural Funds.

The Single European Act 1986 introduced what is now art 159 of the EC Treaty, under which the Guidance Section of the EAGGF forms part of the Structural Funds of the Community, together with the European Social Fund and the European Regional Development Fund. It was suggested above that it is perhaps appropriate that the current legislation in this area, Council Regulation 1257/1999,[73] describes

---

[70] OJ 1981 L197/6. [71] OJ 1984 L44/1. [72] OJ 1985 L197/1.
[73] OJ 1999 L160/80.

itself as being 'on support for rural development from the EAGGF'. Under Council Regulation 1258/1999 on the financing of the common agricultural policy,[74] in principle the Guidance Section finances only rural development measures falling within Objective 1 programmes and the rural development Community initiative. Regulation 1260/1999[75] on the Structural Funds defines Objective 1 as covering those areas where GDP per capita in terms of purchasing power is less than 75 per cent of the Community average,[76] and it is provided that 69.7 per cent of the €195 billion allocated to the Structural Funds for 2000–2006 should go on Objective 1 projects.[77]

Development aid

While it may seem perverse to mention development aid in the context of the EC domestic system of agricultural guidance and structural measures, it may be recalled that the common organization of the market in bananas under Council Regulation 404/93[78] is to a large extent concerned with the situation of ACP banana producers linked to the EC under the Lomé and Cotonou Conventions. As that common organization began to be amended in an endeavour to bring it into line with WTO requirements,[79] it was felt that such modifications would alter the market conditions for traditional ACP suppliers, and might in particular harm the most disadvantaged suppliers. Council Regulation 856/1999[80] therefore established a special framework of assistance for traditional ACP suppliers of bananas, enabling technical and financial assistance to be granted at the request of the ACP to contribute to the implementation of programmes aiming to improve competitiveness in the banana sector, or to support diversification where improvement in the competitiveness of the banana sector is not sustainable.[81] However, although it relates to a common organization of an agricultural market, this regulation was adopted not as a matter of agricultural law under art 37 but as a matter of development cooperation under what is now art 179 (formerly art 130w) of the EC Treaty.

---

[74] OJ 1999 L160/103. [75] OJ 1999 L161/1. [76] Art 3.
[77] Art 4. [78] OJ 1993 L47/1. [79] See Chapter 3 above.
[80] OJ 1999 L108/2. [81] Art 3.

9

Administration of the common agricultural policy

The basic pattern of implementation

Although art 37 of the EC Treaty conferred specific powers on the Commission to make proposals during the early stages of the original transitional period, power to issue agricultural legislation was conferred only on the Council. The exercise of this power is subject to consultation with the European Parliament.[1] In Case 138/79 *Roquette Frères SA v Council*[2] the Court of Justice held that it was a breach of that requirement not to wait for the Parliament's opinion after a proposal had been sent to that body, even if the Council was not ultimately obliged to follow the Parliament's opinion. However, the Parliament is subject to a duty of loyal cooperation, and may not delay giving an opinion on proposals which it knows to be a matter of urgency.[3]

It was noted at the beginning of this book that art 37 provided for qualified majority voting as from 1 January 1966, and can, therefore, be linked to the French failure to attend Council meetings in the second half of 1965, leading to the 'Luxembourg Accords' of January 1966, in which France recorded its view that 'where very important interests are at stake the discussion must be continued until unanimous agreement is reached'. Whilst this view was, in effect, treated as a constitutional convention during the 1970s, although it had no force in law, in 1982 agricultural price legislation was adopted by the Council on a qualified majority vote, despite the fact that the United Kingdom invoked the Luxembourg Accords.[4] Although, subsequently, qualified majorities have not always been sought or obtained where they could have been used, they have become the norm in practice. Indeed, as mentioned in Chapter 1 in the area of health protection, the United Kingdom brought Case 68/86 *UK v Council*[5] seeking the annulment of Council Directive 85/649[6] prohibiting the use in livestock farming of certain substances having a hormonal action, claiming that it should have been adopted under the general harmonization procedure of art 94, which required unanimity, rather than

---

[1] EC Treaty, art 37(2).   [2] [1980] ECR 3333.
[3] Case C-65/93 *EP v Council* [1995] ECR I-643.
[4] For a critical account, see B Hill, *The Common Agricultural Policy: Past, Present, and Future* (1984) 134–136.
[5] [1988] ECR 855.   [6] OJ 1985 L382/228.

by a qualified majority under art 37. However, July 1987 saw the entry into force of art 95 introduced into the EC Treaty by art 18 of the Single European Act, allowing the Council to adopt measures for the approximation of laws by a qualified majority, and, in the current version, in co-decision with the European Parliament, for the purpose of establishing the internal market. More specifically, art 152 of the EC Treaty, as amended by the Treaty of Amsterdam, allows the adoption by qualified majority and co-decision of measures, 'by way of derogation from art 37', in the veterinary and phytosanitary fields which have as their direct objective the protection of public health.

A further aspect of the Community legislative process which is particularly illustrated in the context of agriculture is its sectoral nature: Community agriculture legislation is normally adopted by a Council composed of ministers of agriculture, whose meetings are prepared not by the usual Committee of Permanent Representatives expressly recognized in art 207 of the EC Treaty, but by a 'Special Committee for Agriculture' composed of senior national civil servants responsible for agricultural matters.[7]

Under the regulations establishing common organizations of agricultural markets enacted pursuant to art 37, the Council does generally retain a limited number of powers for itself. While in modern common organizations prices and payments are set for more than one marketing year at a time, in the earlier common organizations the Council used in particular to retain the power to fix the basic target and intervention prices for each marketing year. It is notorious that these price decisions were not always taken in time, so that previous marketing years were often deemed to continue for a while longer, and a particular problem arose in 1985 when it was proposed by the Commission, for the first time, that cereal prices expressed in European currency units should actually be reduced. The Council was unable to reach agreement on the matter by the appropriate date, but, whilst it may be possible to 'stop the clock' when prices are likely to rise or stay the same, and pay the previous year's prices on a temporary basis, much greater difficulty arises if the aim is to reduce the guaranteed prices. If the previous year's prices were to be paid in such a case, producers would be paid an excessive price, part of which would have to be recovered once the new lower prices were agreed. The matter came to a head in June 1985 since, under the version of art 3 of Regulation 2727/75[8] then in force, the intervention prices valid on 1 June in Greece, Italy, and certain regions of France had to be adjusted in the light of the intervention prices fixed for August, which was then the first month of the new marketing year. In the light of the Council's failure to act on its proposals, the Commission, on 20 June 1985, adopted Decision 85/309[9] on 'precautionary measures' with regard to the buying-in of cereals in Greece, Italy, and those regions

---

[7] For the history of this Committee, see E Neville-Rolfe, *The Politics of Agriculture in the European Community* (1984) 208.

[8] OJ 1975 L281/1.   [9] OJ 1985 L163/52.

of France, requiring the Member States to reduce certain of the previous year's prices by 1.8 per cent. This was replaced by Commission Regulation 2124/85,[10] adopted on 26 July 1985 (ie just before the start of the marketing year), applying general 'precautionary measures' (in other words, fixing lower prices) in the cereals sector other than durum wheat. In October 1985, the Commission exercised its express power under art 13 of Regulation 2727/75 to fix import levies on cereals, adopting in Regulation 2956/85[11] levies calculated from the basic prices it had itself enacted. The outline history may be completed by stating that no Council legislation was adopted in the matter until Council Regulation 1584/86 of 23 May 1986,[12] fixing the cereal prices for the 1986–1987 marketing year, which expressly continued some of the prices fixed by the Commission.

In adopting its 'precautionary measures' the Commission declared, in the recitals both to the decision and to the subsequent regulation, that it was acting under what are now arts 10 and 211 of the EC Treaty. Art 10 requires the Member States to take all appropriate measures to ensure fulfilment of the obligation resulting from the action taken by the institutions of the Community, to facilitate the achievement of the Community's tasks, and to abstain from any measure which could jeopardize the attainment of the objectives of the Treaty, whereas art 211 empowers the Commission, inter alia, to ensure that the provisions of the Treaty and the measures taken by the institutions pursuant thereto are applied. Presumably, therefore, the rationale of the Commission's action was that the failure of Member States in Council to fix the cereal prices in due time constituted a breach of their duties under art 10, and that the Commission's duty under art 211 was to ensure the application of the common organization of the market in cereals. What is, however, particularly remarkable is that no direct challenge to the Commission's legislation was mounted either by the Council as such or by any of the Member States, nor does it seem to have been attacked by individual traders or producers through the national courts.

The Commission did show itself willing to follow its own precedent, since in 1987, when it seemed that agreement in the Council was unlikely, the Commission again adopted a series of regulations[13] on precautionary measures, expressed to be without prejudice to the ultimate decisions to be taken by the Council. In this case, however, the Council did reach agreement in July 1987. Be that as it may, it has already been observed that in modern common organizations prices and payments are usually set for more than one marketing year at a time, so the scope for the Commission to take 'precautionary measures' with regard to prices and payments has been considerably diminished.

---

[10] OJ 1985 L198/31.   [11] OJ 1985 L285/8.   [12] OJ 1986 L139/41.
[13] Commission Regulations 1213/87 (OJ 1987 L115/33), 1503/87 (OJ 1987 L141/13), and 1826/87 (OJ 1987 L173/7).

Management committees system

The power to enact most implementing legislation in relation to common organizations is expressly delegated by the Council to the Commission, as authorized under art 211 of the EC Treaty. Hence the vast majority of the thousands of Community agricultural regulations have been issued by the Commission. In practice, the Council has delegated not only powers of simple administration, but also powers requiring the exercise of discretion. In this latter case, however, it has usually required the Commission to consult a committee representing national interests, known as a 'management committee', established for each common organization.

The general rules governing the management committee procedure are laid down in Council Decision 1999/468[14] on the procedures for the exercise of implementing powers conferred on the Commission, which follows the pattern first laid down in the cereals market and currently set out in arts 22 to 24 of Council Regulation 1766/92[15] on the common organization of the market in cereals. It consists of representatives of the Member States (normally civil servants responsible for the particular market), with a representative of the Commission as chairman. The national representatives have votes weighted in accordance with the qualified majority procedure laid down in art 205(2) of the EC Treaty. Where the Commission is required to act under this procedure, it must submit a draft of the measures to be adopted to the committee, which must deliver its opinion within the time limit set by the chairman. A qualified majority as defined in art 205(2) is required for the committee to give either a favourable opinion or an unfavourable opinion. To take as an example the information published in the Commission's 1999 General Report,[16] the various agricultural committees gave in that year a total of 1,618 favourable opinions and three unfavourable opinions, a situation which would appear to be not untypical. If, however, the committee does issue an opinion which is unfavourable, the Commission is not prevented from putting its measures into operation; it must refer the matter to the Council itself, but it has a discretion whether or not to defer the application of its measures. The Council, in turn, may take a different decision by a qualified majority within a month, but if it fails to do so, the Commission's measures remain in force. In practice, this power has hardly ever been used.

The legality of the management committee system was challenged in Case 25/70 *Einfuhr- und Vorratsstelle für Getreide und Futtermittel v Köster, Berodt & Co*[17] on the basis that it interposed between the Council and the Commission a body which was not provided for by the Treaty. The Court, however, held that it formed part of the detailed rules to which the Council could legitimately subject a delegation of power to the Commission. The basis of the Court's decision was that the management committee system was really a method of permanent consultation

---

[14] OJ 1999 L184/23.   [15] OJ 1992 L181/21.   [16] At pp 181–182.
[17] [1970] ECR 1161.

between the Council and the Commission.The committee had no power to take a decision in place of the Council or the Commission, and the system had the beneficial effect of enabling the Council to delegate to the Commission an implementing power of appreciable scope. In the result, similar, if not identical, committees have been established in relation to other areas of Community legislation, and the management committee system is one of the patterns for conferring implementing powers on the Commission recognized in Council Decision 1999/468.[18]

This recognizes three basic procedures: the first, the advisory procedure, merely requires the Commission to obtain the opinion of the relevant committee, the second, effectively, reproduces the 'management-committee' system outlined above, and the third, the regulatory procedure, in principle requires the Commission to obtain the consent of the relevant committee before it can act. On the other hand, the 'safeguard procedure' under art 6 of the decision requires the Commission to notify the Council and the Member States before adopting safeguard measures, and the Council itself may either be empowered to take a different decision by qualified majority, or to confirm, amend, or revoke the decision by qualified majority. In any event, where the Commission is acting under powers conferred by a measure adopted by co-decision procedure, where the European Parliament takes the view that draft implementing measures would exceed the implementing powers under the basic instrument, it may adopt a resolution requiring the Commission to re-examine the measures.

What the Commission may not do, however, is to sub-delegate powers which it should exercise through the management committee system so as, in effect, to circumvent that procedure.This appears from Case 23/75 *Rey Soda v Cassa Conguaglio Zucchero*,[19] where the Court was concerned, in fact, with a sub-delegation of powers by the Commission to the Italian government.The provision in question was art 6 of Regulation 834/74.[20] This provided that 'Italy shall take national measures to prevent disturbances on the market resulting from the increase on 1 July 1974 in the price of sugar expressed in Italian lire.These provisions shall consist in particular of a payment to beet growers of the increased value of stocks.'The action with which the Court was concerned was a reference from an Italian court before which the applicant was seeking to recover the amounts which he had had to pay to the Italian sugar authority under the Italian legislation made subsequent to this provision.

It was held that the Commission should have defined in its regulation what was meant by 'stock' and by 'increased value', but, most importantly, the Court stated that by not specifying the bases of the calculation of the tax in the provision in question, and leaving Italy to choose them, the Commission discharged itself of its own responsibility to adopt the basic rules and to submit them by way of the management committee procedure to the approval, if need be, of the Council; therefore, the article was invalid. On the other hand, many examples can, of course, be found of Community agricultural legislation which directly confers discretionary

---

[18] OJ 1999 L184/23.   [19] [1975] ECR 1279.   [20] OJ 1974 L99/15.

powers on the Member States, particularly in the context of sugar and milk quotas. Indeed, in Cases 103–109/78 *Société des Usines de Beauport v Council*,[21] it was held that Council Regulation 298/78,[22] amending the basic regulation on the allocation and alteration of the basic quotas for sugar, was not of 'direct and individual concern' to the applicants in terms of art 230 of the EC Treaty[23] precisely because that regulation allowed France a discretion whether or not to reduce the basic quotas fixed for sugar producers in its overseas departments, and also as to whether the basic quotas of all or only of certain undertakings were to be reduced.

Control functions of the European Agricultural Guidance and Guarantee Fund and the Commission

The Commission has frequently used its general power under art 226 of the EC Treaty to take enforcement proceedings against Member States with regard to breaches of agricultural legislation. To the extent that the relevant substantive rules apply to agriculture, the Commission may also use its normal methods of enforcing the competition rules under arts 81 and 82 of the Treaty and the state aids rules under arts 87 to 89.

However, a distinctive feature of the agricultural sector is the degree of financial control which may be exercised by the Commission through the European Agricultural Guidance and Guarantee Fund. This arises from the fact that the Member States are responsible, under the system of own resources, for the collection of agricultural levies and Common Customs Tariff duties,[24] and from the fact that the various common organizations make them responsible for the payment of intervention purchases, refunds, aids, and other things. They are also responsible for making the direct payments to producers outlined in the context of the common organizations of the market discussed above.[25] The legal possibilities of this situation were clearly revealed in a group of cases brought by the Netherlands,[26] Germany,[27] and France[28] against the Commission for the annulment of Commission decisions relating to the discharge of accounts with regard to the expenditure of the Guarantee Section of the fund.

The legal basis under which the European Agricultural Guidance and Guarantee Fund (EAGGF) should become liable for agricultural expenditure was

---

[21] [1979] ECR 17.   [22] OJ 1978 L45/1.

[23] See JA Usher, 'Judicial Review of Community Acts and the Private Litigant' in AIL Campbell and M Voyatzi (eds), *Legal Reasoning and Judicial Interpretation of European Law: Essays in Honour of Lord Mackenzie-Stuart* (1996) 121–148.

[24] See Council Decision 2000/597 (OJ 2000 L253/42), art 8.

[25] Council Regulation 1259/1999 (OJ 1999 L160/113) establishing common rules for direct support schemes under the common agricultural policy.

[26] Case 11/76 *Netherlands v Commission* [1979] ECR 245.

[27] Case 18/76 *Germany v Commission* [1979] ECR 343.

[28] Joined Cases 15, 16/76 *France v Commission* [1979] ECR 321.

at issue in the cases brought by the Netherlands and Germany. Council Regulation 1258/1999[29] on the financing of the common agricultural policy, which replaces the similarly worded legislation at issue in these cases,[30] states that the Guarantee Section is to finance refunds on exports to third countries and intervention intended to stabilize the agricultural markets,[31] and provides more specifically for the financing of refunds on exports to third countries granted in accordance with Community rules within the framework of the common organization of agricultural markets.[32] It also provides for the financing of intervention intended to stabilize the agricultural markets undertaken according to Community rules within the framework of the common organization of agricultural markets.[33] The provision invoked by the Dutch and German governments, however, was art 8(2), the first paragraph of which is to the effect that, in the absence of total recovery, the financial consequences of irregularities or negligence are to be borne by the Community, with the exception of the consequences of irregularities or negligences attributable to administrative authorities or other bodies of the Member States. The two governments argued that this provision must be taken to mean that the Community must bear the financial consequences of an incorrect interpretation of a provision of Community law by a national authority where the interpretation was adopted in good faith and was not the 'fault', in the sense of a wrongful action, of that national authority.

After looking at the different language versions of art 8, the Court reached a conclusion which gives rise to concern with regard to the drafting and translation of Community legislation. It found that art 8 'contains too many contradictory and ambiguous elements to provide an answer to the questions at issue'. Looking at the whole of art 8 in its context, however, the Court found that it was concerned with the prevention of fraud and irregularities, and with the recovery of sums wrongly paid. Without going so far as to say, with the Commission (and Advocate General Capotorti), that art 8(2) refers only to irregularities or negligence on the part of individuals, the Court found there to be a general principle common to the Community legal system and to 'most' of the national legal systems that it was not possible to recover from the recipients sums paid in error by the national authorities on the basis of an incorrect interpretation of Community law adopted by them in good faith. From this it concluded that art 8(2) did not apply to such a situation, it being concerned with recovery. On the basis that art 8(2) could not apply, the Court held that the situation should be considered in the light of arts 2 and 3 of the regulation, requiring the Community to finance refunds granted and intervention undertaken 'in accordance with the Community rules'. From this, given that the sums at issue were not only refunds

[29] OJ 1999 L110/13.
[30] Council Regulation 729/70 (OJ 1970 L94/13 (sp edn 1970 (I), p 218)).
[31] Art 1(2).
[32] Art 2(1).
[33] Art 2(2), formerly art 3(1)of Reg 729/70.

or intervention payments, the broader principle was deduced that the Commission could charge to the fund 'only sums paid in accordance with the rules laid down in the various sectors of agricultural production while leaving the Member States to bear the burden of any other sum paid', in particular, any amounts which the national authorities wrongly believed themselves authorized to pay in the context of the common organization of the market. This strict, indeed absolute, rule was justified on the grounds that a Member State should not be able to favour its own traders by a wide interpretation of a provision of Community law, and certainly should not be able to do so with Community finance.

Although a detailed analysis of the items of expenditure at issue in these cases would be out of place, given their highly specific nature, a general consideration of them may furnish useful examples of the way in which the rule was applied by the Court: indeed, only one item was held to be liable to be financed by the EAGGF.

The first item in the Dutch case[34] concerned the release of securities lodged to ensure the export within thirty days of 'sale' of intervention butter sold at reduced prices under Commission Regulation 1308/68.[35] The Dutch government had allowed the securities to be released where the butter was exported thirty days after removal from storage, whereas the Commission took the view that it should have been exported within thirty days of the contract of sale. The Court of Justice held quite simply that 'sale' meant sale and not removal, and hence that the European Agricultural Guidance and Guarantee Fund (EAGGF) was not liable to meet the cost of repayment of the securities. The same point also arose in the German case[36] and was answered in the same way. The second item in the Dutch case involved payments of export refunds for lactalbumin, a product in the milk sector, under legislation which the Court had held in Case 150/73 *Hollandse Melksuikerfabriek v Hoofdproduktschap voor Akkerbouwprodukten*[37] only to apply to ovalbumin, a product in the egg sector. Although it was accepted that there might be doubts as to the exact scope of that legislation, it was found that its incorrect application was not the result of the Commission's conduct. Hence the refunds could not be charged to the EAGGF.

The first item in the French cases[38] involved the payments of aid for skimmed milk powder exported from France to Italy and intended for use as animal feed, where the aids had been paid without the production of the control copies of the Community transit document, as required under the relevant legislation. It would appear that this lapse had later been rectified; but the Court held that aid which has been paid in disregard of a condition that certain formalities relating to proof be complied with at the time of payment is not paid in accordance with Community law and therefore cannot be charged to the EAGGF. The second aspect

[34] Case 11/76 *Netherlands v Commission* [1979] ECR 245.
[35] JO 1968 L214/10.
[36] Case 18/76 *Germany v Commission* [1979] ECR 343.
[37] [1973] ECR 1633.
[38] Joined Cases 15 and 16/76 *France v Commission* [1979] ECR 321.

of the French cases involved the payment of aids for the distillation of wines. The French government had taken the view that the aids payable to this end under Council Regulation 766/72[39] were inadequate, and supplemented them with national aids. The Commission then initiated the procedure under art 226 of the EC Treaty against France in relation to the breach of a Treaty obligation involved in the payment of national aids, but did not pursue the matter when the aids ceased to be paid. However, when it came to the discharge of the EAGGF accounts, the Commission refused to accept liability for the amounts of aid payable under Community law, on the ground that the national measures had had the effect of distorting the distillation operation by extending it. Before the Court the French government claimed that the EAGGF should meet the proportion of the aid granted which corresponded to the rates fixed by Community rules. It was held, however, that it was impossible to ascertain to what extent the total effect of the combined national and Community aid was due to one or other component part, and in particular that it was impossible to establish with certainty what quantities of wine would have been distilled in France if the national measure had not been adopted. With regard to the discontinuance of the proceedings under art 226 of the Treaty, the Court pointed out that such discontinuance does not constitute recognition that the contested conduct is lawful. So, by adding a national element to a Community aid, France found itself having to finance the whole amount.

On the other hand, if a Member State does not add its own national aid, but pays a Community aid to recipients falling outside its scope, the Member State will not necessarily lose the whole aid. In Case 49/83 *Luxembourg v Commission*[40] the Court of Justice held that where a Member State has acted in good faith, it may still obtain reimbursement to the extent that it can prove that the aid was properly paid, although the burden of proof lies on the Member State.

The only item in the trio of cases[41] for which the European Agricultural Guidance and Guarantee Fund was held to be liable to pay involved German expenditure on aid for the purchase of butter by persons in receipt of social assistance. Council Regulation 414/70[42] enabled the Commission to decide that Member States could grant aid to enable, among other things, persons in receipt of social assistance to purchase butter at reduced prices. Its validity was initially limited to 1970, but it was later extended to the end of 1971. Commission Decision 70/228,[43] made under the regulation, enabled Member States to implement the aid by a scheme of individualized vouchers, allowing 0.5 kg per month to be bought at a reduced price. In order to save administrative costs, the German authorities issued vouchers early in 1970 valid for each month of the whole year, and did the same in 1971. However, the Commission decision was repealed with effect from 1 May 1971. Nonetheless, the German authorities continued to allow

---

[39] JO 1972 L91/1.   [40] [1984] ECR 2931.
[41] Case 11/76 *Netherlands v Commission* [1979] ECR 245, Joined Cases 15, 16/76 *France v Commission* [1979] ECR 321, Case 18/76 *Germany v Commission* [1979] ECR 343.
[42] JO 1970 L52/2.   [43] JO 1970 L77/15.

the vouchers to be used until the end of the year, on the ground that by distributing the vouchers it had created a legal position for their holders which it could
not terminate prematurely. The Commission refused to meet the cost of the aid
after 30 April 1971. The Court of Justice held that since the Commission decision
remained in force without any amendment for an indeterminate period after the
period of validity of the enabling regulation had been extended to the end of
1971, it could not be said that the German government had exceeded what it was
lawfully entitled to do to implement the Commission's decision within its territory
by maintaining the system it had initially adopted without making provision for
the possibility of terminating the operation in the course of the year.[44] In this the
Court differed from Advocate General Capotorti, who had suggested that no
Member State was entitled to grant to the recipients, at the expense of the
Community, rights more extensive than those conferred by the Commission decision. It is perhaps the case that this could not at first sight be construed as an
example of expenditure in accordance with the letter of Community law; but the
Court found that the relevant legislation allowed the Member States 'great
freedom' to choose the methods and administrative procedures for its implementation, and that what the German government had done did not exceed the limits
of that freedom. In other words, it was a reasonable exercise of its discretion, at
the time the discretion was exercised.

  In the result, a very simple and virtually absolute rule can be stated with regard
to the recovery of the expenditure of Member States under the common agricultural policy from the fund: a Member State may recover only sums spent in
accordance with Community rules as ultimately interpreted by the Court of Justice,
whatever interpretation that state may itself have put on those rules. Thus, by way
of example, in its Decision 1999/350[45] the Commission excluded from Community
funding £22,807,424 spent by the UK in the beef sector on the 'over thirty month
scheme' for failure to comply with Community rules. The only exceptions are that
where the Community rules grant to the Member States a discretion, expenditure
falling within a reasonable exercise of that discretion may be recoverable, and that
where the incorrect application of Community law is attributable to a Community
institution, the Community should bear the financial consequences.

Introduction of EC agricultural law into the United Kingdom

As is well known, the general provisions of the European Communities Act are
drafted on the basis of a distinction between the rules of Community law which
do not require national enactment in order to be law in a Member State, converted

---

[44] Case 18/76 *Germany v Commission* [1979] ECR 343.
[45] OJ 1999 L133/60.

into what are termed 'enforceable Community rights' and obligations etc under section 2(1), and rules of Community law which do require national implementation, with regard to which section 2(2) enables Orders in Council to be made and enables designated ministers or departments to make regulations.

At the outset, it may be observed that there is not always a clear-cut distinction between provisions of Community law which require domestic implementation in the United Kingdom and those which do not. By definition, an EC regulation is directly applicable throughout the Community and its terms, therefore, do not need national re-enactment; indeed, the European Court has held that they must not receive national re-enactment, since the Community law origin of the legislation might thereby be disguised, and those affected might not realize that Community-law remedies were available in relation to the legislation.[46] Nevertheless, there are many EC regulations which, as the European Court has recognized,[47] expressly or implicitly require domestic ancillary or implementing legislation. Indeed, in the context of the devolved administration of agricultural policy in the UK, it is worthy of note that the Court has recognized that it may be appropriate to adopt a text containing a combination of Community, national, and regional provisions for the sake of coherence and in order to make them comprehensible to those to whom they apply.[48] However, in implementing under section 2(2) what is already law under section 2(1), it is clear that the role of the statutory instruments is to provide machinery to aid the application of the Community law, and not to alter or add to the directly applicable provision.

On the other hand, although directives are defined under art 249 of the EC Treaty as binding only on the Member States to which they are addressed, leaving to the Member States the choice of form and methods to achieve the required result, it is now clear that certain provisions of EC directives may confer on individuals rights enforceable by them before national courts once the time limit for the implementation of the directive has expired,[49] thus falling within section 2(1) of the European Communities Act. Nevertheless, as a matter of Community law the Member States remain under a Treaty obligation expressly to implement such provisions,[50] and may indeed be liable in damages if they fail correctly to implement a directive.[51]

Even where a relevant Community obligation does exist, the powers under section 2(2) and (4) of the European Communities Act do not preclude the use of parallel powers in other legislation or the implementation of Community obligations by separate Act of Parliament, as, for example, the Importation of Milk Act 1983, which was enacted as a result of the judgment of the European Court in

---

[46] Case 34/73 *Variola v Italian Finance Administration* [1973] ECR 981.
[47] eg Case 31/78 *Bussone v Italian Ministry for Agriculture* [1978] ECR 2429.
[48] Case 272/83 *Commission v Italy* [1985] ECR 1057 at 1074.
[49] Case 148/78 *Ratti* [1979] ECR 1629.
[50] Case 102/79 *Commission v Belgium* [1980] ECR 1473.
[51] See Cases C-6 and 9/90 *Francovich v Italy* [1991] ECR I-5357.

Case 124/81, *Commission v United Kingdom*.[52] Conversely, however, a statutory instrument under section 2(2)[53] was used to amend the Merchant Shipping Act 1988
following the Order of the President of the European Court in Case 246/89R
Commission v UK[54] with regard to the registration of fishing boats.

Although directly applicable Community legislation may, as a matter of Community law, render automatically inapplicable any conflicting provisions of national
law,[55] there may still be a Community obligation formally to repeal those provisions,[56] since their apparent maintenance in force may give rise to a state of uncer-
tainty as to the possibility of relying on Community law. Hence, the European
Communities Act itself expressly repealed certain redundant agricultural legislation.

Section 2(2) refers also to the implementation of rights enjoyed by the United
Kingdom by virtue of the Community Treaties. It may be wondered whether the
word 'rights' in section 2(2) is intended in a broader sense than in section 2(1),
where 'rights' are apparently to be distinguished from 'powers', since it would appear
to be far more usual for Community instruments to grant powers or permissions
to Member States than expressly to confer rights upon them. The view appears
to have been taken that art 4(1) of the original Council Regulation 857/84,[57] on
the milk quota system, providing that Member States 'may grant to producers
undertaking to discontinue milk production definitively compensation paid in one
or more annual payments', amounted in reality to a declaration that such compensation would not constitute unlawful state aid rather than a clearly defined right
for the Member States.[58] This scheme was ultimately implemented by a separate
statute, the Milk (Cessation of Production) Act 1985.

In any event, wide as the apparent scope of section 2(2) may be, it is subject to
express limitations in Schedule 2 which may make it necessary to resort to primary
legislation or parallel powers. Section 2(2), as there restricted, does not include
power to make any provision imposing or increasing taxation, or to issue retrospective legislation, for example. The inability to issue retrospective legislation under
section 2(2) is reflected in other enabling provisions of the Act, and the fact that
under section 6(7) agricultural produce could only be taken out of the scope of
section 1 of the Agriculture Act 1957 prospectively led to a retrospective change in
the period of application of United Kingdom guaranteed prices for pigmeat being
effected in the directly applicable Commission Regulation 1822/75.[59]

It may, finally, be observed that the last paragraph of section 2(2) specifies that,
unless the implementation of Community legislation is itself to be by Order in
Council, the minister or department wishing to make regulations must be designated

---

[52] [1983] ECR 203.
[53] Merchant Shipping Act (Amendment) Order 1989 (SI 1989/2006).
[54] [1989] ECR 3125.
[55] Case 106/77 *Italian Finance Administration v Simmenthal* [1978] ECR 629.
[56] Case 167/73 *Commission v France* [1974] ECR 359.
[57] OJ 1984 L90/13.
[58] The aid was originally paid on a non-statutory basis in the United Kingdom.
[59] OJ 1975 L185/10.

for that purpose by an Order in Council. Such designation orders may be broad in scope, and, in the case of agriculture, the European Communities (Designation) Order 1972[60] quite simply designated the Secretary of State and the Minister of Agriculture, Food, and Fisheries with regard to the implementation of the common agricultural policy. Before devolution, regulations concerning the common agricultural policy in Scotland were, therefore, made by the Secretary of State. Post-devolution, if the Scottish example may be taken, the situation is rather more complex. Under the Scotland Act 1998, agriculture in general is not a reserved matter and in principle therefore falls within the competence of the Scottish Parliament and the Scottish executive.[61] While defence is a reserved matter, there is an exemption for enforcement powers in relation to sea fishing,[62] although the regulation of sea fishing outside the Scottish zone is a reserved matter, except in relation to Scottish fishing boats.[63] In principle therefore powers under section 2(2) of the European Communities Act are exercisable by Scottish Ministers under section 53 of the Scotland Act, and to that extent section 2(2) of the European Communities Act is amended by Schedule 8, para 15 of the Scotland Act to disregard the requirement that the ministers should be 'designated'. However, despite this transfer to the Scottish ministers, the powers of ministers of the Crown (ie UK ministers) continue for the purposes of section 2(2) by virtue of section 57(1) of the Scotland Act—quite apart from the special rules which apply under sections 88 and 89 of the Scotland Act with regard to cross-border public authorities such as the Intervention Board. The result is that both Scottish and UK ministers may use section 2(2) of the European Communities Act in relation to Scotland, and the practical consequence is that this matter is dealt with in the Main Concordat between MAFF (as it then still was) and the Scottish executive,[64] paras 21–26 of which lay down procedures for cooperation and consultation between them with regard to the implementation of European obligations.

As well as providing the general mechanism by which Community law becomes available in the United Kingdom, the European Communities Act did itself implement certain substantive provisions of European Community law, or lay down specific mechanisms by which they may be implemented. Formal repeals and amendments of United Kingdom legislation were effected or enabled to be effected by section 4 and Schedules 3 and 4. Part II of Schedule 3 repealed certain legislation relating to sugar, and Part III repealed legislation relating to seeds. Schedule 4, on the other hand, introduced amendments to United Kingdom legislation. On the related matter of food legislation, section 4(1) of the Food and Drugs Act 1955, enabling regulations concerning the composition of food to be made by statutory instrument subject to the negative resolution procedure, was

---

[60] SI 1972/1811.
[61] Scotland Act 1998, ss 29 and 53.
[62] Schedule 5, para 9(2)(b).
[63] Schedule 5 C(6).
[64] Available at www.scotland.gov.uk/concordats/mcmf-01.asp.

amended to allow such regulations to be made if 'called for by any Community obligation', and a new section 123a was added enabling the ministers to make such provision by regulation as they considered necessary or expedient to ensure that any 'directly applicable' Community provision relating to food was administered, executed, and enforced under that Act; in particular, enabling sampling, analysing, testing, or examining to be carried out. This indicates a preference for the use, or extended use, of specific powers, rather than the general implementing power, under section 2(2) of the European Communities Act, wherever possible, and specifically envisaged ancillary legislation where the substantive rules were laid down by directly applicable Community legislation. Similarly, whilst produce subject to Community grading rules (defined as 'directly applicable' Community provisions establishing standards of quality for fresh horticultural produce) was specifically excluded from regulations made under section 11(1) of the Agriculture and Horticulture Act 1964, ministers were empowered to provide for the application of the enforcement provisions of the Act as if such produce were regulated produce. The Plant Varieties and Seeds Act 1964 was amended to broaden the power to issue seeds regulations governing the marketing or the importation or exportation of seeds, seed potatoes, and any other vegetable-propagating material or silvicultural planting material. The Agriculture Act 1970 was amended to enable regulations to be made to control in the public interest the composition or content of fertilizers and of material intended for the feeding of animals, and to apply other provisions of the Act with a view to implementing or supplementing any Community instrument relating to fertilizers or to material intended for the feeding of animals. With regard to animal and plant health, the Diseases of Animals Act 1950 was amended to enable orders to be made excluding prescribed animals imported from other Member States from the requirement of slaughter on landing, and for regulating the exportation from Great Britain to other Member States of animals, or poultry, or carcasses thereof; the Plant Health Act 1967 was amended to enable orders to be made for the control of pests if 'called for by any Community obligation'.

However, the major provision of the European Communities Act with regard to the implementation of the common agricultural policy is section 6, which created the Intervention Board for Agricultural Produce, the role of which will be considered in the next section.

National agencies and producer organizations

In anticipation of the need to provide for the administration at the national level of the common agricultural policy, section 6 of the European Communities Act 1972 provided for the establishment of the Intervention Board for Agricultural Produce. Provision for its constitution and membership was made before accession under the Intervention Board for Agricultural Produce Order 1972.[65] In general, the board is charged with such functions as the ministers[66] may from time to time determine in connection with the carrying out of the obligations of the United Kingdom under the common agricultural policy.[67] Under the Main Concordat between MAFF and the Scottish executive it is envisaged that there should be a subject-specific concordat between all four UK Agriculture Departments in respect of the Intervention Board.[68] Levies on the export of agricultural goods are specifically required to be paid to and recoverable by the board.[69] On the other hand, levies on agricultural imports, which were in practice far more important, were to be levied, collected, and paid as if they were Community customs duties,[70] even if as a matter of law they were not. However, as noted earlier, the Uruguay Round Agreement as implemented by Council Regulation 3290/94[71] has converted agricultural import levies into real customs duties. Their collection is therefore entrusted to the Commissioners of Customs and Excise.

Regulations may be made to provide for the charging of fees in connection with the discharge of any functions of the board,[72] as well as regulations modifying or adding to the constitution or powers of any other statutory body concerned with agriculture or agricultural produce either to enable it to act for the board or to require it to discontinue activities prejudicial to the proper discharge of the board's functions.[73] The 1972 Order specifically enabled the board, with the ministers' approval, to arrange for the performance of any of its functions by another such statutory body.

A delegation of powers was effected[74] before accession under the Intervention Functions (Delegation) Regulations 1972[75] to the Home-Grown Cereals Authority and to the Meat and Livestock Commission. It was there provided that the Home-Grown Cereals Authority should have power to carry out in the United Kingdom such of the functions of the Intervention Board for Agricultural Produce with respect to wheat, barley, oats, rye, maize, and oilseed rape as the board might with the approval of the ministers and the agreement of the authority delegate to the authority in writing. This is of some legal interest in so far as, under Community law, oilseed rape falls within the common organization of the market in oils and fats rather than under the common organization of the market in cereals. It was similarly provided that the Meat and Livestock Commission should have power to carry out in Great Britain such of the functions of the Intervention

---

[65] SI 1972/1578.

[66] Including, within the scope of their competence, Scottish ministers, under the Scotland Act 1998 (Cross-Border Public Authorities) (Adaptation of Functions) Order 1999, SI 1999/1747, Sch 15.

[67] European Communities Act 1972, s 6(1).

[68] Para 54.

[69] European Communities Act, s 6(4).

[70] Ibid, s 6(5).

[71] OJ 1994 L349/105.

[72] European Communities Act 1972, s 6(2)(b).

[73] Ibid, s 6(2)(a).

[74] ie under the European Communities Act 1972, s 6(2)(a).

[75] SI 1972/1679.

Board with respect to livestock and livestock products as the board might with the approval of the ministers and the agreement of the commission delegate to the commission in writing. This policy was repeated, inter alia, with regard to the Milk Marketing Boards[76] until their elimination under the Agriculture Act 1993.

Against this background of split responsibility, it may be observed that art 1 of Council Regulation 3508/92[77] establishing an integrated administration and control system for certain Community aid schemes, as amended by Council Regulation 1593/2000,[78] requires each Member State to set up an integrated administration and control system applying, in particular, in the crop sector and the livestock sector. However, what Council Regulation 3508/92[79] means by an integrated system comprises a computerized database, an alphanumeric identification system for agricultural parcels, an alphanumeric system for the identification and registration of animals, 'area' aid applications, and an integrated control system.[80] The computerized database is required to record, for each agricultural holding, the data obtained from the aid applications, though in the UK's state of devolution it may be observed that under art 3(2) the Member States may set up decentralized databases on condition that these, and the administrative procedures for recording and accessing data, are designed homogeneously throughout the territory of the Member State and are compatible with one another. The alphanumeric identification system for agricultural parcels must be based on land registry maps and documents, other cartographic references, aerial photographs, or satellite pictures or other equivalent supporting references, or on the basis of more than one of these elements.[81] The system for the identification and registration of animals to be taken into account for the granting of aid governed by the regulation was required to be set up in accordance with Council Directive 92/102[82] on the identification and registration of animals.[83] Finally, art 7 of the regulation provides that the integrated control system is to cover all aid applications submitted, in particular as regards administrative checks, on-the-spot checks, and, if appropriate, verification by aerial or satellite remote sensing.

The development of producer organizations on the other hand is often regarded as essentially a structural or guidance measure,[84] but it has usually been achieved by authorizing such organizations to effect certain guarantee measures, such as operating a withdrawal system, withdrawing goods from the market when prices fall below a certain level. This appears to have been first introduced in relation to the markets in fruit and vegetables in Council Regulation 159/66,[85] and is continued in Council Regulation 2200/96[86] on the common organization of the market in fruit and vegetables, art 18 of which enables fruit and vegetable producers' organizations to extend their marketing and withdrawal rules to non-members

[76] Intervention Functions (Delegation) (Milk) Regulations 1982, SI 1982/1502.
[77] OJ 1992 L355/1.   [78] OJ 2000 L182/4.   [79] OJ 1992 L355/1.
[80] Art 2.   [81] Art 4.   [82] OJ 1992 L 355/32.
[83] Art 5.   [84] See Chapter 8 above.   [85] JO 1966, p 3286.
[86] OJ 1996 L297/1.

in certain defined circumstances. Similar provision may, for example, be found in the common organization of the market in fish products under Council Regulation 104/2000,[87] under which non-members may be required to abide by the rules of producer organizations.

Legal consequences of national administration of the common agricultural policy

Although agricultural levies and Common Customs Tariff duties form part of the Community's own resources,[88] their collection is expressly stated to be the responsibility of the Member States. Hence in references made in criminal proceedings relating to fraud in the context of the export and import of agricultural products, the Court of Justice held that it was for the Member States to take the necessary criminal or civil proceedings to enforce or recover agricultural levies.[89] This view was taken further in a ruling given in 1977 on a reference in criminal proceedings before an Italian magistrate,[90] where the Court held that the Community institutions are not empowered, in the present state of the law, to take proceedings before national courts for the purpose of claiming payment of Community revenue constituting own resources. On the other hand, the implementing legislation[91] provides that the Commission may be 'associated' at its request with measures of control carried out by Member States. It was pointed out by the Court of Justice in Case 267/78 *Commission v Italy*[92] that this does not enable the Commission itself to carry out measures of control and that it does not, for example, alter national rules as to the secrecy of criminal investigations and of documents related thereto. While art 280 of the EC Treaty requires the Community and the Member States to counter fraud and other illegal activities affecting the financial interests of the Community, art 280(4) provides that Community measures may not concern the application of national criminal law or the national administration of justice. A convention between the Member States on the protection of the financial interests of the Communities was signed in 1995. Given the fact that the convention and its protocols had still not been ratified by all the contracting parties, in September 2000, the Commission put forward a proposal for the creation of a European Public Prosecutor responsible for prosecutions in national courts.[93]

---

[87] OJ 2000 L17/22.
[88] Council Decision 2000/597 (OJ 2000 L253/42).
[89] Joined Cases 178–180/73 *Belgium and Luxembourg v Mertens* [1974] ECR 383.
[90] Case 110/76 *Pretore of Cento v Person Unknown* [1977] ECR 851.
[91] See now Council Regulation 1150/2000 (OJ 2000 L130/1), art 18.
[92] [1980] ECR 31.
[93] DOC/00/27. This proposal was not however taken up in the Nice Intergovernmental Conference in December 2000.

Conversely, there is a series of judgments holding that an individual trader who wishes to recover agricultural levies which he thinks the national authorities have wrongly charged him must bring his action against the national authorities rather than the Community, even though the levies may constitute the Community's own resources. This was first clearly stated in Case 96/71 *R and V Haegeman v Commission*,[94] where an importer brought an action against the Commission for recovery of charges levied by the Belgian authorities under Commission legislation on imports of Greek wine. It was held that since the collection of own resources was basically the responsibility of the national authorities, disputes concerning the levying of such charges should be resolved by the national authorities or before the national courts, subject to the possibility of referring any question as to the interpretation of Community law to the Court of Justice. It may be noted that in subsequent cases it has not always proved easy to distinguish between actions for the recovery of agricultural levies and actions for damages for harm caused by the wrongful acts of Community institutions.

Just as traders seeking to recover agricultural levies must in principle act against the national authority which collected them, so also a trader seeking payment of sums due under Community agricultural legislation must act against the national authority entrusted with making such a payment. The clearest example of this is perhaps Case 99/74 *Société des Grands Moulins des Antilles v Commission*,[95] where the applicants were claiming export refunds and carry-over payments due under the relevant Community legislation in relation to cereals respectively exported from or stocked in French overseas departments. It was held that their action should be brought against the national authorities, even though their refusal to pay arose because the European Agricultural Guarantee and Guidance Fund in turn refused to finance such payments in relation to overseas departments, since by art 299(2) of the EC Treaty the benefits of the fund did not automatically extend to overseas departments. A similar approach was followed in Cases 89 & 91/86 *Société l'Étoile Commercial*,[96] where the national authorities required the applicants to repay a subsidy following the Commission's refusal to recognize it as chargeable to the EAGGF. It was held that the Commission's decision related solely to the relationship between France and the Commission, and it was the responsibility of the national authorities to recover aid unduly paid; the action should therefore be brought against the national authorities. On the other hand, where the Community legislation fails to provide for the payment claimed, and this is alleged to be a wrongful act, an action may be brought directly against the responsible Community institution, as was confirmed in 1979 in the *Ireks-Arkady* case,[97] one of a group of cases in which damages were for the first time awarded to applicants harmed by Community legislation which seriously breached a superior rule of law for the protection of the individual. This distinction between claims for

---

[94] [1972] ECR 1005.   [95] [1975] ECR 1531.   [96] [1987] ECR 3005.
[97] Case 238/78 *Ireks-Arkady GmbH v Council and Commission* [1979] ECR 2955.

sums due, which are to be brought before national courts, and actions for compensation for loss resulting from the alleged unlawfulness of the EC legislation at issue, which falls within the jurisdiction of the Court (or, more often, the Court of First Instance), was expressly asserted and recognized in Case 281/84 *Zuckerfabrik Bedburg v Council and Commission*.[98]

Particular problems may arise in considering whether a trader has suffered harm as a result of the action of the Community authorities or as a result of the action of the national authorities implementing the Community legislation. In Case 133/79 *Sucrimex v Commission*,[98] it was held that where the application of the relevant Community rules was a matter for the national authorities it was their actions which should be treated as harming the applicants, even though they had acted on the basis of a (non-binding) telex from the Commission. A similar approach was taken in Case 12/79 *Wagner v Commission*,[100] where the dispute related to the refusal by the German authorities to allow the applicant to cancel a sugar export licence on 1 July 1976. The German authorities thought they were acting on the basis of a Commission regulation which purported to come into force on 1 July 1976. It transpired, however, that, because of a strike, the copy of the *Official Journal* containing the regulation was only published the next day, and it, therefore, could only enter into force on that day. The view of the Court was that it was the German authorities which had, thus, acted unlawfully in the absence of binding Community legislation, and the legality of their conduct should be challenged before the national courts.

However, in Case 175/84 *Krohn v Commission*,[101] where telexes sent by the Commission to the German authorities were interpreted, in the context of the legislation in question, as instruction to the German authorities, it was held that the alleged unlawful conduct was to be attributed to the Commission itself, and an action for damages could, therefore, be brought against the Commission.

It is now clear that where the national authorities might have been able to prevent or alleviate the consequences of Community acts only by using powers which were neither appropriate nor provided for that purpose, any harm will be regarded as having been caused by the responsible Community institutions. This appears from Cases C-104/89 and C-37/90 *Mulder v Council and Commission*,[102] which were actions brought by dairy producers who had not been granted any milk quota when the quota system was introduced in 1984. These producers had agreed to give up dairy production for a period of five years under an earlier Community scheme and therefore had not produced any milk during the year (1983 in their case) taken as the base year for calculating the quotas, and the legislation did not make any provision for their situation. The Commission and Council nevertheless argued that the national authorities could have allocated quotas to these producers under their (rather limited) powers to make certain transfers and

[98] [1987] ECR 49.   [99] [1980] ECR 1299.   [100] [1979] ECR 3657.
[101] [1986] ECR 753.   [102] [1992] ECR I-3061.

adjustments. However, the Court held that the national authorities were not required to allocate quotas to these producers under powers that were neither provided for that purpose nor appropriate for their situation. Any unlawful conduct must therefore be regarded as emanating from the Community institutions, which were liable for any harm suffered.

Enforcement by and against national authorities

It is in the context of the common agricultural policy that most of the basic principles have been laid down concerning the enforcement of Community law by and against national authorities.

With regard to the enforcement of Community law *by* national authorities, the basic principle is that, in the absence of specific Community rules, the national authorities must enforce Community law by national methods, but that, in so far as the national authorities have wrongly paid out Community moneys, they enjoy no discretion as to whether they should attempt to recover such moneys;[103] on the other hand, it would appear to be permissible for the national courts to protect a bona fide payee who did not give wrong information, where such a payee would be protected in relation to an incorrect payment under national law. [104] The fundamental rule, however, is that the power to recover sums due to the Community under national law must not be more restricted than the powers granted to the same authority in relation to sums due under national law.[105] Finally, whilst Member States may not fill a lacuna created by Community legislation, as where a regulation failed to provide for the recovery of a deposit where its release was obtained by fraud,[106] they remain under a duty to take any available national criminal proceedings with regard to such conduct.

Where an individual or trader wishes to enforce Community law *against* national authorities before national courts, the basic principle remains that in the absence of any relevant Community rules, normal national remedies should be used, provided that they do not make it practically impossible to exercise enforceable Community rights,[107] and that these national rules are non-discriminatory[108] and subject to the overriding obligation on national courts to protect directly

---

[103] Cases 205–215/82 *Deutsche Milchkontor v Germany* [1983] ECR 2633.

[104] Case 265/78 *Ferwerda v Produktschap voor Vee-en-Vlies* [1980] ECR 617.

[105] Cases 66, 127, and 128/79 *Italian Finance Administration v Salumi* [1980] ECR 1237.

[106] Case 117/83 *Koenecke* [1984] ECR 3291.

[107] Case 33/76 *Rewe v Landwirtschaftskammer Saarland* [1976] ECR 1989, Case 45/76 *Comet v Produktschap voor Siergewassen* [1976] ECR 2043, Case 826/79 *Mireco v Italian Finance Administration* [1980] ECR 2559, Case 130/79 *Express Dairy Foods v Intervention Board* [1980] ECR 1887, Case 199/82 *San Giorgio v Italian Finance Administration* [1983] ECR 3595.

[108] Case 130/79 *Express Dairy Foods v Intervention Board* [1980] ECR 1887.

effective rights under Community law.[109] Hence, the relevant national limitation periods apply[110] if they comply with these conditions. However, national limitation periods cannot be invoked to prevent an individual claiming rights under a directive against a defaulting Member State;[111] in such a case, in the view of the European Court, time only begins to run when the directive has been implemented, on the basis that the private citizen is only likely to become aware of the rights which should have been conferred on him or her once implementation has taken place. On the other hand, it would appear that it is possible for the Member State to limit the period for which compensation is payable.[112] However, whilst in a claim for restitution of sums paid to the national authorities the national courts may take account of the fact that those charges were actually passed on to the applicant's customers so as to prevent the unjust enrichment of the applicant, if national law so provides,[113] they cannot impose an excessive burden of proof that such charges were not passed on to the customers, even if such a burden would be imposed in relation to an analogous claim arising under national law alone.[114] On the other hand, if it is possible to recover an overpayment on grounds of equity in relation to a national tax, it should also be possible to recover an overpayment made under Community law.[115]

The effective implementation of Community law has however required United Kingdom courts to ignore what was thought to be a national rule which precluded interim relief being granted against the Crown, as was held in C-213/89 *R v Secretary of State for Transport ex p Factortame*[116] in the context of preventing the entry into force of the provisions of the Merchant Shipping Act 1988 laying down nationality requirements for the registration of fishing boats which breached the EC Treaty rules on freedom of establishment. Furthermore, in Case C-271/91 *Marshall v Southampton AHA (No 2)*,[117] the European Court held that the duty to give full effect to Community rights may require a national tribunal to ignore the predetermined financial limits on its jurisdiction.

With regard to the enforcement of Community agricultural legislation against the public authorities in the United Kingdom, the aspect of judicial review most frequently involved is the action for a declaration. Actions for a declaration have been used in two separate ways: either to challenge the validity of UK acts in the light of Community law, or to challenge the validity of Community acts. In the first category was Case 118/78 *Meijer v Department of Trade*,[118] where a declaration was sought that the United Kingdom was no longer authorized to control

---

[109] Case 61/79 *Denkavit Italiana* [1980] ECR 1205.
[110] Case 33/76 *Rewe v Landwirtschaftskammer Saarland* [1976] ECR 1989, Case 45/76 *Comet v Produktschap voor Siergewassen* [1976] ECR 2043.
[111] Case C-208/90 *Emmott* [1991] ECR I-4269.
[112] Case C-410/92 *Johnson* [1994] ECR I-5483.
[113] Case 130/79 *Express Dairy Foods v Intervention Board* [1980] ECR 1887.
[114] Case 199/82 *San Giorgio v Italian Finance Administration* [1983] ECR 3595.
[115] Case 113/81 *Reichelt* [1982] ECR 1957.
[116] [1990] ECR I-2433.   [117] [1993] ECR I-4367.   [118] [1979] ECR 1387.

the importation of potatoes from other Member States. The second category includes the English isoglucose cases,[119] where declarations were sought to the effect that a series of Council regulations were void and of no effect and that the United Kingdom government was not entitled to implement those regulations. Hence, the action for a declaration provides a very attractive method of avoiding the restrictions on actions for the annulment of regulations brought by private individuals under art 230 of the EC Treaty.

Whilst the application for judicial review may, in general, involve a consideration of the law rather than of the facts, it was held in *R v MAFF ex p Irish Dairy Board*,[120] where the applications sought both declarations and mandamus with regard to the designation of exclusive ports of entry for UHT milk, that the court was entitled to consider whether, and to what extent, the detailed measures of control were capable of constituting an impermissible restriction on intra-Community trade[121] under art 28 of the EC Treaty, on the basis that where, in a matter of public law, the application for judicial review was the only available form of proceeding, the United Kingdom should not be left in a situation where those persons with rights under European Community law should be denied the means of enforcing them.

That a breach of Community law giving rise to rights enforceable by individuals before national courts may constitute the tort of breach of statutory duty under English law was indicated by the House of Lords in *Garden Cottage Foods v Milk Marketing Board*,[122] which involved an alleged abuse by the Milk Marketing Board (MMB) of its dominant position in the milk market, with regard to its policy on the sale of bulk butter. After referring to the judgment of the European Court in Case 127/73 *BRT v SABAM*[123] holding that 'as the prohibitions in arts. 85(1) and 86 tend by their very nature to produce direct effects in relations between individuals, these arts create direct rights in respect of the individuals concerned which the national courts must safeguard', Lord Diplock concluded that a breach of art 86 may be categorized in English law as 'a breach of a statutory duty that is imposed not only for the purpose of promoting the general economic prosperity of the Common Market but also for the benefit of private individuals to whom loss or damage is caused by a breach of that duty'. The majority of the House of Lords concurred in this view, although Lord Wilberforce, in his dissent, regretted that the House should take a position on the point in interlocutory proceedings. These proceedings concerned the activities of the MMB as an 'undertaking' in the context of the EC competition rules, rather than as a statutory organization. However, a similar view has been taken in proceedings where the pricing system adopted by

---

[119] Cases 103 and 145/77 *Royal Scholten-Honig v Intervention Board, Tunnel Refineries v Intervention Board* [1978] ECR 2037.
[120] [1984] 2 CMLR 502, per Forbes J.
[121] A form of words borrowed from Case 132/80 *United Foods v Belgium* [1981] ECR 995.
[122] [1984] AC 130.
[123] [1974] ECR 51.

the MMB was alleged to breach the EC regulations governing the common organ-ization of the market in milk and milk products.[124] It was held that, although the price system may be a matter of public law, EC regulations which had direct effect created direct rights in private law which national courts must protect, so that a common-law claim for damages should not be struck out. The same approach was also followed at first instance in *Bourgoin v MAFF*,[125] where damages were claimed in respect of the revocation by the Ministry of Agriculture of a general licence to import turkeys from France, later held by the European Court to constitute a breach of art 28 of the EC Treaty.[126] Notice was taken of the case law of the European Court holding that art 28 produces direct effects and creates individual rights which national courts must protect,[127] and it was held that no differentia-tion could be made between the direct effects of art 28 and the direct effects of art 82, which had been at issue in the *Garden Cottage Foods* case, so that the state-ment of claim did disclose a cause of action for breach of the statutory duty imposed by art 28. It was, further, held in this case, however, that for a minister (or other official) to do something which he had no power to do under Community law, where he knew that he had no power so to act and that his act would injure the applicant (in this case French turkey producers and traders), could also give rise to a cause of action for 'misfeasance in public office'.

The Court of Appeal was in agreement with regard to the question of misfea-sance in public office, but the majority invoked the case law of the European Court on the liability of the Community institutions under art 288(2) of the EC Treaty to pay damages for harm caused by legislative acts as a justification for limiting the circumstances under which liability may occur when Community law is breached by a United Kingdom minister. Their view appeared to be that, where the minister acted in good faith, judicial review was the appropriate remedy, and that this mere breach of art 28 did not give rise to an action for breach of statu-tory duty, unless an abuse of power was involved. Whatever the merits of this view, the matter did not get to the House of Lords, since the case was settled on the basis that the French turkey producers would be paid the sum of £3.5 million.[128]

With the benefit of hindsight, the English Court of Appeal can be seen to have been correct in making a connection between the rules governing the liability of the Community itself under art 288 of the EC Treaty, and the liability of a Member State for breaches of Community law. On the other hand it can be seen to have been incorrect in the criteria it adopted for determining whether a breach was sufficiently serious to give rise to liability. The European Court had the opportu-nity to clarify this situation in judgments delivered in 1996,[129] which raised the

---

[124] *Irish Dairy Board v MMB* [1984] 1 CMLR 519 and 584.
[125] [1985] 3 All ER 585.
[126] Case 40/82 *Commission v UK* [1982] ECR 2793.
[127] Case 74/76 *Ianelli and Volpi v Meroni* [1977] ECR 557.
[128] *Hansard*, vol 102, no 156, col 116 (23 July 1986).
[129] Cases C-46/93 *Brasserie du Pêcheur* and C-48/93 *Factortame III* [1996] ECR I-1029.

issue of liability in damages for harm suffered as a result of breaches of basic Treaty freedoms involving national legislation. The leading cases involved a claim by a French brewery that it had suffered harm as a result of German rules on the marketing of beer which breached art 28 of the EC Treaty on the free movement of goods, and a claim by Spanish trawler owners that they had suffered harm as a result of UK legislation on the registration of fishing vessels which, inter alia, breached art 43 of the EC Treaty on freedom of establishment (the same legislation as had been at issue in the action for an injunction to prevent its being brought into operation, mentioned above). Both these Treaty freedoms have long been held to be directly effective, and it was argued before the Court that the liability to pay damages was relevant only where the provisions breached were not directly effective.[130] This argument was rejected by the Court, which stated that the right to rely on directly effective provisions is only a minimum guarantee, and asserted that 'the right to reparation is the necessary corollary of the direct effect of the Community provision whose breach caused the damage sustained'. The Court also rejected an argument of the German government that a general right to reparation of individuals could only be created by legislation, holding it to be a matter of Treaty interpretation falling within the jurisdiction of the Court. It also repeated the view it had expressed in Cases C-6 and 9/90 *Francovich v Italy*[131] that state liability for loss and damage caused to individuals as a result of breaches of Community law is inherent in the system of the Treaty, adding that this applied whatever the organ of the state responsible for the breach, so that it made no difference that the breach complained of was attributable to the national legislature.

With regard to the conditions under which a Member State could incur such liability, the Court accepted that they must in principle be the same as those governing the liability of Community institutions under art 288 of the EC Treaty taking account in particular of the margin of discretion left to the author of the act at issue. However, while under art 288 a Community institution which enjoys a wide discretion does not incur liability unless it manifestly and gravely disregards the limits on the exercise of its powers, which was the approach the English Court of Appeal had also taken with regard to the liability of a Member State for a breach of EC law in the *Bourgoin* case, the European Court pointed out that Member States do not systematically have a wide discretion when acting in fields governed by Community law. The Court nevertheless held that in the two cases at issue the Member States did enjoy a wide discretion (whereas it enjoys no discretion as to whether for example to implement a directive) and indicated the criteria governing liability in such circumstances: the provision breached must be intended to confer rights on individuals; the breach must be sufficiently serious; and there must be a direct causal link between the breach of the obligation on the state and the damage sustained by the injured parties.

---

[130] See Cases C-6 and 9/90 *Francovich v Italy* [1991] ECR I-5357.
[131] [1991] ECR I-5357.

There was no doubt that arts 28 and 43 met the first condition. With regard to the seriousness of the breach, the Court suggested that account should be taken of the clarity and precision of the rule breached, the discretion it left to national or Community authorities, whether or not the infringement and the harm caused was intentional, whether or not any error of law was excusable, whether a position taken by a Community institution had contributed to the breach, and whether national measures or practices contrary to Community law had been adopted or retained. In particular, the Court emphasized that a breach of Community law will be sufficiently serious if it persists despite a judgment finding that there is an infringement, or where there is a preliminary ruling or settled case law making it clear that the conduct in question does constitute an infringement; in *Factortame III*[132] it also suggested that account might be taken of the views expressed by the Commission at the relevant time. On the other hand the Court held that there was no requirement to show fault, a concept which in its view had different meanings in different legal systems, on the part of the national authorities other than a sufficiently serious breach of Community law. It will be seen that these criteria have now been followed by the English Court of Appeal and the House of Lords.

The Court repeated its view that the procedural rules for such an action for damages are left to national law, and should not be less favourable than those relating to parallel national remedies or make the action virtually impossible. However, in the particular context of *Factortame III* it emphasized that the requirement of English law, as laid down in *Bourgoin*, that state liability in relation to a policy measure should depend on proof of misfeasance in public office or abuse of power was such as to make it impossible or extremely difficult to obtain reparation, at least where the breach was attributable to the national legislature, thus in effect overriding the view of the majority of the English Court of Appeal in *Bourgoin v MAFF*. The Court also noted that total exclusion of loss of profit as a head of damage could not be accepted; although this was stated in the context of the German reference in *Brasserie du Pêcheur*, it would appear also to be relevant in the context of the English concept of the non-recovery of economic loss in cases of tortious liability. In effect therefore, a substantive rule of English tort law is overridden in the context of liability for breach of Community law—in this particular case where the breach was legislative in nature. On the other hand it was held that where exemplary damages would be awarded under national law, they must also be awarded in the context of breaches of Community law.

A situation has therefore arisen in which the European Court of Justice has laid down the criteria to be applied by domestic courts in the context of liability for breach of Community law, and done so largely in an agricultural and fisheries context. Nevertheless, to the extent that the provisions of EC law at issue are directly effective, such liability could conceivably be categorized as breach of statutory duty. However, it is clear from Cases C-6 and 9/90 *Francovich v Italy*[133] that

---

[132] [1996] ECR I-1029.   [133] [1991] ECR I-5357.

there are circumstances under which a Member State may be liable in damages for harm caused by its failure to implement a directive even where the provisions of the directive do not give rise to directly effective rights against the state, thus giving rise to a liability in damages for a failure to exercise legislative powers. Italy had failed to give effect to Council Directive 80/987 on the protection of employees in the event of the insolvency of their employer, and the Italian government was therefore sued for damages by a number of people who had been employed by firms which had become insolvent and who had not received the payments guaranteed to them under the directive. On the question of direct effect, the Court held that while it was clear that the directive imposed a guarantee of payment and how much was to be paid, it was not clear that the state itself was the debtor against which the guarantee could be enforced. Nevertheless, the Court went on to hold that the full effect of Community law rules could be undermined if individuals whose rights were harmed by a Member State breaching Community law could not obtain damages, and reparation was indispensable where the full effect of Community law depended on the action of Member States, as is the case with directives. In so doing, it invoked the principle of Community solidarity in art 10 of the EC Treaty, stating that it imposed an obligation on the Member States to wipe out the illegal consequences of a breach of Community law. It concluded that there was a liability to pay damages to compensate for the harm caused by failure to implement a directive subject to three conditions: the directive should require rights to be conferred on individuals, the content of these rights should be identifiable from the provisions of the directive, and there should be a causal link between the obligation imposed on the Member State and the harm suffered by the applicant. While the procedural rules for such an action for damages are left to national law, and should not be less favourable than those relating to parallel national remedies or make the action virtually impossible, there could hardly be a starker illustration of the relationship between Community law and national law.

The Court has subsequently maintained its view that where harm has been suffered as a result of the failure of a Member State to implement a directive, the appropriate remedy is that the Member State should be liable in damages rather than that the directive should be enforced against a private trader.[134] However, while it would appear that a total failure to implement a directive will always constitute a sufficiently serious breach[135] of Community law for the Member State to incur liability, the same will not necessarily be true where the Member State does implement a directive, but the implementation is incorrect or based on a wrong interpretation of the directive. In such a case, account is to be taken of the clarity and precision of the rule breached. Thus when the United Kingdom incorrectly implemented a provision described by the European Court as imprecisely

---

[134] Case C-91/92 *Faccini Dori v Recreb* [1994] ECR I-3325, Case C-192/94 *El Corte Inglés v Blázquez Rivero* [1996] ECR I-1281.

[135] Cases C-178–9/94 and 188–90/94 *Dillenkofer v Germany* [1996] ECR I-4845.

worded, and reasonably capable of bearing the interpretation given to it in good faith by the United Kingdom, at a time when no guidance was available from case law of the Court as to the interpretation of the provision at issue, such incorrect implementation could not be regarded as a sufficiently serious breach of Community law to give rise to liability in damages.[136] It should however be emphasized that this liability is separate from the question of direct effect: where a provision in a directive gives rise to enforceable rights, these rights may be invoked against the relevant national authorities so as to prevail over national legislation based on an incorrect interpretation of the directive, irrespective of the reasonableness or otherwise of their conduct.[137]

In both *Garden Cottage Foods* and *Bourgoin*, the view was taken that given the availability of the established action for breach of statutory duty, the formulation of a cause of action as being for the commission of an innominate tort was obsolete. This would also appear to make redundant the suggestion of Lord Denning MR that breaches of arts 81 and 82 of the EC Treaty might constitute new heads of tort in English law.[138] However, while the concept of breach of statutory duty may be appropriate where the liability to pay damages arises from the infringement of directly effective Community law rights converted into enforceable Community rights by section 2(1) of the European Communities Act 1972, it may be doubted whether the same is true where the liability to compensate arises precisely because the Community obligation breached is not directly effective, as in the *Francovich* case. It may be suggested that here the duty of the UK courts to award damages arises more from their duty to follow the case law of the European Court under section 3(1) of the European Communities Act 1972, or as a right which itself is an enforceable Community right under s2(1), rather than a statutory right which has been breached. It may therefore be submitted that the appropriate response in English law might be to follow the suggestion of Lord Denning MR that breaches of Community law might constitute new heads of tort in English law. Indeed one of the leading modern textbooks on public law[139] suggests that the private law action in damages is available where the claim is based on a recognized tort *or* (emphasis added) where a right conferred by Community law has been infringed.

In their most recent judgments in the matter, given in the continuing saga of the Spanish-owned fishing boats in *R v Secretary of State for Transport ex p Factortame Ltd and Others (No 5)*,[140] the English Court of Appeal and the House of Lords

---

[136] Case C-392/93 *R v HM Treasury ex p British Telecommunications plc* [1996] ECR I-1631.

[137] See eg Case 103/88 *Costanzo v City of Milan* [1989] ECR 1938.

[138] *Application des Gaz SA v Falks Veritas Ltd* [1974] Ch 381. This view was doubted by a differently constituted court in *Valor International Ltd v Application des Gaz SA* [1978] 3 CMLR 87, but reasserted by Lord Denning MR in *Garden Cottage Foods Ltd v Milk Marketing Board* [1982] QB 1114, [1982] 3 All ER 292.

[139] A Le Sueur and M Sunkin, *Public Law* (1997) 627.

[140] [1999] 2 All ER 640 (though a fuller report may be found in *The Times*, April 28 1998) [1999] 4 All ER 906.

appear to have concerned themselves more with the application of the criteria for liability laid down by the European Court of Justice rather than with categorizing the claim in terms of the traditional heads of tortious liability—in itself an interesting illustration of the interaction between EC law and domestic law in this area. It was agreed that mere breach of Community law by a national legislative act would not be enough to fix the state with liability for damage caused thereby. On the other hand, it was accepted that a submission that liability was fault based contained inherent ambiguities inasmuch as the concept of fault was too uncertain to be of any assistance. In particular, the view was rejected that no liability for compensation could be attached to the state unless the state deliberately intended by its act to do something which it knew was undoubtedly against Community law.

It was also argued that if the relevant provision of Community law was not clear then no liability for compensation could be attached to the state. This argument was rejected, though it was accepted that lack of clarity was a relevant factor. A further submission that where the view of the law which was held by the Member State was one which could reasonably be held then no liability could attach was also rejected, although it was accepted that the fact that the state held a view which could reasonably be held was a relevant factor when deciding whether to attach liability.

Finally, both courts did agree with the submission that the Commission's view as conveyed to the government that the UK Act of Parliament at issue breached Community law was not legally conclusive of the question whether or not liability should attach. However, it was stated that having regard to the Commission's role in the Community, any Member State should regard the views of the Commission as being worthy of great respect. A Member State always had the choice between proceeding on its course despite the opinion of the Commission or defending its action until the legality of what was proposed had been clarified, and it was emphasized that where there was doubt about the legality of any proposal, a failure by a Member State to seek the views of the Commission or, if it received them to follow them, was likely to lead to any breach being regarded as inexcusable and so manifest.

In what appears to be a clear break from traditional principles of domestic tortious liability, it was held that a breach of Community law could be manifest and grave so as to make it sufficiently serious to give rise to liability in damages on the part of the state without it being intentional or negligent. The lack of the intention to commit the breach or negligence or fault were, in the view of the Court of Appeal, relevant circumstances, but their presence was not a condition precedent to a breach being sufficiently grave or manifest, although Lord Slynn in the House of Lords referred to 'the deliberate adoption of legislation which was clearly discriminatory'.[141] It was agreed that in a case in which the legislative

---

[141] [1999] 4 All ER at 923.

discretion of a Member State was involved, as here, a basket or global approach involving weighing the relevant considerations was the required approach so as to avoid an excessive 'chilling factor' defeating that discretion. Nonetheless, where what was relied on in support of an application for damages was a direct breach of the fundamental principle of the EC Treaty forbidding discrimination on the ground of nationality, that would almost inevitably create a liability for damages.

This case law clearly illustrates the extent to which EC agricultural law may influence even basic principles of tortious or delictual liability in domestic law.

Bibliography

Barents, R, 'The System of Deposits in Community Agricultural Law: Efficiency v Proportionality' (1985) EL Rev 239.

—— *The Agricultural Law of the EC* (Dordrecht: Kluwer, 1994).

Cardwell, M, *Milk Quotas* (Oxford: Clarendon Press, 1996).

—— 'Milk and Livestock Quotas as Property' (2000) Edinburgh Law Review 168.

Churchill, R, 'Scope of National Fishery Measures' (1982) EL Rev 412.

—— 'The EU as an International Fisheries Actor: Shark or Minnow?' (1999) European Foreign Affairs Review 463.

Coffey, P, *The European Monetary System: Past, Present and Future* (2nd edn, Dordrecht: Kluwer, 1987).

Dony, M, 'Towards a Pan-Euro-Mediterranean Integration: A Survey of Issues in the Agricultural Sector' in M Mareseceau and E Lannon (eds), *The EU's Enlargement and Mediterranean Strategies* (London: Palgrave, 2001).

European Commission, *The Agricultural Situation in the EU: 1998 Report* (Brussels, 2000).

—— *The Agricultural Situation in the EU: 1999 Report* (Brussels, 2001).

—— *The Agricultural Policy of the European Community* (3rd edn, Brussels, 1982).

Evans, A, *The EU Structural Fund* (Oxford: Oxford University Press, 1999).

Fennell, R, 'Community Preference and Developing Countries' (1997) European Foreign Affairs Review 235.

Garcia Bercero, I, 'Trade Laws, GATT, and the Management of Trade Disputes between the US and the EEC' (1985) Yearbook of European Law 149.

Green, N, Hartley, T, and Usher, J, *Legal Foundations of the Single European Market* (Oxford: Oxford University Press, 1991).

Hiester, E, 'The Legal Position of the European Community with Regard to the Conservation of the Living Resources of the Sea' [1976] Legal Issues of European Integration 55.

Hill, B, *The Common Agricultural Policy: Past, Present, and Future* (London: Methuen, 1984).

Hudec, R, *The GATT Legal System and World Trade Diplomacy* (2nd edn, London: Butterworths, 1990).

Krenzler, H, and MacGregor, A, 'GM Food: The Next Major Transatlantic Trade War?' (2000) European Foreign Affairs Review 287.

Lane, R, *EC Competition Law* (London: Longman, 2000).

Le Sueur, A, and Sunkin, M, *Public Law* (London: Longman, 1997).

Loyant, B, 'La Force majeure et l'organisation des marchés agricoles' (1980) Revue trimestrielle de droit européen 256.

McGovern, E, *International Trade Regulation* (1982; 2nd edn, Exeter: Globefield Press, 1995).

McMahon, J, *The Development Cooperation Policy of the EC* (Dordrecht: Kluwer, 1998).

—— *Law of the Common Agricultural Policy* (London: Longman, 2000).

—— *European Trade Policy in Agricultural Products* (Dordrecht: Nijhoff, 1988).

—— *Agricultural Trade, Protectionism and the Problems of Development* (Leicester: Leicester University Press, 1992).

—— 'International Agricultural Trade Reform and Developing Countries' (1998) ICLQ 632.

—— 'The EC Banana Regime, the WTO Rulings and the ACP: Fighting for Economic Survival' (1998) Journal of World Trade Law 101.

Meyer, K, Pedersen, D, Thorson, N, and Davidson, J, *Agricultural Law, Cases and Materials* (St Paul, Minn: West Publishing, 1984).

Neville-Rolfe, E, *The Politics of Agriculture in the European Community* (London: Policy Studies Institute, 1984).

OECD, *Agricultural Policies in OECD Countries: Monitoring and Evaluation 2000* (Paris: OECD, 2000).

Peers, S, 'Banana Split: WTO Law and Preferential Agreements in the EC Legal Order' (1999) European Foreign Affairs Review 195.

Pescatore, P, Davey, W, and Lowenfeld, A, *Handbook of GATT Dispute Settlement* (Irvington-on-Hudson, NY: Transnational Publishers, 1991, and subsequent looseleaf editions).

Pischel, G, 'Trade, Treaties and Treason: Some Underlying Aspects of the Difficult Relationship between the EU and the WTO' (2001) European Foreign Affairs Review 103.

Scott, J, 'On Kith and Kine (and Crustaceans): Trade and the Environment in the EU and WTO' in J Weiler (ed), *The EU, the WTO and the NAFTA: Towards a Common Law of International Trade* (Oxford: Oxford University Press, 2000).

—— 'Tragic Triumph: Agricultural Trade, the CAP and the Uruguay Round' in N Emiliou and D O'Keeffe (eds), *The European Union and World Trade Law* (Chichester: John Wiley & Sons, 1996).

Snyder, F, 'The CAP in the Single European Market' in *Collected Courses of the Academy of European Law,* vol ii, book 1 (Dordrecht: Kluwer, 1992).

—— 'European Community Law and Third World Food Entitlements' (1989) German Yearbook of International Law 87.

—— 'EC Law and International Economic Relations: The Saga of Thai Manioc', EUI Working Paper 93/2 (Florence, 1993).

—— 'The Taxonomy of Law in EC Agricultural Policy: A Case-Study of the Dairy Sector', EUI Working Paper 95/3 (Florence, 1995).

Strauss, R, 'The Economic Effects of Monetary Compensatory Amounts' (1983) JCMS 261.

Tridimas, T, *General Principles of EC Law* (Oxford: Oxford University Press, 1999).

Usher, JA, 'Judicial Review of Community Acts and the Private Litigant' in AIL Campbell and M Voyatzi (eds), *Legal Reasoning and Judicial Interpretation of European Law: Essays in Honour of Lord Mackenzie-Stuart* (London: Trenton, 1996).

—— 'Agricultural Markets: Their Price Systems and Financial Mechanisms' (1979) EL Rev 147.

—— 'The Effects of Common Organisations on the Powers of a Member State' (1977) European Law Review 428.

—— 'The Common Agricultural Policy and Commercial Policy' in M Maresceau (ed), *The European Community's Commercial Policy after 1992: The Legal Dimension* (Dordrecht: Kluwer, 1993).

—— 'Common Policies and Common Prices? From Units of Account to Euros in

Common Organisations of Agricultural Markets' (2000) Legal Issues of Economic Integration 119.

—— *EC Institutions and Legislation* (London: Longman, 1998).

—— 'Uniform External Protection: EEC Customs Legislation before the European Court of Justice' (1982) CML Rev 389.

—— *General Principles of EC Law* (London: Longman, 1998).

Vasey, M, 'The 1985 Farm Price Negotiations and the Reform of the CAP' (1985) CML Rev 649.

—— 'Decision-Making in the Agricultural Council and the "Luxembourg Compromise"' (1988) CML Rev 725.

Wallace, H, 'A European Budget Made in Strasbourg and Unmade in Luxembourg' (1986) Yearbook of European Law 263.

White, R, 'Fishery Rights of Non-Member States in Community Waters' [1982] EL Rev 415.

Index